MW00377580

Regarding Victory:

Adventures in Entrepreneurship Led Back to Love

Joshua Wallack

Dedication

This book is dedicated to Elida Christine, Brett Jonah, and Mia Alexandra, with whom I will always place my whole heart.

Acknowledgment

I would like to acknowledge my wonderful family – Florence (RIP), David, Judi and David, Barbara, Blaze, Laurie (RIP), Tracey, Andy, Matt, Ben, Gabby, Wendy, Dan, Zack, Lexi, Janna, Josh, Claire, Miles, Max, Shep, Kevin, Rachel, Violet, and Sophie.

I would also like to give special thanks to Pam, Pops, Carl, Dylan, Peaches, Zack, and Jeremy.

I am also so grateful to Richard P, Boris F, Bruce W, Juan E, Carlos R, Joel N (RIP), Elliot N, Michael N, Bill A, Angel DLP, Alejandro P, Hal K, Trippe C, Robert F, Harris R, Marco M, Jerry L, Ceci V, Randy R, Nikki C, Mike C, Thornton W, Greg MB, Rick W, Alan H, Mike C, Michael K, Marlo C, Monika E, Jack P (RIP) Ambrish B, Roger Z, Derek W, Steven S, Michael M, Abdul M, Adrian J, Jason S, Adam R, Jesse P, Steve P, Eric F, Steffan A, Matt K, Izzy M, Jason T, Mike P, Kiki P, Edith R, Mauricio C, Thomas B, Claudio C, Frank C, Sergio S, Natalie C, Shelley M, Rabbi G Glickstein, S Ben-David (RIP), S Montaine, L Lynn, D Ricke, P Boyle, E Cobin, C Dreeson, Jeff N, Isam W, Robi D, David L, David P, Carlos G, Terry B, Ron H, Alberto V, Bobby P, Mark D, Chris R, Mick K, Paul S, George K, Josh D, Claire B, Jodi B, George A, Dr. Y Wang and Gary S.

Contents

About the Author

Orlando Business Journal's 2017 *CEO of the Year*, Joshua Wallack's life of service to his family and communities in Miami Beach, Florida, and Orlando/Orange County, Florida, spans a career of nearly 25 years. When Wallack departed Miami Beach in 2013, he was *Vice Chairman* of the Miami Beach Chamber of Commerce, *Commissioner Appointee* to the Miami Beach Convention Center Advisory Board, and *VP of Community Partnership and Executive Committee* of Mount Sinai Medical Center Foundation.

In Orlando, Joshua received the *Orlando Business Journal's 40 under 40, C-Level Honoree, CEO of the Year,* and a 2022 *Power Player*, and is a *3x Orange County Mayoral* appointee to the I-Drive Improvement District *Board of Directors* and the International Drive Resort Area Chamber of Commerce *Board of Directors.*

Joshua serves as COO of Wallack Holdings and is *Development Manager* of The Estates at Juggler Meadow, an 80-acre redevelopment of the Yankee Candle Mansion in Leverett & Amherst, Massachusetts. He lives with his wife and two children in Orlando, Fl.

Preface

"No matter what level of success, wealth, or achievement you may attain, none of it matters at all if you don't bring it home to a house full of people you love and who love you."

"If you're content with solitude and your kids' resentment, then working religiously around the clock might suit you. But remember, you'll become the 'Cats in the Cradle' guy, alienated from your grown children who won't want to know you."

"This type of extreme dedication, while often necessary for an entrepreneur at certain key junctures in short bursts, is not for always, and will lead to family losses if not tempered and controlled. You can't redline indefinitely; something in the engine will blow up."

"Merely providing financial support doesn't correlate to being a good husband and father. Any ex-spouse who barely or never sees his kids can fulfill some financial obligation by sending a check somewhere. It doesn't make them any less of an asshole."

Chapter 1:
The Impossible is Possible:
The '80s in Miami

For most people, childhood is the most enchanted stage of life, filled with boundless curiosity, creativity, and infinite originality. My self-created adventures during those years as the eighties engulfed America were extraordinary, at least to me. Timeless recollections of my youth, when I explored the world through guilt-free eyes, and how those days shaped my perception of the world and perpetually altered my faith in the potency of dreams, inventiveness, and the mind's eye. More than anything, witnessing events once thought to be impossible became real before my eyes and changed everything.

Running the streets of old Miami Beach, either on my Huffy dirt bike or a Metro Bus bound for anywhere, I didn't adhere to boundaries. My parents, very busy all the time, mostly didn't know where I was at any given moment, and I spent countless hours trying to be as adventurous as I could. I knew I had a stronger purpose than others my age; I knew it and felt it. The bedroom I shared with my younger brother Kevin evolved into a portal of sorts to these wondrous realms as I dreamed and schemed, exploring outlying possibilities. Nothing seemed too far out of reach, and I gravitated toward innately badass friends. We just thought we were cool kids in those days in Miami; every day held the potential for a new journey.

I don't know why some things happen the way they do; sometimes it hits you so hard that *BAM*...it changes your whole life. My world was changed forever over a few weeks in January 1984. A confluence of events hit close to home and happened so quickly that I was hooked on a feeling. I knew I loved it; I just didn't know until later what was washing over my heart and mind. It felt like a suit of armor.

In the last days of 1983, Miami was a 'Paradise Lost' (as Time Magazine's cover so eloquently put it). The fallout from Mariel, race riots, lootings, and shootings engulfed the city. The film Scarface glamorized the drug trade, and all the real Cocaine Cowboys started emulating the movie. Those days were not safe; truly the entire Medellin cartel led by Pablo Escobar was using Miami as the main entry point for all their product entering the US. My parents used to have friends they stopped talking to as soon as they heard someone was making a ton of money out of nowhere. Many professionals in our community were now making fortunes, helping launder houses full of cash you couldn't bring to the banks. No one went to Downtown Miami; it was a slum, and even on Miami Beach and Ocean Drive, where our family business was and still is, we had to put bars on all the windows. It wasn't safe to walk to the car, and after South Beach photographer Andy Sweet was murdered in his apartment a few blocks away, my father grew even more concerned. Our city was divided, unsafe, and suffering.

It only took one day into the new year to change everything for Miami and set off the most memorable month of my childhood. On January 2, 1984, with the city awash in racial violence and crime, David faced Goliath in front of the entire world. I was at a New Year's Weekend party at my cousin's waterfront home on Allison Island, complete with all the accouterments of a Jewish deli spread. We ate all day, but the cousins of my generation there, who were much older than my sister and I, drank like a fish and kept going outside and coming back smelling very funny. They also kept going to the bathroom together. I was eight and too young to understand the partying that was going on. All I saw were people there having a blast.

That night, in our Orange Bowl Stadium, the 50th Annual edition of the Bowl Game, the undefeated Nebraska Cornhuskers, some calling the greatest college football team ever, were 11-point favorites over the upstart #5 Miami Hurricanes. The Canes lost the first game of the season, benched their quarterback, and put in a freshman to replace him. They reeled off 10 straight wins to find themselves in the Orange Bowl. They were playing in their home stadium against the 12-0 Huskers. #1 Nebraska was on a 22-game winning streak, averaging 52 points a game, and their RB Mike Rosier had just won the Heisman Trophy. The cousins and some of their degenerate friends who kept coming and going were betting aggressively all day on the games, not one of them taking Miami. The consensus was the game would be over at halftime, a total blowout, possibly without the Hurricanes scoring at all.

All of a sudden, the stakes skyrocketed. #2 Texas, who, if they had won the Cotton Bowl, could have argued for a share of the National Title, lost 10-9 to Georgia. #4 Illinois got crushed by unranked UCLA, and #3 Auburn did end up beating Michigan, but the game was boring and unimpressive.

Something incredible was going on; the energy through the living room became insane. Twelve high teenagers and their equally bombed parents realized that even though it was a huge longshot, the Miami vs. Nebraska Orange Bowl, which seemed like lambs to the slaughter earlier in the day, had become the outright National Championship Game of College Football.

All of a sudden, everyone in the room became rabid, wild Canes fans. They were screaming and yelling about how our speed and athleticism may match up with Nebraska's power and that we had home-field and crowd advantage in the Orange Bowl. The cynical adults laughed at the idea that Nebraska wouldn't demolish us. More bets were made.

In what seemed at the outset like just a formality, the unbeaten Nebraska team that had blown everyone's doors off all season ran onto the field. They looked huge and so confident. Surely, 18-year-old Canes QB Bernie Kosar would be no match for this juggernaut, but shockingly, at the end of the 1st quarter, Miami led 17-0. We were freaking out.

The bewildered Cornhuskers countered with a gimmick play called a "fumblerooski," where offensive lineman Dean Steinkooler picked up an intentional fumble and lumbered 19 yards for a touchdown. Still, Miami led by 7 late, and when a low tackle injured Rosier and knocked him out of the game, Nebraska tried a rare deep pass. The room went crazy again when WR Irving Fryar dropped a wide-open touchdown, and when QB Turner Gill had his next attempt batted away, Nebraska was down to its last gasp, a 4th down and 8, with less than a minute left.

Echoes of the yelling and cries of the party are imprinted in my mind; everyone knew if Miami could stop this last play, they would take over the ball. Gill took the 4th down snap and took off in triple option formation, but before he was crushed by a Miami tackler, he elegantly pitched the ball to Rosier's replacement RB Jeff Smith, who quieted the Orange Bowl and our wild room up as he weaved through the field and was tackled in the endzone for a touchdown. The play brought the score to 31-30 Miami, with the extra point to come. The Huskers had found a way, it seemed, and their sideline exploded.

The room went silent, and a sick sensation entered my body. All Nebraska had to do was trot their kicker on, hit the extra point, and the game would have ended in a tie. There was no overtime, so Nebraska would have finished the season unbeaten and as National Champ. Their legendary coach, Tom Osbourne, however, had other ideas.

"What are they doing?" the announcers gasped as they saw the Nebraska coaching staff surround QB Turner Gill. Then Osbourne sent his offense back out.

The TV announcers began with a monologue I'll never forget as long as I live, "I have not seen the kicker come on the field, and I don't think he's coming on the field. I think that they've got things going their way, Tom Osbourne made this decision a long time ago, don't think this situation caught him by surprise; he's decided to go for 2 and take a shot at winning. I commend him for it."

If I thought I had seen wild throughout the day, this was 20 times that. The girls were now in it, too, even the grandmothers and aunts; everyone was freaking out. My cousin Pauline buried her face on her husband's shoulder and couldn't watch. Nebraska's offense lined up to attempt a 2-point conversion and go for the win.

With people losing their minds all around me, my heart was racing, and this was it. The NBC announcer bellowed to America, "This is for the National Championship for Nebraska."

It was an out-of-body experience; I couldn't breathe, and our family's energy was jacked up to the moon. I could barely see, so I ran to another spot around everyone crouched in front of the TV. Gill snapped the ball, but instead of a triple option running play to gain the 2 yards, he rolled out and threw a short pass to Jeff Smith, who was in the endzone. In the most legendary moment in Miami sports history, a moment that seemed to last forever, Miami defensive back Ken Calhoun dove toward Smith from 6 feet away, fully extending his body and reaching with everything he had. Calhoun deflected the pass with the tip of his fingers, which bounced off Smith's pads and fell to the turf.

"Incomplete!" rang from the TV. I was then knocked over by my cousin's drunk friend. As the room exploded, the Orange Bowl exploded, and the City of Miami, down and out for so long, exploded.

The victory was shocking. Everyone then started crying in joy and ecstasy. The Miami Hurricanes, an impossible underdog, nowhere near this moment when the day started, defeated #1 Nebraska in the Orange Bowl to win the National Championship.

Now Miami was #1.

Later that night on the news, people were reveling in the streets, thousands of residents of Little Havana were out banging their pots and pans, and the *Miami Herald's* morning headline boasted, "The Dream Comes True." The whole city was elated. Weeks of joyful celebrations were set off that helped bring the city of Miami together.

The next few weeks were a treasure trove of pride. We all had Hurricane National Champions shirts, and no one could stop talking about it, re-living the game and where they were or how they felt when Nebraska missed the 2. The impossible was indeed possible. Through the lens of youthful exuberance, I felt no boundaries, limitless. For the next two weeks, the massiveness of the Canes title win and how the energy of Miami had turned around changed my perspective.

Just a few weeks later, three straight days happened with similar exhilaration. I didn't think anything could top the Orange Bowl, but there was more to come, powerhouse events that again shook me, America, and the World.

First was Super Bowl Sunday, January 22, 1984, a memorable day as we sat on a mattress on the floor at my father's girlfriend's lake house, not knowing why she didn't have a couch. It was a very hippie-friendly place, a place of dreams. They were growing pot in the backyard, and I fished all day in the lake that seemed to have endless largemouth bass action. I was, of course, wearing my Hurricanes National Champions shirt, which was already starting to fall apart.

As twilight fell, the Super Bowl between the defending World Champion Washington Redskins and the villainous LA Raiders began. This was a more chilled-out crowd than the wild scene at Cousin Gene's the prior time; no one here drank, this group was just all high. The few casual sports fans there, the announcers, and most of my friends at school assumed Washington would win back-to-back titles. The Silver and Black had other plans.

Unlike the Cane's legendary win, which came down to the wire, this was anything but; it was another kind of victory, domination. A beatdown, a humiliation, an ass whipping. The Raiders just smashed the Redskins in every way, including two iconic Super Bowl touchdowns that were replayed over and over for years. Redskins QB Joe Theisman threw a simple screen pass to the flat and, like a savage, linebacker Jack Squirek leaped in front and intercepted it in the air, landing in the endzone to score with only 12 seconds left in the half. The pick 6 demoralized the soon-to-be ex-champions.

I was so pumped. The Raiders were notorious for doing anything it took to win, and their bravado and relentless attacking style were pulverizing Washington. Then, on the last play of the 3rd quarter, star RB Marcus Allen took a simple handoff, and to avoid getting tackled, he reversed his field and exploded through the heart of the Redskin defense for a 74-yard touchdown, then a Super Bowl record. The demolition ended 38-9; another champion was crowned stunningly.

Something also happened between the 2 TDs, something that struck me like thunder. Apple Computers aired a commercial that came on in the 3rd quarter called '1984,' named after George Orwell's dystopian novel. It heralded the coming of the Macintosh, "where 1984 would not be like 1984." Being a computer guy who was an Apple 2 user, I was dumbfounded.

The next day, Jan 23rd, everyone was talking about the Raiders, but more so, the Apple commercial. I requested our computer teacher, Mrs. Lynn, to see if we could watch the unveiling of the Macintosh at Apple's presentation, which was the next day and would be aired on PBS. She agreed and said she was going to try. That was enough for me because that night, I had other plans. Big plans.

My next-door neighbors, Diego and Eddie, two brothers whose yard backed up to mine, had their house equipped with certain high-tech gadgets that ours just wasn't. Their mother, Esther, was a sweet Cuban lady who always took care of me like a 3rd son when I would come over. We took fire from Esther's mother, Gladys, who we called "Aba," which was short for Abuela. I'm not sure how, but Aba could target us like a ninja and, if we weren't quiet during her novellas, could whizz a shoe and hit you with it without ever missing. Aba was lethal with those *chancletas*, but always a very sweet lady.

That night, we were there for serious issues. Esther had the coveted "HBO Box" on their set, which was a really big deal. Beyond its hype as first-generation cable TV, the HBO Box had access to the MSG Network, which aired live sports from Madison Square Garden. It was mostly for New York Knickerbocker fans in the mid-Atlantic region who wanted to watch NBA games. It wasn't any Knick game we were interested in that night, though, because another title was on the line once again.

Hulk Hogan, who played Thunderlips in the movie Rocky 3, was about to wage World War III against the nation of Iran. We had studied the hostage crises in 1980, and the bombing of the Marine barracks in Beirut was still a hot topic in school. To add insult to injury, Iran, the sworn enemy of the United States, was on top of the wrestling world. The WWF World Heavyweight Champion was none other than the Iron Sheik.

The Sheik spat on the American flag, with xenophobia being exploited in full swing. There was only one man who could save us, and Madison Square Garden was on its feet the entire match.

However, all was almost lost as only a few minutes in, The Hulkster was locked in the Sheik's signature hold, the camel clutch. This move would snap anyone else's back, but this was Hulk Hogan, and he was fighting for America. Shockingly, Hogan erupted out of the Sheik's camel clutch and crushed him into the corner, sending the Sheik crumbling to the mat. Madison Square Garden, seeing the Iron Sheik lying prone on the canvas, was going ballistic, and so were we. Again, my heart was in my throat; it was like I was flying. Hogan raced across the ring into the ropes and came down with his crushing leg drop. We were all dying as Hogan hooked the Sheik's leg in a pinning cradle; it was the biggest moment we had ever seen.

The referee slammed his hand down to the mat, 1...2...and the 3rd time he hit, history was made. Hulk Hogan was crowned the new WWF World Heavyweight Champion, and fans were absolutely going berserk. We had witnessed the United States defeat a bitter rival at their own game. Maybe it wasn't the 1980 US Hockey defeat of the USSR at the Olympics, but it sure felt the same.

Even Diego and Eddie's stepdad, Michael Bienstock, a federal prosecutor working for the legendary Janet Reno, came downstairs in his underwear with all the commotion, and he too ended up dancing with joy at the new World Champion. Hulkamania had set America on fire. We ordered Steve's Pizza, which was the only place open that delivered and celebrated. My parents knew I was just next door and didn't mind that it was past midnight.

To me, sports became characterized by moments of brilliance created by tactical and strategic planning. Seeing the adaptation of technique on the fly to gain any advantage helped create an innovative mindset. I realized embracing change and being adaptable in the moment was essential in order to do what I was becoming obsessed with, which was to win.

The next day, January 24th, Hulkamania was running wild at North Beach Elementary. Everyone was talking about it. Some of us believed Hulk would be able to keep the belt for a long time, while others thought the Sheik could take the title back in a rematch.

After lunch, we returned to our classroom to find a theater setup in front of the TV, a huge old box sitting on a black iron cart. The teachers had worked through lunch, and with the help of the school maintenance guy and some tinfoil antennas, they got PBS working and clear.

As we sat down, all thoughts of Hulk Hogan quietly went on pause as I stared at the screen, which read "1984 Apple Shareholder's Meeting," and a countdown clock was running.

While we stared at the countdown, all of us started buzzing about the Super Bowl commercial and its announcement of this new computer called Macintosh. We were well-versed in Apple 2 and felt lucky to be seeing this happen.

As the counter went to zero, PBS went live to the theater, where a huge crowd was in the audience. Steven Jobs, the young CEO of Apple Computers and inventor of the Apple 2, came out wearing a suit and green bowtie. I remember thinking how weird the bowtie was, as I had never seen anyone wear one unless they were in a tuxedo. But Jobs also wore something else that caught my eye and attention: it was the look on his face, so confident, dominant, and captivating. The look said, *"I'm going to kick your ass, IBM."* Shortly after, he pulled out the bag that had the Mac in it and put the computer on the table.

Steve then told the crowd he had something in his pocket, and he casually pulled out a floppy disk and slid it into the Mac. An epic version of 'Chariots of Fire' began playing, and the Mac began displaying different images, programs, fonts, and games. When it told us itself that it was "Insanely Great," the crowd at the event went crazy. The applause didn't stop for five straight minutes.

Then, Jobs quieted the crowd, whose energy could have powered not only the little town of Cupertino but the entire City of San Francisco, and said, "for the first time," he would let Macintosh speak for itself. The Mac, in a cool, 80s alien voice, said, "Hello, I'm Macintosh. It sure is great to be out of that bag. Unaccustomed as I am to public speaking, I'd like to share with you a maxim I thought of the first time I met an IBM mainframe. Never trust a computer you can't lift. Obviously, I can talk, but right now, I'd like to sit back and listen. So, it is with considerable pride that I introduce a man who's been like a father to me...STEVE JOBS."

The crowd erupted even louder, and while we were all so young, we even saw our teachers marveling at what we were watching. Again, history was being made right before our eyes, and so many things that we had talked about, dreamed of, and seen only in movies were now actually happening.

Those three days are tattooed into my mind, where everything I thought could never be, was. Dreams turned into reality, fiction became fact, and the impossible became possible. The Miami Hurricanes and the Raiders dethroned unbeatable champions, Hulk Hogan saved America by winning the World Title, and Apple launched a new computer that would rocket us into the future.

My mind was overblown, but being the analytical kid I was, it raised a whole bunch of new thoughts and questions. What if nice guys do finish last? What if being a badass like the Canes and Steve Jobs is what gives you the edge you need? What if you had to do whatever it took to win? That's what I was seeing; that's what was happening.

That span of only a few weeks in January 1984 shaped me, gave me quiet confidence, and made me feel a part of something. I remember lying in my bed, unable to sleep for a while the next few nights. I didn't understand that it was adrenaline, and what I was feeling, more than anything else, was an association with victory.

My journey from being a young boy mesmerized by these powerhouse moments to a serious businessman comes down to the power of focus. Witnessing intensity, perseverance, and what they yielded kindled an entrepreneurial spirit within me. The lessons I was learning became the driving force behind my thoughts, empowering me with the notion to create a vision and pursue it relentlessly with powerful, deliberate action. The influence of sports further demonstrated how the pursuit of greatness in any field can transcend boundaries and open doors to success.

As I started to grow up, I tended to venture more toward the activities that would make money. This included leadership, teamwork, resilience, and creation. I craved as much independence as I could get from my father and parents, who were baby boomers very much preoccupied with their own lives.

I just didn't want to hear "no" or "we can't afford it" anymore, especially from people who got themselves anything they desired anyway. I didn't want conflict, I just wanted to have my own money to go to the mall and buy whatever I wanted, eat wherever I wanted, and go wherever I wanted.

My first venture began in 5th grade, a VHS dubbing operation in my room with VCRs double stacked. My father did it all the time with rented movies (both hits and X-rated), and his technique was to be flawlessly organized with everything, including clear labeling; so, I followed his model. SP gave you 2 hours; EP gave you 6 hours. I spent whole weekends on the bus across metro Miami, hitting video stores from Broward to Kendall and building a library of WWF and NWA VHS tapes. Many times, the video store owners knew me and cut me deals. My sister Wendy, who was a freshman at UM, found a great store in Coral Gables that sold me over 20 tapes in one shot at $15 each. It was a monster score for me; I was dubbing the tapes at every waking hour. My mind became a clock as if I knew when to come back up and find both VCRs automatically rewinding because they were finished. I would then load in a new blank and start all over. I soon had most of the World Wrestling Federation home video series, which was like absolute gold. You had an elementary school full of rabid Hulkamaniacs who rented or bought my videos, and most of them paid every day.

I did have some kids that I extended credit to based on their allowance, and often, comped friends I knew didn't have the money. Venturing on this entrepreneurial path, I uncovered a natural skill for marketing and enterprising. I guess I was defying some age barriers, impressing teachers who saw that half my knapsack was full of videotapes. While most of my peers were engrossed in typical childhood activities, I found delight in attending to everyone's needs, which basically was identifying consumer behavior and market trends. It was during this experimental phase that I discovered a lot about myself and then, serendipitously, met my match.

In the middle of my 5th-grade year, it was 1985, and I was 10, already a business guy. My teacher, Mrs. Brown, was a sweet lady from Jamaica who showed certain kids, including me, a lot of favoritism. On the Monday after Thanksgiving, a new student in our class had just moved from Buffalo, NY, to Miami Beach. His name was Jason, and he had an earring and an Adidas tracksuit on. The girls started giggling, and it was clear another cool kid was checking in. Jason sat down near me, and at lunch, we started talking.

It turned out Jason's family rented a home three blocks down from ours on the same street. His new house was pink, so of course, I made fun of it when I came over that afternoon, and he laughed at my joke without being embarrassed at all. He actually put his arm around me, too. Right then, I knew he was a great guy. Then he opened the door.

Inside, in the living room of the new rental, Jason had three full-sized arcade games, including the brand-new Super Mario Brothers. I couldn't believe my freaking eyes. Everyone was talking about Super Mario; lines of people were waiting to play it at the mall, and this kid had it in his living room. His mother, Janice, had a barstool set up in front of it and was playing when we walked in.

"Mom," Jason said without saying hello, "this is my friend Josh." It was clear right away Jason ruled the roost, at least with his mom, and Janice immediately quit playing and turned and smiled brightly at me. She was so happy her son had made a friend on his first day.

"Did you go to the market?" Jason asked her. I remember thinking that as a sign he was from out of town. My mother never called the grocery store 'a market.'

"Yes, sweetie, what do you want?' Janice warmly asked.

"Do you like pizza? Wait, dumb question," Jason joked at me.

"Mom! Make the Stouffer's French bread pizza with pepperoni and make it in the oven so it's crispy!" Jason directed. Janice was so happy, even as he kept asking for things. I was enthralled; his mind moved as fast as mine did. He somehow knew my answers to questions before I said them.

We started playing Super Mario Bros, and Janice brought oven-toasted Stouffers and cut them into pieces so we could play and eat at the same time. Yoo Hoo bottles with straws. Man, this was living! While we were playing, and it was clear Jason was a few weeks ahead of me on Mario skills, he asked about my tapes.

"You have all the WWF videos, right? Where did you get all those?" I let him know about the bus rides, the video stores, and my dubbing laboratory. He was surprised at me taking the bus everywhere, as it was clear that Janice would drive him wherever he wanted to go. As he played, he asked, "Do you think Hogan can slam Big John Studd?" Right at that moment, I knew we were going to be best friends. I sometimes lay in bed at night, thinking about the same thing.

We went upstairs, and Jason showed me his WWF tape collection, which was meager compared to mine. I looked around his room; he had a Poison poster and 3 Buffalo Bills posters. This was another source of ribbing, as the Dolphins had just made it to the Super Bowl, and I was a member of the 'Marino Corp.'

"The Dolphins suck," Jason mocked, "they got friggin waxed in the Super Bowl. Montana tore them a new ass." Though he was clowning my team, I marveled at this new vocabulary I was learning. Nothing phased Jason, absolutely nothing; he would just laugh and then have a great comeback for everything. I pulled out a copy of Hulkamania, one of the first WWF tapes and my most popular seller and rental.

"Want to watch this?"

"Hell yeah," Jason said, more great answers.

As we got up, I noticed dozens of long boxes stacked on his shelves and piles of scrapbook-like folders on the floor of his newly moved-in room.

"What is all that?" I asked on the way downstairs.

"My baseball card collection," Jason said proudly. We didn't have a baseball team in Miami, and I was so into the Hurricanes and Dolphins I never really thought about it much. I liked the Yankees and knew all about Babe Ruth, Mantle, Aaron, and the other greats. We went down and watched Hulkamania and then played more Super Mario Brothers.

I got home at almost 11 p.m. My mother was furious; I had not come home for dinner and forgot to call. She lambasted me for scaring her and kept reminding me about Adam Walsh. I asked her to please calm down, which only made her more upset. At that point, I wanted to pack a bag and go back to Jason's. She relaxed when I told her I'd made a new friend and went to his house. I lied and said I fell asleep on his couch, and that's why I was late. After a few minutes of hearing the story about the new friend, she went back to her room. I smiled and was happy I got away with it. My mom knew very well about my abilities and told me all the time she thought I'd either be President of the United States or Lex Luthor.

Over the next several weeks, Jason got into the video business with me. He came over to my house only a few times; there was no one to wait on us there. He marveled at the VCRs going at all hours, and I showed him a few things on my Commodore 64. But who wanted to play Pitfall or Oregon Trail when we could be playing full-sized arcade games at his house?

I didn't meet Jason's father for a few weeks. I honestly hadn't given it much thought or asked. Janice was really sweet, and he had a younger sister named Tiffany, with whom she was totally smitten. Everything worked in their home; there was nothing wrong with any of it. I definitely was enjoying it there.

One night, when we were hanging out, Jason's father, Richard, entered through the front door. There were smiles all around as he gave Janice a big kiss. That was something I had never really seen before. When I was six months old, my biological parents got divorced, and they genuinely loathed one another. When I was two, my mother married my stepfather, David, her 2nd David, and they couldn't have been more opposite guys. In our house, it was much more old-fashioned, basically my parents' way or the highway.

It was slightly different at Jason's. Richard joined us and, before dinner, pulled out his giant brick cell phone and ordered Flora's, a pizza joint on 79th Street Causeway, for a large pie and garlic rolls to supplement the spaghetti Janice was making. She was thrilled to serve all of it together, which continued to stun me. My mother would never allow a pizza on a dinner table of food she made.

Then, as we ate, Richard said to Jason, "I got you that thing." Jason shot up, "You did?" Richard smiled sharply at his son and reached down beside him. I hadn't seen my new best friend ever so submissive; he looked, finally, like a little boy. Richard popped up with a box and handed it to Jason.

"Is this from Mister Mint?"

"Of course," Richard said, "he met me at the airport."

I was in awe as Jason opened the box to reveal a thick glass frame with a single baseball card in the center. Jason's demeanor changed back to normal Jay. "Hell yeah," he yelled, smiling ear to ear, and got up from the table to run upstairs. I followed him.

Jason stood before his closet door, holding the 1948 Leaf Jackie Robinson Rookie he had just received. He paused, then turned to me. "Don't tell anyone about this, OK?" Holy shit, now I was really freaking out.

Jason opened his closet door like an arc, and on the ground below his clothes, there were no shoes. There was a Buffalo Bills blanket that covered something large. He pulled away the blanket, and under it, he had a 6' x 4' glass case that was locked. He retrieved the key from his bedside and unlocked it, and it opened like a car hood. Now I had seen the top layer of Jason's baseball cards already, fully sealed Topps sets going back years, Fleer sets, Donruss sets, and looked through his albums where he tried to make full sets out of packs he opened. But it was clear I hadn't seen a damn thing yet; this was his real collection.

He had a place clear for the Jackie Robinson rookie set up, right next to his Brooks Robinson rookie. Then, I peered across the rest. Some piles of glass-cased cards were more recent and not on display: Rickey Henderson, Roger Clemens, Daryl Strawberry, Dwight Gooden, Mike

Schmidt, Wade Boggs rookies. They were stacked in the case, but afterthoughts. No, there were at least 15 cards in heavy glass that were single-laid in just the way Jason wanted them. That being the Mickey Mantle rookie, Ty Cobb rookie, Hank Aaron rookie, Roberto Clemente rookie, Sandy Kofax rookie, every single major rookie card, graded. And next to the Mantle rookie, Babe Ruth. Jason had a freaking Babe Ruth 1933 Goudy Gum. This was almost the holy grail. "I don't have a Honus Wagner, *yet*." It was intoxicating. Jason's secret baseball card collection was the most amazing thing I had ever seen.

Over the next weeks and months, we started hanging out more with Jason's dad. My mother couldn't stand Jason; she thought he was obnoxious and compared him to "Eddie Hascal," she said, because of the way he asked her for things. It was always a party at his house, and we ran over to mine to switch tapes from time to time. He started to get used to it; it was business for both of us. He was renting and selling my tapes to some older kids I wasn't friends with, so we were seeing more money. Jason's family moved into a new house they bought a few more blocks away, which was much nicer than the rental. His new room was a suite, with an outer room with built-in shelves and an inner bedroom. All our tapes and his baseball card sealed sets now adorned the shelves; the secret case, however, was always hidden on his closet floor.

Jason's father soon started taking us to themed arcades in Miami called Pirates, which had a pizza stand and were packed with people from all walks of life. He instructed us to wait while he entered the back office as we made our way in. He would then appear in a flash, handing one of us a burlap sack. The sack was so heavy to carry that it must have contained at least $200 in quarters. While Richard was at work, we played and ate like kings for hours; Jason ordered a big pizza, and we had infinite quarters. We frequently performed this twice consecutively at two Pirates arcades. I had no idea, nor did I care, what Richard did while we played.

One time, however, there was one area in the back of Pirates that was kind of a DJ booth, so it was noticeably exposed. I happened to glance through the plastic, and Richard was in there seated, counting a mountain of cash. There were stacks in front and a huge pile beside he combed through, separating bills. I assumed it was money from the arcade, as it was well-known he owned all the video games in Pirates.

Richard also took us to the James L. Knight Center, a Hyatt Hotel in Downtown Miami, several times. Jason told me his dad "promoted fights" there on Closed Circuit TV. The "Superfight" between "Sugar" Ray Leonard and "Marvelous" Marvin Hagler may have been at Caesar's Palace in Las Vegas, but if you wanted to see it in Miami, you had to buy a ticket to the Knight Center. There were

3,000 people there going crazy watching the 12-round war on giant movie screens. Jason lost his mind when Ray Leonard won the split decision and the Middleweight Title.

A few months later, as time went by, Jason's dad bought the hottest place for kids in all of Miami, Hot Wheels Skating Center, a roller-skating rink in West Kendall. It was a freaking palace. Hot Wheels had a huge rink with disco lights and a live DJ, a massive arcade bigger than any Pirates, and a café that had pizza, burgers, and good ice cream shakes and sundaes. I wasn't the best skater, but I learned fast so I wouldn't look like a loser. Older kids from all over Miami poured in like crazy.

It didn't matter that we had the run of the place, free tokens, and all-you-can-eat pizza. We were still young, and the older, pretty girls were all with boyfriends who had cars. Eventually, we started going on Monday after school, when it would be nearly dead. Jason liked it more packed, and I liked the quietness and feeling like we ran the place again, but now I realize Richard wanted to count money from the massive weekends. He would bring the deposit bag out and put it in the trunk of his Porsche, which I had to squeeze into the back of while Jason rode shotgun.

I had never cared about how Richard did all these things until suddenly, he disappeared. No one asked, and no one talked about it. Then, one day, the Miami Herald carried a story about a massive marijuana operation that had been busted. The article detailed the multi-million-dollar empire, which was washing money in arcades and other ventures. And there it was, the kingpin of the whole thing was Richard.

Everyone was talking about it, and my mother forbade me from hanging out with Jason anymore. I was so pissed. This was my best friend, my partner in our tapes and baseball cards; he was like my brother. And now we were banned. We tried to work around the ban, but she demanded I be home from school every day. We had spent nearly every weekend and every day after school day and night together since his first day, and now our relationship had been suspended. I resented the shit out of this, and now on Friday nights, I was home, watching movies by myself or with my little brother. Over time, Jason and I seemed to grow apart, and I had lost my match. I missed him and his family. I now knew what Richard was involved in, but they were always so great, and I really didn't care. It was what it was, and my friend was gone. I felt alone and didn't want to be at my parent's house that summer.

There was an alternative for total freedom again. The sun-washed avenue called Ocean Drive is one of the most famous streets in the world. In the summer of 1989, I moved into The Eastern Sun, my father's nursing home that he and our family had created out of my grandmother's beachfront motel ten years earlier.

Time passed slowly at The Eastern Sun, making it a very interesting place. About 40 elderly people, a few of whom were still married, occupied 20 apartments, in both single and double occupancy. Numerous Holocaust survivors lived there. Some of them had Alzheimer's disease and various forms of dementia, and their children had essentially abandoned them. They were rarely visited by relatives.

My father was going through a very creative period in his life since divorcing my mother. This included living in a commune in Coconut Grove and experimenting with all kinds of things. He was having fun and living freely.

At the time, my dad was working on his music and running the ALF with my grandmother at his back. The Eastern Sun was really a magical place. It was 24 hours a day, with something always going on, always staffed with some level of our people.

Firstly, when I was staying with my father, I would wake up early and go downstairs to meet Chef Max, who was a fun and sweet guy. Max would pull out two massive pots in the kitchen, and we would make giant vats of Cream of Wheat and Quaker Oatmeal. Then, he would poach and make 40-50 scrambled eggs so they could be served to the residents who were allowed to still have them. There was challah bread that was delivered by a Jewish bakery in the area that we would slice and give toast to those who desired. They ate in the dining room, many of them dressed up in suits, sports jackets, dresses, anything they considered their fine clothes.

After breakfast, they would go and sit down and find a place to rest for the mid-morning. In many instances, we brought out the bingo game and handed out cards, got on the little handheld PA system, and called bingo to the residents. Sometimes, when my sister Janna would visit, she would bring her girlfriends, and they would put on whatever performance they were working on in their dance school for the residents, who just sat there smiling in their chairs. I would bring some of my VHS tapes that were great movies, certainly not the wrestling stuff, and put them on for them to watch. The Wizard of Oz, Star Wars, Jaws, The Empire Strikes Back, and Raiders of the Lost Ark – all the movies that I really loved.

I played them in the den, which had seating that had heavy plastic over the couches for those who were incontinent, sometimes in the afternoon and in the evening, and they sat there simply enthralled.

I didn't realize it at the time because it was a family business, and I was living there and getting to do what I love to do all the time (roaming the streets of South Beach, going to the beach myself and swimming, wakeboarding and body surfing), but it was in fact, scheduled work. I woke up early, made oatmeal, fed residents, and provided entertainment for them. At one point in the summer, I said that I was working for free.

My dad told me he didn't have money to pay me, but he would do something that I wanted to do later in the summer if I could put it together. I told him that I wanted to go bass fishing on Lake Okeechobee, which he agreed to. We actually did drive up there, stayed at a dingy motel, and were awakened at 4 a.m. by a talented, redneck bass captain who took us out on his boat while it was still dark. We cast live shiners out, and we were catching monster bass, some of the biggest I'd ever seen.

My dad was always so into whatever he was doing, whether it was hanging out with his friends, his music, or whatever woman he was seeing at the time (there were many of those), and good weed. Sometimes, he would go to Jamaica for days at a time, and I was there at The Eastern Sun. When I was by myself, I felt comfortable with the staff, who treated me very well; everybody there was very sweet.

My dad lived on his own terms, without regret, just showing me his example that way. Being with him, it was always an 'anything can happen day.' Creativity abounded, and when we were together, Janna, he, and I had great fun.

My stepfather, a different type of man, also taught me through his example, which was through a contrasting lens: how to shave, tie my tie, and dress like a preppie. He took me to Brooks Brothers and bought me a suit, expecting me to dress appropriately for special occasions. He was an attorney in Bay Harbor Islands, and even though he didn't have much fun doing kids' stuff, we sailed on his boat, which was very adventurous. We had dinner at the table like a family where he called Trivial Pursuit questions while we ate, and it was just a different scene in their house than in my dad's wilder world. Both experiences yielded very unique perspectives.

That was the end of elementary school and a lot of innocence; as we started teenage years back then, you had to grow up very fast. In junior high, they were already partying and having sex, and my sister's friends were two years older and were always around our house. I saw how the older kids behaved.

Being a freshman at Miami Beach Senior High, you were thrown headfirst into the deep end of the pool. The seniors there were already adults; everybody had their own car. Immediately, the pretty freshmen girls that we thought were in our league started dating older guys with cars. From what I had seen from my sister's experience, it was clear that it wasn't going to be easy to get a car in 10th grade unless I earned my own money, as usual.

I was never ever able to replace what I had with Jason, but I did have another friend who had been close to me my entire life and was in a similar situation with his dad. I had been friends with Israel, or Isy as everyone called him, for most of elementary school and junior high, and now we were all freshmen. Isy lived in a gigantic mansion on North Bay Road, much more so than any rock star fantasy house. It was the Maharaja's house in Miami Beach, 50,000 square feet, and the first time I slept over there, I simply couldn't believe it.

Isy's father was a wild and crazy Peruvian man named Zigmundo Markevitz, who went by Ziggy. He was very rarely there, just like Jason's father, and when I went over to Isy's house as we started to get closer in ninth grade, it was literally the home of a Bond villain.

The kids lived in the former servant's ward, which was the northern wing of the mansion. It was the shabby part of the house, on the other side of the kitchen and the Butler's pantry. We mostly played Nintendo games in the children's wing because we were never allowed to pass the kitchen. Fortunately for us, we grew more ballsy, and when his dad would travel for weeks at a time, we ventured over to the other side of the house.

There were huge, luxurious rooms that no one ever used. They were just showplaces for all of Ziggy's riches. One time, I guess really boldly, Isy said, "Do you want to see something crazy?" and I said, "Of course I do," so we went across the polar bear, cheetah and leopard skin rugs, past the marble floors, incredible tapestries, paintings and sculptures and a $100,000, 30-foot-long table from China that no one ever ate at, into a side of the house where there was a wall with a keypad on it. Isy punched in the code, and a door opened like something on a military base. We entered his dad's space-age office, which looked like Tony Montana's from Scarface. He had an exact replica of the Resolute Desk that was used by the President of the United States in the center of the room.

Then we went up the back stairs of the office to his dad's palatial bedroom. Isy explained the bed was a California King, which I had never heard of before, but it looked like six people could sleep in it.

Ziggy had a locked drawer, and Isy knew where the key was. He opened it, and I remember it being just like the first time that I saw Jason's card collection, as we laid our eyes on Ziggy's watches. I had never in my life seen anything like it, not in a jewelry store, not anywhere.

Rolex, Cartier, Piaget, Audemars Piguet, Bulgari, Chopard and Patek Phillipe. He had the most amazing watch collection you could imagine. Most pieces, as Isy explained to me, were one-of-a-kind, encrusted with diamonds, rubies and emeralds. The Cartier and Patek Philippe pieces he had were going for $200,000, even at that time. We tried some of them on, and I was absolutely hooked. I couldn't believe how glamorous it felt wearing a Rolex Presidential, being 15 years old, in this massive mansion. I wanted to have my own watch just like it. I didn't need 35 of them like Ziggy had, just 1.

We walked back to the other side of the house, and I couldn't stop thinking about the watches, especially the Rolexes, which I had a personal affinity for. I liked Cartier and Patek Phillip a lot, but I felt like those were much fancier with their leather bands, and I didn't think people would notice if you were wearing one of those versus some cheaper Gucci watch from Macy's. But everyone would know if you were wearing a Rolex. It was clear. So, we talked about it, and Isy mentioned to me that in New York, in Chinatown, they sold all kinds of phony Rolexes that looked just like the ones that his dad had. Isy had one in his room.

His knockoff Rolex was really nice. Isy said he really didn't have anywhere to wear it, "but I got it if I need it." That was always Isy. He was so much humbler than Jason. His dad was abusive, whereas Jason's dad was kind and sweet, so while he had some of the things that Ziggy had, Ziggy never allowed him to wear or enjoy them. It was Ziggy's show, always.

Isy and I decided to look around and see where we could find a fake Rolex because I wanted one for myself, for personal use. I never thought this was going to become a new business for me like the videotapes were.

In the driveway, Ziggy had an Austin Martin Lagonda, which no one in the United States had at the time, a bulletproof Mercedes with curtains on the windows and police sirens, a Rolls-Royce Phantom, a Bentley Turbo R, and many other luxury vehicles for himself, while the maids and kids drove around in a Clark Griswold-style station wagon that they nicknamed 'The Survivor' because it broke down so many times. Ziggy had the finest of everything in the world, and we, on the other side of the house, had the bare minimum. Luckily, he was never there, and there was always loose cash lying around so we could get a pizza, Burger King, or whatever.

On a random day, when his dad's worker was around, Isy asked him where we could get a Rolex like his. He mentioned that there was a Travel Mart near Miami International Airport where he would go and get things for Ziggy all the time, that he had seen Rolexes like that and would take us there. Later that day, we drove all the way out to *MIA*.

We parked the car at a Marriott hotel with a convention center portion of it called Miami International Mart, and when we walked in, it was like a flea market of imported goods. Products from all over the world had been flown into Miami and brought over to that place to be sold wholesale to various retailers throughout Miami.

We came upon one guy who did have a bunch of Seikos and other watches out in front, so we walked over. His name was Abdu, not Abdul, *Abdu*. I said, "These are nice, but do you have any Rolexes?" and he said, "No. No Rolex." I said, "The ones like from Chinatown," and he said, "Oh, those Rolex." I said, "Yeah." Immediately, Abdu cut to the chase. "You have money?" I had $300 in my pocket, which I showed him, and he said, "Come with me, Boys."

We went through a curtain where Abdu kept his stuff behind his little stand, and he pulled a blanket from over about 12 phony Rolexes, which he said "had Seiko guts," and if I didn't swim in the water with them, "they'd last a long time." Immediately, I looked at the stainless-steel submariner. I didn't want to get something yellow gold

35

because my mom would freak out. Abdu asked me for $200 bucks, and I paid him and walked out of there with the Rolex that I wanted on my wrist.

I wore my new watch to school the next day, and everybody was going crazy over it. They had known me to always have money in my pocket and be kind of a businessman, so they assumed that the watch was real. It certainly looked real. Everybody inspected it, and the watch didn't tick; it rolled like every Rolex is supposed to, and I heard, "Wow, this is beautiful" over and over. That was all I really needed to hear.

The next weekend, after selling some of my stuff, including some VCRs and a whole lot of tapes, I also cashed in some of the bonds that I got for my bar mitzvah. I put together about $1800 and went back to Abdu's place in the Miami Mart.

He said, "You back already?" and I said, "Yeah, I want to get some watches." He took me in the back and showed me what he had, and it was clear he didn't have anything new. I spent $1500 buying about 8 pieces out of the 10 that he had. Abdu was over the moon to have that much cash coming at him from a kid.

The next day, I entered my school with all 8 watches in my backpack. I had an eye out for some of the teachers and one security guard who had been so vocal and saying how much they liked my watch before. I asked them to go into their classrooms and close the door, or I met them at lunch and laid out the watches for them. Not only did they not turn me in, but they also looked at what I had and said, "Wow, these are incredible!" Obviously, teachers don't carry around a lot of money, so I allowed some teachers to take them on credit. Another told me to bring their choice back tomorrow, and they'd bring the money.

I charged $200 more than I paid, and by the end of the week, I had sold four of the eight watches for $400 each, which doubled my money per unit. I had recovered my investment and still had four watches to sell.

I also wanted to increase my distribution because I could see how badly people who didn't have a lot of money really wanted one. I started going to the medical building that I went to as a child for the dentist and just walked into the offices of various doctors, lawyers, tax accountants, anybody who would let me in. When they said, "Can I help you?" I would open my little pillow where I had the watches. "I have some really nice Rolexes that are not real, but they're very good quality," that's what I said to every single person who saw them. Immediately, they started calling other people from the office to come out.

I remember the first time a doctor actually left a patient that he was examining sitting in the room to come out and take a look at the watches, and ended up buying one for his son while he still had his rubber gloves on. I accepted a personal check from him because I figured I could cash it right there at the bank right across the street. After a short time, I had sold the rest and was sitting on close to $3 grand. Right away, I wanted to return to Abdu to get more inventory.

The next weekend, I took the bus there, almost 3 hours to get out to the airport, and he only showed me he had one watch left, which was for a woman. I told him I needed more inventory. "It's easier if you pay in advance," he said. "You want me to give you money upfront?" I asked. "I need money; I don't have it to lay out," he said.

I bought the one watch for a lady, and I ended up giving Abdu $1000 more than the payment for the watch. I don't know why I trusted him, but there was something there I could feel instinctively. Usually, you don't trust a guy who's working in a flea market to do anything but rip you off, but I just had a really good vibe from him. He told me to come back on the 10th of the month, which was two weekends from then.

When I returned, Abdu looked very happy to see me. I walked into his back room, and he pulled away the rag, and I saw double the number of watches that he had originally. Different kinds, there were Submariners, GMTs, Presidentials, Datejusts, two-tone, all steel, all gold, some with diamonds. All knockoffs, of course, but they looked great.

REGARDING VICTORY: ADVENTURES IN ENTREPRENEURSHIP LED BACK TO LOVE

With my thousand-dollar credit and another $2500, I bought as many as I could, and Abdu was very kind in giving me a slight discount per unit because I was spending so much money. I think he saw me as someone who was going to keep coming back, as it was already my third visit. I left the Mart with more than 15 watches. The next week, I did the same thing again. Some of the teachers who had gotten watches in the first round told their teacher friends, so everybody was now asking for watches. Some gave me personal checks, some had cash ready, and some gave me $100 today and $100 the next week, taking a month to pay me off. The teachers who were on credit owed me favors, and then there was the straight bartering.

My Driver's Ed instructor, one of the football coaches, told me that for a watch of his choice, he would give me a waiver that I had completed the full course and could just bring the paper down to the DMV. I obliged, and he wrote me a pink waiver, which I immediately turned into a driver's license the day I turned 16.

For my Spanish teacher, I had kept aside a very nice lady's Rolex two-tone Datejust just for her. She said she couldn't pay me, but "maybe I wanted a little help with my grade" because I had really been screwing up in her class. She told me that I was going to get a D that semester, which I had never received in my entire life. Happily, I told her I would take care of her, no charge. She took care of me, too, and wore her new watch the next day and every day thereafter.

When I got my report card, I received an A 3 D in Spanish. I'll never forget my mother's reaction when she saw I had gotten an A 3 D, which was going to be a D 3 D. She had changed my academic grade as agreed but forgot to change the effort and conduct sections.

"Who the hell gets an A 3 D, I had 3 kids before you, and I've never seen anything like this," my mom said, puzzled. I told her not to worry because, after all, I got an A, and colleges didn't look at conduct grades. She didn't argue the point back but stared at my report card and then glared at me with her President of the United States or Lex Luthor look.

The phony Rolex business was the most money that I had ever made. I was walking around Aventura or The Omni Mall with thousands of dollars in my pocket. I bought Edwin jeans, Air Jordan sneakers, and whatever else my heart desired. I also took my brother Kevin with me many times, and we would eat at the nicer sit-down restaurants in the mall when everybody else was at the food court. I wanted to take care of my brother, get him his school clothes, and get him the shoes he wanted, too. He was like my baby. I hadn't really had a best friend like Jason since the demise of our relationship, and was now kind of a loner, maybe because of the fact that I was spending hours on the weekends on a bus when other people were going to games or out on the boat with their parents.

REGARDING VICTORY: ADVENTURES IN ENTREPRENEURSHIP LED BACK TO LOVE

Throughout my journey, I constantly faced skepticism from people who doubted my capabilities. I simply refused to let negativity in. Instead, I channeled it into motivation, striving to prove my worth and be free of much of the bullshit I saw all around me.

Some may see the journey of a teenage boy who took charge of his world as a testament to the boundless courage that lies within young minds. Perseverance, ability to confront major adversity, and commitment to achieving whatever my goals were continued transforming me.

The impossible was becoming more and more real. I was doing exactly what I wanted to do, going exactly where I wanted to go, and being exactly who I wanted to be. At the time, that, to me, was victory.

Chapter 2:
Love Makes a Kid into a Man

The summer of 1997 had passed much like the previous three. I was engrossed in classes at the University of Florida; my days punctuated mostly by hanging out with friends. Trips to Miami were rare, my parents had sold the house and moved to an apartment prior to their relocation to the Berkshires in Western Massachusetts. My father resided in a room above Mango's, which he had lived in since the club opened. The prospect of a possibly vacant hotel room at Mango's seemed my only free option, or I could pay for another hotel.

There was just no place to call home in Miami at the time. I found solace in staying in Gainesville, where I felt in command of my life. Just before my fall term, I found myself in Miami for a few days between semesters. Hanging at Mango's, I visited with my grandmother Florence, who counted money there in the early days.

That afternoon, Grandma gathered her purse early and asked, "Care to join me?" Inquiring about her destination, I learned she was headed to my cousin Blaze's dance recital for her summer camp. Normally, I would have declined, but the allure of time with my grandma drew me in. Our lunches together were always pleasant affairs.

"Sure, I'll come with you, Grandma," I replied, and thus, I accompanied her down to the car, which was parked on Ocean Drive. The dance school, Peaches School of Dance, was in North Miami Beach, about a 25-minute drive. I sat, radio on, as my grandmother smoked cigarettes. Despite being 21, I was still a kid, oblivious to the life-altering experience that was about to happen to me.

Entering the dance school, owned and primarily taught by a talented woman named Leslie (she was called "Peaches" by everyone in her life), we joined the rest of the families to witness the summer camp's final show. My cousin, 8 at the time, partook in two of the roughly 20 performances. Amidst the showcase, a breathtaking girl graced the stage to perform a solo. Mesmerized by her execution, she enraptured the audience, even cradling her two-year-old nephew mid-performance.

Her dance was exquisite, revealing not just her incredible skill but her character through movement. As the summer sun cast its final glow, little did I know that my fate was intertwined with hers and that this moment would forever change my life.

With her nephew in her arms and the youthful energy of the kids around, the scene seemed to radiate an enchanting aura. I learned that this mesmerizing dancer was Peaches' younger sister, and she was 24. At 21, I felt a substantial gap between our ages, convincing myself that any connection between us was improbable. She was too beautiful, too incredible to be interested in me.

Yet, she seemed to think differently. As I headed toward the door to leave, she emerged and stopped me in the hall. "Are you Blaze's cousin?" Turning around, I greeted her back, kids were peering at us, giggling, a sign that something had transpired before this. Here she was, making sure I didn't depart without meeting.

I complimented her performance, expressing how it had really captivated me. Her eyes and smile were amazing, and at that moment, I yearned to kiss her. That was not like me at all. Something I thought would never happen, I felt myself falling for Elida Jarvis, affectionately called "Toops" by the kids and her family and friends.

She gave me her number when I asked, suggesting I call her. That evening, I consulted my 8-year-old cousin for any information I could get. After the obligatory three-day wait, I called her when I was back in Gainesville. We spoke for hours.

Seizing the moment, I asked her out, and we made plans for that Friday. I drove to Miami for our date, my thoughts consumed by her. Carwash, haircut, and a new shirt later, I picked her up from her mother's house in Miami Shores. Dinner in Aventura followed, alongside a movie, my choice, the forgettable "Mimic."

Hand in hand, we sat through the film, humorously regretting my pick afterward. Exiting the theater, thoughts of the lousy film disappeared, and a pressing desire to kiss her took hold. Back in the car, our eyes met, and an embrace led to our first kiss. I was oblivious to the fact that the girl I was kissing would be the love of my life, my future wife, and the mother of my children.

Upon returning to Gainesville, Toops completely dominated my thoughts. We spoke for hours on the phone every night, and the fraternity and social aspects of my initial college years lost their allure.

As an upperclassman, it was time to focus on a major leading to a profession or grad school. However, my chosen major left me dissatisfied as the tech boom overtook America. The world of computers, technology, and stories of burgeoning dot-com startups raising millions and usually led by people maybe five years older than us captured my imagination. I felt the energy of this once-in-a-lifetime period, to be part of the entrepreneurial wave sweeping the nation. Also, back in South Beach, nightlife dominated the scene and the whole area was scorching hot, leading Mango's to start making real money after the lean, pioneering years.

Amidst it all, Toops remained the constant in my mind; I wanted to spend as much time with her as I could. That fall, an all-encompassing love bloomed between us, setting the stage for an unforgettable journey. By the

45

holidays, my presence in Miami outweighed my time in Gainesville, despite my supposed commitment to school.

All I yearned for was to be by her side every day and night. Having a hotel room at Mango's initially granted us the luxury of sharing incredibly romantic nights, even with the pulsating salsa rhythms outside. Mornings were a revelation, gazing at her sleeping, my growing love for her, and the desire to commit to her fully left me breathless. Gradually, I immersed myself in her family life, bonding with her two nephews, Dylan and Zachary, who affectionately dubbed me Uncle Joshy.

The transition from a college student to a grown-up figure happened rapidly, overwhelming at times. A crucial choice lay before me. Older, wealthy suitors constantly pursued her with flashy cars and extremely rich daddies. Yet, their superficial gestures left her wanting. My love for her was passionate, and our connection intense. We mirrored each other's emotions deeply; every touch, every kiss, and every shared moment felt like merging into one.

Leaving her side was always a challenge. Returning to a place I had once yearned for now flipped in my priorities. The next year, we oscillated between Miami and Gainesville. There were instances where my dedication to her led to knowingly procrastinating my schoolwork, and the online support systems students have today were a distant future then. You had to be physically present or risk being out of the loop. My attempts to keep up were valiant,

but a medical withdrawal to reclaim tuition oddly felt
liberating that fall semester. It gave me the freedom to
spend endless days in Miami with her.

A vision began taking shape, a dream of returning to
Miami. We grappled with the reality that a long-distance
relationship had its limits, especially after a year and a half.
A plan was formed one summer day when we were at a
Disney hotel; we would move in together and share an
apartment, a symbol of our commitment. An idea I had
conceived years ago, when I first started working at
Mango's in high school, began to rekindle. I contemplated
creating a career there, a place that had been part of my
life's journey from the start.

With each passing day, the idea of the plan grew
stronger, painting a future where I could be with her
unfettered, no longer restricted by distance or anything for
that matter. And so, as my time at UF faded into the past,
my heart and mind surged forward, driven by love, hope,
and the promise of a life shared with her.

In mid-1999, Toops and I ventured to a property
manager on 163rd Street near her dance studio. This
office managed an apartment building in Bay Harbor,
Florida, the quaint Blue Fountain. We came across a
$900-per-month gem, a charming apartment with wood
floors, a living room, and a spacious one-bedroom with a
canal view.

Mango's had become my workplace, but I didn't yet have the required, provable income, so Toops's check stubs from Peaches Studio qualified us to lease the apartment. Moments like these illuminated the truth: stepping up was more than just posturing as a mature individual. In many ways, I had to become a better man to keep this extraordinary woman by my side. I felt the pressure every day to evolve beyond my college student identity.

We welcomed our new abode at the Blue Fountain, extremely excited. I secured a substantial, no-interest credit line from Rooms to Go, asking my Aunt Barbara to co-sign. With about $7,000 in credit, we went furniture shopping together as a couple. Hand in hand, we picked out an exquisite bedroom set (her choice), a soft king mattress, couches, tables, accent chairs, and a dining room ensemble.

The following day, all the furniture arrived, and within just half an hour, our home was transformed. Her joy was amazing; it was her first apartment at 24, having previously lived with her mother. Once the furniture was in place, we celebrated with dinner and ventured to some stores to look for paintings, picture frames, and decorative pieces for our walls and shelves.

My own wardrobe was limited, mostly college football gear and Nike shorts. In contrast, she possessed a stunning wardrobe of clothes and shoes, and I was content to give 95% of the closet space to her.

I discussed my aspirations with my father at Mango's, which was experiencing the first real peak of South Beach's transformation after early years and growing pains. The rise of lavish hotels like the Delano and Gianni Versace's Ocean Drive mansion nearby, even after his tragic murder, painted a vibrant picture. The hottest clubs in the country were all around us, frequented by celebrities strolling alongside the general public. Paparazzi captured moments that mirrored Hollywood, from Madonna to Sylvester Stallone and Will Smith taking over the dance floors. Smith's hit song "Miami" had a whole verse about Mango's, the "salsa merengue melting pot...hottest club in the City and it's right on the Beach," which became my claim to fame in my last days in Gainesville.

I was drawn to the floor of Mango's rather than an office role as I had in high school when we first opened. In the office, options were limited to desk jobs and answering phones, work I'd done at 13. Desiring financial success over telephone duty, I yearned to join the action on the floor, perhaps trying my hand at bartending for the cash that was sloshing around the vibrant South Beach nightlife scene.

I engaged with Frank H, the bar manager, to go on my journey as a bartender at Mango's. Frank and I agreed on a plan for me to start as a barback for 2 weeks, learning the intricacies of a fast-paced club before assuming the role of a bartender and, eventually, bar manager. I embraced the plan and also enrolled in a prestigious bartender course to rapidly bolster my skills.

Once on the floor, the relentless nature of the business became apparent. The day's rhythm began at 5 or 6 p.m., and the momentum persisted until 5 a.m., followed by cash-outs, breakdowns, and cleanup—on a seven-day cycle. There were times when I didn't leave until 8 a.m., walking out into the bright morning light. At that juncture, Mango's generated less than $10 million, yet my father's financial progress was extraordinary. He had acquired his dream house and cars, basking in his newfound, long-deserved success.

When I would see him at Mango's, he acknowledged my presence with a wink, a gesture of encouragement, as he moved toward his office. On the floor, I was a mere barback and an aspiring bartender, maneuvering through shifts that stretched for 14 hours in the lively open-air nightclub environment. The atmosphere, while electrifying, was often sweltering as I heaved ice, cases of beer, and bottles of liquor, lurking through swarming crowds.

My meals came from the kitchen, and with an eagerness to explore Mango's menu offerings, I inadvertently expanded my waistline, so I switched back to chicken breasts and white rice. Coming home at dawn initially tested our relationship, but the joy we derived from our new home helped bridge any gaps. I maximized my days off together with Toops, ensuring our connection remained strong.

Within a month, I ascended to the role of Mango's bartender. My earnings ranged from $400 on slower days to as much as $800 on better ones—all in cash. Exhausted, I'd leave the cash on the table at home, a visual testament to my late-night endeavors. Eventually, the stack of money grew so large that it became a spectacle. My neighbor's astonishment at the money pile one day was embarrassing, prompting me to discreetly start depositing my earnings in a night deposit box at the bank, incrementally building my savings.

Being a bartender at Mango's had its challenges, as it was tailor-made for young people seeking excitement on South Beach, as many of my coworkers did. This atmosphere, while enticing, also introduced some issues, particularly for our relationship. Toops began to question if she could envision a future with "a bartender." Unsupportive friends cast doubt, questioning the feasibility of our relationship. Yet, Toops reiterated her love for me, the happiness she felt when I was home, and the importance of these factors. Still, it was clear that a decision needed to be made.

As time went on, the repetitive nightly routine at Mango's became second nature. The bartenders began their shifts by retrieving their cash drawers from an upstairs closet conveniently located next to the drop safe. My proficiency in procedures became such that I asked the managers if I could assist in cashing people out, a request they eagerly granted. For them, having a Wallack doing intricate work was a blessing, as they all always harbored concerns about upsetting my father. My evolving role eased the tension.

I transitioned from a bartender's role to managerial responsibilities. Frank intended to promote me to bar manager, and I accompanied him in strategizing ordering from suppliers and inventory/deliveries during the early morning hours. However, I found myself disliking the role. Frank was unhappy all the time, and I didn't want to be in that position either.

As I began attending management meetings, a glaring issue emerged that became my opportunity and direction. Mango's had a daytime operation managed by two individuals: Ron McLane, an older gentleman, and Claudio Carneiro, a Brazilian dancer and actor. The friction between Ron and Claudio was evident. Claudio, a talented choreographer and samba dancer, was popular among staff, while Ron lacked rapport. He was a nice guy, very sweet, but somewhat of a fish out of water. His tenure seemed to be short-lived.

Although the vibrant, 14-hour nights brought me encounters with people like Bill Gates, Harrison Ford, and Wyclef Jean, I recognized the need for change. My relationship with my girlfriend was extremely important, and I didn't want to create problems where there were solutions on the table.

I presented a proposition to Arnie and Mary, the head managers. The plan was to remove Ron from his mismatched role and appoint me as the head daytime floor manager. I knew the procedures inside out and could ensure the smooth opening of the venue, from the kitchen to the bars and cash drawers. Claudio readily embraced the idea, and our camaraderie contributed to its success.

The day came when Ron was let go. Though I felt empathy for him, it was purely a business decision. The following weekend, Claudio and I devised a schedule that allowed both of us to manage the 7 daytime shifts. I proudly told Toops about the change over dinner, explaining that I would now be home in the early evening, enabling us to essentially be on the same hours. Her dance classes ran late, sometimes until 7 p.m., and our new workdays aligned perfectly.

As our routines converged, we found ourselves arriving at the apartment at the same time three or four times a week. Despite the fatigue, we were on the same schedule at last, and our relationship blossomed in harmony with our newly synchronized lives.

Not being able to spend weekends with Toops during the day while everyone else enjoyed the beach or boating was challenging, but we managed. She was also happily spending time with her sisters and her third nephew Jeremy, born in 1999. Her family and the children held a tremendously special place in her heart.

On Mondays and Tuesdays, my days off, everything was carefully planned. We'd begin with a leisurely morning at home, followed by a lunch outing, and then we'd immerse ourselves in various activities such as shopping days or attending special events. This allowed us to make the most of our time together, even if it was on weekdays.

I quickly established a rhythm, recognizing that the daytime atmosphere on South Beach needed a more laid-back vibe compared to the energetic nights filled with Latin music. I started each day by playing albums by artists like Bob Marley, Peter Tosh, and Jimmy Cliff on a loop using CDs and CD players (all we had at the time), creating a cool and inviting ambiance. This attracted people seeking a relaxing lunch on iconic Ocean Drive. Despite being a day shift, we began seeing impressive sales numbers, even during weekdays, with weekends showing a very intense level of activity.

The addition of live bands transformed our daytime shifts into total beach parties. The talented group of dancers and staff members the daytime shift amassed contributed to the instant, sustained success. Arnie, the head manager, was often stunned by the wild scene when he walked in. Our weekend daytime numbers skyrocketed to nearly $30,000 before 6 p.m., providing a significant head start to the evening's sales goal.

Although there were occasional clashes between Arnie and me, rooting from him offering prime night shifts to

54

staff I had trained, I learned to view decisions through a broader lens. The bigger picture involved considering what was best for Mango's, not just my personal goals. This mindset resonated with me strongly, and I felt a deep sense of responsibility for the overall operation.

Starting with a $45,000 salary for the daytime managerial role, it became evident that my efforts were driving sales and amplifying the overall enjoyment. I understood the importance of contributing to the success of the entire team and the business. This perspective guided my decisions, and I began to see myself as an integral part of Mango's thriving ecosystem, responsible for its continuous growth.

My father was very happy with my dedication to Mango's, which was his first priority. Recognizing the commitment and results, I earned a raise to $65,000 per year. This was the highest salary I had ever earned in a job, and along with it came health insurance and various other perks, such as treating friends at Mango's with substantial table comps.

This advancement within the company, coupled with the faith of the managers and my father, inspired me to consider taking my relationship with Toops to the next level. After cherishing and adoring her for three long years, I felt the time was right to gauge her feelings. I turned to Boris, my father's close friend and Mango's cover charge 'door guy', who was renowned for his decades of pawn shop ownership and vast inventory of jewelry and valuables.

I inquired if he had an engagement ring or a diamond I could explore. Boris knew his extensive collection outright and asked me what level of ring, of which I said, "Stunning." Right away, he revealed he had a beautiful, amazing center-cut diamond he brought to show me the next day that made my knees weak, surpassing my expectations in size and beauty. He asked me for $10,000, an offer that was likely a modest reflection of the diamond's actual worth, which I estimated at around $25,000. Considering my financial constraints, I suggested making monthly payments, and Boris, in his benevolent manner, agreed to flexible terms.

With $500 cash in my pocket, I made the initial payment to him and obtained the ring right there, promising to make timely payments every month. This gesture of Boris's, though seemingly simple, held a profound significance. While the diamond could have sat in his inventory forever, it was now a symbol of a future I was eager to embrace.

That night, as I continued to work at Mango's, I found myself with the ring in my pocket and a mixture of excitement and nervousness. Seeking a female perspective, I entered the manager's office where Mary was. Opening the box, I revealed the ring and asked for her opinion. Mary rarely smiled and was hard to know, but she beamed, blushed, and said, "It's beautiful," and her genuine admiration lifted my spirits, confirming my belief that I had the right ring.

Toops and I had just moved from our apartment to a house we rented in Surfside, a remarkable upgrade for just $200 more per month. This new home provided us with much-needed room and comfort. My goal was to eventually purchase the house when finances allowed, but for the time being, we were content renting it.

My optimism was fueled by my progress at Mango's. I believed that with my course, another substantial raise was perhaps only six months away. As I figured out my burgeoning career and relationship, I felt a sense of empowerment and purpose, ready to seize the opportunities that lay ahead.

That night, as we lay in bed together, I mustered the words, "I love you so much." It was one of those enchanting moments never to be forgotten. Then, with a sense of anticipation, I revealed that I had something to show her. I took the ring case from the drawer and hid it behind my body as I crawled back onto the bed. I showed her the closed case, and as her hands covered her mouth in astonishment, I slowly got down on one knee, unveiling the diamond ring.

Overwhelmed with emotion, she couldn't hold back her tears. In a heartfelt moment, I professed my love and expressed my desire to share every day with her. "Will you marry me?" I asked. Without hesitation, she responded with an enthusiastic "yes," slipping the ring onto her finger; our bond felt stronger than ever. We held each other and drifted off to sleep, embracing the significance of our first moments as an engaged couple.

Things had truly taken shape. In a short span, I had transformed from a college student driving down from Gainesville to be with my girlfriend into someone with a shared home and a promising career at my family's multimillion-dollar business. And now, we were engaged and planning a wedding.

This extraordinary time was cherished and savored, but the journey had its share of challenges. The following year, our initial wedding date coincided with the tragic events of 9/11. However, as odd as it might sound, we were relieved that our honeymoon plans were thwarted, as we would have been stranded in Jamaica due to the travel restrictions that followed. We rescheduled the wedding for the following spring, choosing the third week of March, Saturday night, March 23, 2002.

As we faced the financial responsibility of a beautiful wedding, I made the decision to sell the house we had bought. Watching the Twin Towers fall on TV there, I realized I didn't want it to be our first home. Toops's uncle, in his final days, gave her a $12,000 tax-free gift, which she contributed toward the wedding costs. When I closed the sale of the house in Surfside, we used some of the proceeds to fund the remaining costs of the party.

After the incredible wedding, we found ourselves in a beautiful rental apartment in Aventura. With work thriving, our marriage solidified, and our love flourishing, happiness enveloped us. Despite life's challenges and uncertainties, we remained steadfast in our commitment to each other, ready to face whatever came our way. It was a truly amazing time.

Life was wonderful on all fronts, and I don't think either of us had ever been that happy. Around a month after our wedding, Toops woke me up one morning and asked me to make a trip to Walgreens to pick up a pregnancy test. I sprung out of bed like lightning, raced over, and bought three different types of tests. To our amazement, every single one showed a positive result. Just one month into our marriage, she was expecting our son Brett, who would eventually be born in January 2003.

Our journey had taken us to a new and wondrous phase, that of an upcoming new family. I had purchased a house in Miami Shores that we intended to fix up and rent out, which we changed to moving in ourselves and preparing for the baby. When we brought Brett home, our hearts overflowed with joy. We reveled in the newness of parenthood together for two weeks, cherishing every moment.

Mango's continued to be a pillar of support for our growing family, providing not only a career but also a strong foundation. Yet, the demands of the job were substantial. Days off were rare, and at times, working with family could be challenging. Despite this, the bond within our family was unbreakable.

As Thanksgiving approached, my mother, now living in Great Barrington, Massachusetts, extended an invitation for us to visit with the baby. Eagerly, we agreed, looking forward to our first holiday season as parents. In moments of reflection, I realized that falling in love with Toops had been the most beautiful and perfect thing to ever happen to me. Her presence inspired me to become a better man every day, every way. Now, with Brett in our lives, that aspiration extended to our little family as well. With the holiday looming, we prepared to take our baby on a road trip to the Northeast.

Chapter 3:
The Fast Lane:
Amtrak & Hertz

For any young entrepreneur, it all starts with a *big idea*. Big ideas can really be anything: product, service, any kind of business, technology, or innovation. It's that general concept that may enhance some small, trivial thing all the way to an idea that possibly changes the world. Big ideas are always the key to an entrepreneur's beginning, the genesis of the quest. I had my first big idea in 2003 when my wife, who didn't love to fly, and I were preparing to drive to my mother's house in Massachusetts with our 8-month-old baby, Brett.

I remember looking up, at the time, on MapQuest to see how long the drive was and trying to piece together a plan. It seemed like one fleabag hotel after another on the side of the road of I-95 as you got out of Florida, something we just weren't interested in with the baby. Then it occurred to me that I knew of an Amtrak train that ran daily out of Orlando, and it would take us up to Washington, D.C., *with our car*. It was called the Amtrak Auto Train. My wife thought it was a great idea because she, in fact, loved trains. So, I called Amtrak, as it was about 9 in the morning. They said that we had to be in Sanford, Florida, with the car by 3:00 p.m. at the latest so that they could load the car onto the train. We packed up, and I booked a sleeper car for us. We soon left, driving to the Sanford Auto Train station, which was about four hours from our house.

When we got there, the station was very busy. A valet took our minivan, and we watched them put it into a rail car. We boarded the train and asked to have dinner in our room. I took care of the sleeper car attendant with $50 to bring our food in because we didn't want to bring the baby to the dining car and to help us turn down the room early. Brett hadn't taken his nap yet, so he was exhausted. I had some coffee after dinner, so when they went to sleep, I was still up and a little wired.

I was just like, what is there to do here on this thing for the next 16 hours? I mean, I walked down to the bar car, and a few people were drinking. The real action was a movie that was being played and watched by at least 20 or 30 people.

I thought, okay, this is what everybody's doing. Well, it was a crappy TV with even crappier sound. I don't know what the movie was, but one could barely hear it. One could barely see it. And many more people were trying to jam their way in than there was space. I thought to myself, "Amtrak needs to rent DVD players and DVDs" in order to let people just watch movies in the room and enjoy the trip, as I had done in many airports at a company called InMotion Entertainment. The notion really hit me like a thunderbolt, and I started to think about it deeply. Little had I realized that this was a big idea.

I loved the long-distance train trip, but I could see the endless hours wearing on people. Most are used to flying and getting somewhere in two hours. This is 20 hours or more, and I really felt, at some point, the average rider would be like, "Let me watch a movie and break through some of the monotony."

We continued up to my mother's house, and I was making conversation on the rest of the drive, talking about the idea with my wife. She thought it was a good idea too, because my son at the time loved watching his videos on the portable DVD player we had in the car. When we got back, I went to BrandsMart and bought the most high-end Sony portable DVD player on the market as a sample.

With additional feedback from others I trusted, I knew it was a big idea. I decided that I obviously had to contact Amtrak and see if they'd be interested and eventually maybe work out some kind of a deal for us to do this together.

I thought about the first steps and decided that I really needed a very professional business plan in order to be taken seriously. I was 27, and I knew that as a young entrepreneur who had spent a couple of years managing Mango's, I felt like I was pretty seasoned and could do this. I went on Google and searched for 'business plan firms,' and a sponsored link came up called "Growthink," a think tank/consulting firm in Los Angeles made up of a very bright bunch of UCLA Anderson MBAs who did this for a living.

Their business was to receive calls from entrepreneurs all the time with ideas and hear them out so they could hopefully get to the essence of what the idea was. A lot of times, people are wild-eyed with their new concepts, and ideas or visions are all over the place. What these guys would do is deeply listen to you, then hone in and shape your idea into something that they think is a viable business plan while meeting your proposed vision.

They'd give you a quote for services, and after you pay their fees, they'd help craft an executive summary and, eventually, a full business plan with financial modeling. Usually, this meant showing how much money you would need to raise in order to launch the business, get into the market, and get to break even, and, eventually, profitability. And so, they would help you end up with a very professional, impressive business plan.

I started to work with the two main principals at Growthink, Dave Lavinsky and Jay Turo. As I worked with both Dave and Jay, there was just great synergy the whole time. I loved talking to those who were extremely entrepreneurial and analytical anyway, and they certainly fit the bill. They helped me cultivate this baby idea that I had in my head into something much more mature. They'd chip away the rough edges, which would inspire me, and together, we could all see the breakthrough concepts emerge.

Right from the beginning, they loved the idea of renting DVDs and DVD players on Amtrak because it was working in airports all over America on much shorter trips. We soon had a business plan and called the company "Railway Media." I was dedicated to Amtrak and wanted them to see that the service was devoted to them. Once we had a strong draft of the plan, I felt it was time to contact the Railroad.

At the time, Amtrak's CEO was a guy named David Gunn, a talented railroad executive from Nova Scotia. The word on Gunn was he was really brilliant but wasn't a big talker. I decided to send him a letter describing Railway Media's mission to work with him, which went unanswered. I was looking for a window and wasn't seeing it, which was frustrating.

One afternoon, I was home with Brett, who was napping, and I ended up watching a new film that, out of nowhere, was life-changing for me. It hit me hard and shook up my thoughts.

Called 'Startup.com,' which debuted at the Sundance Film Festival in 2001, I watched it fairly riveted. It was from the director of the War Room, Jehanne Noujaim, and was a documentary about two friends who started an internet company in the later stages of the dot-com bubble. The one in charge, Kaleil Isasa Tuzman, ended up being the 'star' of the film as a former Goldman Sachs banker who became CEO of his best friend's startup. Their big idea was to change the way regular citizens interacted with the government, allowing people to pay for traffic tickets, driver's license renewals, and other things online from various cities and municipalities around the country. The first part of the film brimmed with optimism as Tuzman led a financing roadshow to the top venture capital companies in Silicon Valley and New York City, eventually raising close to $50 million for GovWorks.com. They failed spectacularly by the end, but I was overwhelmed by the energy that this guy, Kaleil, had created.

I felt as if I had a strong business plan, and my situation was similar to what his had been in the film. I thought I had to go on a roadshow and raise capital, too, but my product wasn't like his. I wasn't inventing anything; I was creating a service on Amtrak, where there was certainly a market demand for movies. I could get right into business if given the chance, but I wasn't getting a proper response from them. At this point, I assumed they were looking at me as just a solicitor.

Some read about the people they see on FOX, CNN, and CNBC, and they think these people are a world away, when sometimes they're really just a phone call or an email away. I never had a problem reaching out, so I contacted Kaleil Tuzman directly. His energy in the movie had continued to inspire me, and I thought it would be cool if we connected.

I emailed his new company, Recognition Group, which he formed after GovWorks.com failed. Recognition Group was a merchant bank that made small investments in early-stage companies. He would also then go and raise more money for these firms, help them grow, and then exit.

I didn't think he was going to be interested in my business in the beginning, but I was excited when he invited me to come up to New York City and meet about "my very cool plan." I put on my best suit, flew up to NYC, and went to his office on Wall Street. It just felt so different, like I was in another world. Being there, I felt 10 feet tall, and suddenly, I felt like getting through to Amtrak was possible.

Kaleil asked me for $17,500 a month to represent Railway Media, try to help me get a contract with Amtrak, and other advisory services, including financing. He said he would introduce and help me pitch the Company to investors in New York. I didn't negotiate the number. I was young, somewhat starstruck, and felt like once we got funded, it was off to the races.

And so, after shaking hands on our arrangement, I wrote him the first check for $17,500. I had a line of credit on my house, as I had bought it on a very low basis. I resolved to use the second mortgage funds to make the business happen.

Being 27, I was throwing the ball down the field. The whole time I was building Railway, I kept my job at Mango's, giving maximum effort. I did not ever leave my day job because I had a wife, a child, a mortgage, and other responsibilities. Railway Media work was done at night and on days off.

I would always go up and come back the same day because of my wife and son, waking up at 3:30 a.m. and leaving the house by 4:30 to catch a 6 a.m. flight out of Fort Lauderdale on Spirit or JetBlue, landing in LaGuardia at 8:30 a. m. so I could be at the office by 9:30 in New York City. I'd have a full day of work there, a dinner meeting, and then a 10:30 p.m. departure. I was paying a ton of money to this firm and making progress, so I believed, as Kaleil had a very sharp analyst named Isam Walji, whom I became close with, to help enhance the business plan and create a strategy to pitch Amtrak when I was more refined.

Kaleil introduced me to a couple of possible investors and took me to some other interesting meetings and gatherings in the city. Then, one day, he said, "There's somebody big who's interested in what you're doing, and he wants us to meet him today." The meeting was at the legendary 'Sky Club' in the MetLife building on Park Avenue.

For someone from Miami who hadn't spent a lot of time in New York City yet, here I was in a private elevator to Sky Club, which was full of Wall Street executives and bon vivant millionaires who ate breakfast at 2 o'clock in the afternoon. It had a beautiful buffet, fresh flowers everywhere, and a busy bar. We were there to see a man named Jeffrey M. Nugent, rock musician Ted Nugent's older brother, who had just left as CEO of Revlon, Inc. It was staggering to think his last job was leading a multi-billion-dollar company, where he had just signed Halle Berry as their spokesperson.

So, we all sat down, and I started to talk to Jeff, who I thought immediately was a great guy. I had my portable DVD player and put really good headphones on him. I then put on the best scene from Braveheart, the Battle of Stirling, and he was going crazy. It was clear that Nugent was not just into the movie; he was way into the experience, too. When he pulled off the headphones, he said, "I didn't even remember that I was here." Seemed like a great sign.

He actually then came back with us in the cab to Kaleil's office. All the while, we talked about Railway Media, Amtrak, and the business plan. Here I am, this guy from Miami paying these people to help me with my thing, and suddenly, we're talking to the former CEO of Revlon.

When we got back, Jeff went into Kaleil's office with him and closed the door. They came out 20 minutes later, and Jeff shook my hand, said he'd be in touch and left.

Kaleil glared at me with this perplexed look on his face and said, "Come in, I need to talk to you." I went into his office, and he blurted out, "I don't know what's going on here, but Jeff just said he wants to be CEO of Railway

Media." To say I was shocked was an understatement. The former Chief of Revlon, a multi-billion-dollar Fortune 500 executive, wanted to be the CEO of my startup.

Kaleil then said there was no way we couldn't raise money now if he was involved. "Now that I have him, we're going to get funded, and we're going to start to execute." Tuzman boasted. I just couldn't believe it. The risk of paying the fees had paid off!

I went back home, and I told my wife about what happened. She thought it was amazing, too, but with all our family and baby responsibilities, it just seemed like a world away from her. She was very busy with our son, who was nursing. Brett was a great baby but was very needy at night and often slept with us in bed. With the 24-hour feedings and fewer quiet moments alone, there was only so much time I would take discussing these crazy things at home.

I came up with a stock structure giving Nugent a big chunk to incentivize him to take Railway Media to the moon. I also decided to give Kaleil 10% because I wanted him involved too, mostly for fundraising. It was as if this fantasy of mine was coming true. We started talking to several wealthy investors, and a lot of people were interested. We also started to have business brainstorming sessions where Jeff led the meetings, and it was just a different world. It was my big idea, I was the founder of the Company, but Jeff was in charge.

We got connected to people at Amtrak, and David Gunn began responding to us. He finally delegated Amtrak's Chief of Customer Service by the name of Matthew 'Matt' Hardison (who is still a great friend) to work with us and explore the opportunity.

Matt and his staff asked us to come down to Washington, D.C., and meet at Amtrak Headquarters in Union Station. We took the *Acela* First Class from New York down to D.C. and met with them in a kickoff meeting. We started to talk through some of the logistics of what we wanted to do, and it was clear Amtrak operated as more of a government organization than a for-profit company, which irked Nugent right away.

I told them that we should probably start on the Auto Train because it was a nonstop train that everyone was overnight on. We said it would be a perfect opportunity to see the feasibility, as we were still far away from putting together a national contract where we could roll the thing out. Matt concurred.

Things seemed to be moving along, but one day soon, back in Miami, I got an email as my wife and I walked out of the supermarket with Brett sleeping in his stroller. I just wasn't ready for this one, with a car full of groceries on a rare day off. The email was from one of Matt's staff, Leonard Jeffords, and the main text of the note had a link in it to click with a subject line that read, "How is Jeff Nugent going to do your company?" The link then directed me to an online press release by a company called Insight Pharmaceuticals, which owned brands like Nix Lice and Bayer Aspirin. It announced that Jeffrey Nugent had just been named president and CEO of Insight Pharma and was set to grow and expand the Company. He certainly hadn't told me about it. Maybe he didn't think it was going to happen. I had spent countless hours scheming for his management to lead us, and now that seemed to have evaporated.

I called Nugent on the phone, and Jeff said, "Josh, I'm sorry, my friend. Your thing is awesome, but this came, and I have to take it. I'm out." I had this sick feeling in my stomach. My star CEO had bolted.

That same night, Brett had a pretty bad round of colic and a lot of gas. My wife was so tired and asked me to take him for a walk because sometimes the night air helped him fall back asleep. I put his blanket over my shoulder, picked up the baby, and took him for a walk around our block a few times. It was 2 a.m. when we set out.

I was burping him, and he went back down; meanwhile, I was thinking about what to do. While I was clearly the founder, I had painted myself in the background while Jeff Nugent was the front end. Now, that dynamic was dead.

I just looked up at the sky, and it was a dark night with a lot of stars that were shining very brightly. I then said to myself, "Man, these stars have been around for billions of years, and I'm only going to be here in this little world for maybe 85 years. My life is so insignificant, meaningless in the grand scheme of things. We really are just ants on a rock, traveling through space. Why should I be afraid of anything? Why should I be afraid to do anything in this life?"

It was a true turning point, as that night, holding my baby, I decided not to be afraid, not to be in the background any longer. The next morning, I replied to Leonard and said I knew about Jeff, which was not true. "I just wanted to let you know that I am now the president and CEO of Railway Media." And I pressed send on the email.

I didn't know what was going to come back at me. I didn't know if they were going to reply with, "Well, that doesn't work for us anymore." I was terribly anxious to see their response. It turned out that Leonard wrote back to me pretty quickly with Matt cc'd on it, and the subject line said, "Thank Goodness."

"Thank goodness that you're the CEO, Josh, not the big Fortune 500 guy. You've been the driving force the whole time." I was emboldened beyond belief by their confidence in me. From that moment on, I was the boss; I'd be the one at the helm no matter what.

That helped me to really understand, from a corporate standpoint, what *being a driving force is*, because in any company, they're always the key person. I officially became the president and CEO and went up to Union Station the next week. I told them exactly what my battle plan was going to be. I'd share what phase 2 would be if the Auto Train pilot was successful after further time in the field. Strangely, I was really interested in the long-distance trains that ran out of Chicago to the West Coast, full of tradition and Americana. I felt like there were a lot of people on those trains who would want DVD players and movies, too. Then, of course, there was the massive Northeast Corridor where all their traffic was. D.C. to New York and New York to Boston were both three and a half or four hours. So, it was a perfect time for a movie with either one of those.

I told Kaleil that I was going to end my advisory services at Recognition Group because Nugent was out, and it was clear that I was going to be in charge of raising the money myself. Frankly, I hadn't seen any action from them since Jeff had left. I figured they lost interest after that because they were going to use him as the catalyst to get the money. The parting was amicable, and afterward, I remained in touch with Isam.

I spent hours scanning the internet, looking for different opportunities and direction to raise money, and came upon a story about a baggage handler from Tacoma, Washington, named Bill Boyer, who had invented a new, revolutionary portable media player. Called *digEplayer*™, the movies were preloaded onto the device's hard drive. It was the first player the Hollywood studios approved because of the encryption that it had on its firmware, where the content couldn't be pirated or stolen. At the time, DVD was still king, so this was state-of-the-art.

Boyer invented the digEplayer while working for Alaska Airlines, where he sold his units for their market debut. Immediately, it was a big success, and he was already doing really well when I got in touch with him. Bill was a very nice guy, and he revealed he had just completed a 100% sale of his company to an aviation parts conglomerate called Wencor. He mentioned the CEO of Wencor was a multi-millionaire who was very into in the inflight entertainment space and that he might be interested in talking to me because "they were looking for other opportunities to roll it out." So, when I hung up with Boyer, that's precisely what I did. I called Wencor and spoke immediately to their CEO, whose name was Brent Wood. It turned out they were located in Springville, Utah.

Brent loved my story right away and asked me to speak to his in-house attorney, Eric Vernon. Apart from getting his law degree at BYU, Eric was also a Yale MBA, and I liked his demeanor. I asked if we could get together in New York City and talk about my business plan.

I decided to overwhelm them with Gotham sophistication. In many instances prior, I would have meetings in the lobby of the *Waldorf Astoria Hotel*. I'd go to the 2nd floor, set up a meeting area with chairs and a table, and take care of the doorman so no one would bother us.

My people would come in, they'd sit down, and we'd be having a meeting in one of the finest hotels in the world, and it didn't cost me anything.

It was great, but this was a different animal. I was obsessed with securing Wencor as an investor, a strategic partner, and getting the digEplayer for Railway Media. So, instead, I rented what they call *"The Chairman's Office"* in the legendary *New York Palace Hotel*. This used to be Joe Kennedy's private office, and it was a truly awesome place. It looked like the library from the Clue Mansion with a large fireplace. I think it cost me $1700 for a couple of hours. I asked them for a huge, roaring fire and for it to be dark and intimidating. Jeff and Isam were also there for backup as friends. We were waiting for Eric and Russ from Wencor to walk in.

I had positioned myself with my back to the door holding a novel, like Moby Dick or something that was on the wall, and was just reading whatever random page when the guys opened the door. We sat down and began chatting, and it was clear the plan was perfect; they were very taken with the elegant surroundings and gushed about how incredible everything was. We had a great meeting, where I described the Amtrak system and the overall plan.

They told me to come out to Utah two days later. Clearly, things were in fast forward. I felt like I was on my way;

these guys had both a one-of-a-kind product and investment capital.

I flew out to Salt Lake City, rented a car, and drove to Springville, which is a little suburb of Provo. Eric met me at their headquarters first, then he said it was lunchtime and took me out.

As we were driving around, he told me the trip to New York really shook them in a good way, and they were very impressed. He started to tell me a little bit about himself, how it was in Utah, and what his life was like in the LDS Church. He had never tried alcohol, cigarettes, drugs, or even coffee in his entire life. I felt like a complete degenerate in comparison; it was quite a cultural shock for me. I was very interested in listening and learn from Eric what it was like to be part of the Mormon Church out of both respect and curiosity. One thing was certain, though: despite any differences, the executives at Wencor loved to make money. We surely had that much in common.

Coming back from lunch, we walked the entire operation, and there were hundreds of people working. Essentially, they were like a one-stop online shop for airlines all over the world that needed thousands of different parts to fix their planes. Brent also had offices in 6 countries, including one in Miami, which I thought was really cool.

It was clear that they all liked me right away, and they were interested in the company. I continued explaining my plan, that we were going to get a contract with Amtrak for the entire national system and would begin by opening two kiosks in the Auto Train stations and start renting digEplayers there.

Eric then said, "If you can do that, I think Brent would really be interested in doing something with you." So, we went into this large conference room for the big meeting with Brent Wood.

The funny thing about Brent was, when you met with him, you also met with 10-15 other people too, as he always surrounded himself with his executives. When I entered the room, he had his president, his lawyer, his son, his VP of sales, and at least a dozen others waiting for me.

It was clear Brent was very high on buying digEplayer and was enthralled with everything I was saying. "Here's the Amtrak system," I showed them all on a large, system-wide map, "It's the entire country; people are riding for an average of 15 hours, and they have nothing to do."

It hit me like a thunderbolt: I was now the guy from *Startup. com.* I was sitting in this room with strong capital. I had brought these guys to New York City and sold them on the big idea, and here I am, closing the deal at their headquarters in Utah. I then laid out what was a gigantic investment and strategic partnership for Railway Media.

Brent smiled at Eric, nodded, and then said he had another meeting and left. I got the message, and my heart was racing. Eric turned to me and said, "Well, I guess you got your backing. Go forth, go for it." Unbelievable!

All the things that had to be done operationally to actually start up were in my head for over a year. Now, I had a checkbook and was to submit all reimbursements to them. I was to create an invoice every two weeks with receipts, and they would fund it. So immediately, as I drove back to the airport in Salt Lake City, I called Jason Sobel, my best friend during college. He was working as a bartender at a hotel in Miami and had previously worked for me at Mango's.

I said, "I have a real job for you. I'm going to make you a vice president of my company. I just got venture financing!" We talked about it for a couple of minutes, and then he walked right over and quit his job on the spot. I really needed him there with me to bounce things off, so the next day, we got together at his house; I was on a mission and was bringing him with me.

I negotiated a salary for him of $55,000. Jay, at the time, was just making tips as a bartender, so $55,000+ benefits a year was his first real salaried job. Brent had asked us to go down to the Wencor building near the Miami International Airport, and in retrospect, we maybe should have taken some free space there, but there wasn't a whole lot of room. Instead, we signed a cheap lease close by and started setting up our office.

The first thing we did was get a large whiteboard, as I always do everything with one. It helps me to get everything out of my mind, like a data dump. Then, I can organize all of my thoughts into outlines and action items. You need to get raw thoughts out of your head and write them out before you can start really prioritizing them, especially with other people also giving valuable input. This style of brainstorming I have always found to be the most synergistic and collaborative.

We did everything that first day to create a full plan; it was Roman numeral one, Roman numeral two, and all these different subheadings of what we needed. There were paychecks, bank accounts, cell phones, a website, email addresses, legal for the Amtrak contract, a travel fund process, credit cards, and so much more. So, we put down all these issues and transcribed everything that had been in my head and the business plan for so long onto the whiteboard. Then, we just started to pick them off, one at a time. This was now a Company.

For payroll, I remembered someone I'd met in the 'employee leasing business.' I had heard this was a really good way to compile payroll, insurance, withholding taxes, all these different things together, as we didn't have the infrastructure to do it manually.

I brought the guy over, and he gave me his pitch. We contracted his service right away, and within one day, the Company had a solid backbone that could hire properly with full payroll and benefits. At the time, I hired a 3rd employee, Adam Roth, who was a dear friend. He was also doing another job that he didn't like either, so we got his good energy going. I had another friend from college, Adrian Johnson, who was a brilliant technologist; he was going to work on the website and other software we would need. We began to build a fabulous website we kept behind a password.

All this time, I relentlessly pursued a contract with Amtrak, who was finally ready to do the deal. The President of the United States, George W. Bush, had appointed a man named Floyd Hall to the Amtrak board of directors. Hall was another guy like Jeff Nugent; he was the former President and CEO of Kmart. Bush put him on the Board of Directors to help Amtrak commercialize better and look for opportunities to make revenue.

I thought it was perfect and decided to try to meet with Floyd Hall. It turned out that he was a big ice hockey guy and owned his own hockey team and ice arena up in Montclair, New Jersey. I contacted Hall and told him I had a big idea for Amtrak and wanted to come see him. He told me to come up, so I flew to Newark, rented a car, and drove out to his arena.

Our meeting was stellar. I put the digEplayer in front of him, just as I did for Jeff Nugent, with a great pair of headphones. He turned it on and started going through it. Immediately, he saw the whole shebang.

Guys like Floyd Hall get the whole picture in seconds. *"Video on demand, huh?"* he smiled brightly, impressed at the device. I said, "Yeah," with a confident grin. Then, he put the headphones back on for a few more moments and then took them off. He glanced over and threw me a look that said, 'You did it, kid.' He smiled again, and then he continued playing around with it some more. I had demoed the digEplayer for a lot of people, but never saw anyone as into it as Floyd Hall. I took it as a great sign.

I received an email from Amtrak four days later, saying that they were ready to have a meeting to talk about the contract. Floyd had called them up and slammed his fists on the desk for delaying the opportunity. Apparently, they assured him they were going to bring me in to try and make the deal.

I thought about who to hire as an attorney. I had looked at the former Secretary of Transportation of the United States under Bill Clinton, Rodney Slater, at a prestigious D.C. firm called *Patton Boggs*. Jay thought Secretary Slater would've been the best attorney, but it turned out that he wanted $10,000 a month to be more of a lobbyist, and I needed an attorney to simply negotiate the big-time contract. So, I went to see a second attorney, who was a very strong guy from the law firm *Latham & Watkins*. His name was Rick Bernthal, and he had worked for President

Reagan as a younger attorney. He was well-known in business and transactional law in Washington, D.C. I hired Rick, and I believe the retainer I gave him was five grand. I was well aware of Bernthal's reputation, and I believe he gave me a break on his typical retainer ask because he thought it was a very interesting deal to work on.

I liked Rick; I felt like he was the one who was going to help me get a signed contract. We had our meeting at Amtrak, and as we put together the framework of a 5-year deal, I watched closely how Bernthal negotiated with them. He said what he wanted very calmly, and then he just crossed his arms, made a face like stone, and didn't even blink. He didn't say a thing until they either agreed to or countered each point, if needed, he'd defer to me, and then, in unison, we'd come to a compromise. Bernthal was masterful, and it wasn't long before we had a fully executed contract between Amtrak and Railway Media.

I hired a kiosk company to build two units for the Auto Train endpoints. They fabricated the kiosks, installed the first in Lorton, and then drove to the other station in Sanford and installed the second. We used QuickBooks POS, which was tied into our QuickBooks accounting software. Adrian, who served as our Chief Technology Officer, found an equipment rental program we could buy a license to for $10,000. Then, he used his coding ability to go in and modify the program just for us. It worked perfectly within our POS system so that we could scan a barcode and know exactly which digEplayer it was, what content it had on it, who was renting it, and what the credit card number was of the customer. It was perfect.

The *Auto Train* pilot was great, especially since we began during the holiday season. We hired people on both sides and launched the program, and even with some technical glitches we debugged, each kiosk rented every player it had on the first day.

Day 1, we had 170 players out at $25 each. That was $4,250 for our first day. Then we began adding extras. If you wanted an extra pair of headphones, we gave you a splitter, which allowed two people to watch the same film. That was an extra $5 for the splitter and $5 for the 2nd headphones.

It was November 2, 2005, I was 29 years old, Brett was a toddler, and Mia had just been born that July. I couldn't believe I had a wonderful wife, a 2.5-year-old son, and a brand-new baby daughter. I also had a brand-new business that I had started by myself. At the time, I had been away so much with the setup, and the kids were so important to us that I was trying to spend more time with them. Instead of being just a workaholic for a new business, I had to try to run the company somewhat virtually because we were based in Miami. We didn't live in Lorton and Sanford, so I depended on our station managers and regional management for day-to-day issues. I wanted them to be good managers that didn't need micromanagement and overbearing scrutiny. How could anyone grow under those conditions?

Brent was very impressed with the way that things had taken off, and he asked me to come out to Utah and meet him at a hotel to talk. When I arrived, I was told we were there to talk about "mergers and acquisitions."

I don't know if Brent made a specific offer, but he was about in the $5 million range for this thing, and I asked him for a moment if I could use the bathroom. I called my wife and talked to her, and said, "They want to buy the company!" She seemed very excited about it. I said, "I'm going to ask for $15 million because I could take some time off with you and the kids, and we'd nearly be set for life if I get $15 million."

I went in there and threw that number out, but I think I had gone a bit too far with what they were willing to do. If they were at $5 million, I probably could have gotten them up to $7-8 million, but certainly, the 15 was more than they were thinking. We didn't get into a term sheet. After what I had just gone through, I certainly didn't want to just give it away unless it was for a big enough number that made it worth my while. So, I went back, and the Auto Train was still cranking. Everybody was excited. More money came in every day: expansion time, seize the momentum.

I had gone to see locations in Washington, D.C. Union Station, where we picked out this little space in the passenger waiting area for a kiosk, the same in New York Penn, which Amtrak owned outright in the middle of the City. Then, I took the train all the way out to Boston South Station. This was the endpoint of the Northeast Corridor, and Amtrak just leased their area there. So, I had to talk to the company that owned the station that did the leasing, but they seemed interested in giving me a little kiosk for the Amtrak program.

In retrospect, the plan made sense because not only was monster traffic coming through the Northeast Corridor, but people who were traveling between the two endpoints of it via New York had time to see a movie while they were on the train, so it would've turned and burned. We could have rented the same player two or three times a day, perhaps $10-15 for 3 hours.

It would have been great. However, I also had gone out to Chicago because if you looked at the Amtrak route map, every single train ran through the Windy City.

Trains were coming from D.C. to Chicago called the *Capital Limited*. The *Lake Shore Limited* came from New York to Chicago, and from Chicago out west, you had the gigantic Superliner trains that took two days or more to get out to the West Coast. The *Empire Builder*, one of the most famous trains in the system, ran from Chicago to Seattle up through the northern part of the country. The *California Zephyr* went through the Rocky Mountains from Chicago to the town of Emeryville, which is just outside of San Francisco. The *Southwest Chief* ran through the desert from Chicago to Los Angeles. I was really into those incredible lines and their stories. When I went to Chicago to see what it was all about, because we had done so well on the Auto Train, I thought it might be a risk that maybe people in the Northeast Corridor were too busy at work to enjoy a movie, and that we should stick with the model of long-distance trains and the leisure traveler.

The late Fred Nardelli, who ran the *Auto Train* for Amtrak in those years, made sure my national staff was welcome when I brought them to Lorton before the nationwide launch. Everybody worked, and then I directed half of them to put their stuff on the Auto Train, and we rode down to Sanford. After working the next day in Sanford, I took them all back on board, and we rode back to Lorton again.

I then repeated this with the 2nd group. We brought everybody down, and then we brought everybody back the next day. When we were all back in Lorton and the new managers had passed through training, we had one more meeting and a special team dinner together at Old Ebbitt Grill in D.C. Then, everybody flew back to their cities to prepare to open.

On June 20, 2006, Amtrak put out a press release that they were launching the digEplayer nationwide, based on the success of the Auto Train. I had a very high hope for what was about to happen.

I liked the initial staff we hired, even though it was hard to find people in cities where you didn't have operations yet. Some of them were a little quirky, but I like quirky, and all of them loved movies, which was required. It was a very fun job in a new company. And, truly, everybody was excited about it.

We were getting great press, which I kept sending back to Wencor. The *Auto Train* was still doing great business. We would send them expense reports for all these flights, dinners, and rental cars, and we would get a reimbursement check. Everything was solid, and everyone was feeling great about the deal.

We launched the full system simultaneously, and on the same day, started renting players in Chicago, Seattle, Portland, Emeryville, and LA. I hoped that we would have the same success as the Auto Train, but it didn't take long to see that the Auto Train was a closed loop, and there were several new issues, some we anticipated, some we had not. The Auto Train was a system where you got on in one city, and you got off on the other. On these other trains, however, there were 20-25 stops in the middle. Less than half of the people were traveling from endpoint to endpoint. So, how did you deal with people who were getting off in Kansas, Nevada, Oklahoma, or Minnesota and still wanted to rent a player? We put a prepaid FedEx pack inside the digEplayer cases that would come back to us directly. We passed that on as a charge, and I tried to make a little money on the shipping, as the player would be out of service while it was in transit.

We also felt with some of the passengers, it was a slightly different customer than was traveling on the Auto Train. If you're taking Amtrak from Chicago to some small town in coach, you might be paying $100 for the ticket. Some people either didn't have a credit card or they came and looked, and I immediately could see that it was harder to convince a portion of them to rent the players the way we were doing it on the Auto Train, where it was nearly automatic.

Don't get me wrong, plenty of passengers rented them, but it was absolutely clear to me that, day after day, things in these cities were different. I called the other managers and said, "Look, the passengers are not used to this. We have to let them know how great the service is and make sure that we have plenty of movie posters up." We had sent posters to all the different stores of the films we were showing. Also, all locations had players running in the display cases, so people would see what they were getting.

We started having to be flexible on the pricing and on the deposits. We were trying our best to push the service out there, and I asked managers to continually send me pictures of the kiosks. If there was an issue, if things looked messy, if they hung up their posters crooked, I'd try to uplift and train the manager to do better. It wasn't easy to just fire someone and replace them 3000 miles away. Routinely, I drove to Sanford, took the Auto Train up to Lorton, and took the *Capitol Limited* from D.C. to Chicago. Then, I flew from Chicago to Seattle to see the Seattle operation, took a train down to Portland and then rode the *Coast Starlight* to Emeryville and eventually LA. It took nearly a week and a half or longer to tour my stores in one round.

One day, I arrived in Emeryville and met our manager, Glenn, a very nice guy. I walked up to see him for the first time since the *Auto Train* experience, and he was down underneath the kiosk fixing something with his behind up in the air with his underpants coming out of the back. I just thought to myself, "Oh my God, this is indicative of what's going on here."

I said, "Glenn, how many players did you rent today?" I just saw that the *Zephyr* had left.

He said, "Two," and I said, "Two!? Are you kidding me? We have the best first-run movies in the country!"

"Yeah, there were only 12 people that left outta here today to Chicago," he told me.

"What is going on here?" I asked myself. It was clear that people loved to take these long-distance trains in the summer months. But we found that seasonally, during much of the year, a lot of the clientele, save for the sleeper car riders, didn't have the money and credit cards to do this, even though it was the best product. There had to be a better way.

I knew a few things were wrong; I could see very clearly. There was the issue of getting the players back. We would rent a player to someone, they had their shipping bag in their pack, and then they'd leave the player on the train. They said they shipped it, but we never received it. They'd ship it missing equipment, they'd ship it back late, and when we tried to charge their card for additional fees, it would decline. So, there were holes in the system that we were working to solve. I knew some things had to change right away. My thoughts immediately went to augmenting the model. What was Amtrak doing to help us sell the service? We were in all the endpoint stations with fantastic product. Where was the cavalry?

I immediately turned to Amtrak and said, "Look, we're positioned at the key stations. We've rolled out strategically. We can hit all these trains. Why don't you put one of these digEplayers in every sleeper car and give it to the rider free as a premium service? Railway Media can get some sort of wholesale fee, like a voucher program." That was my pivot because Amtrak was our partner, and it was their system and ridership. I tried to get them to take on some of the sales responsibility because, frankly, it was in their best interests to help us, and they could really ramp things up if they wanted to.

Amtrak took a while to consider. They always took a while to do everything. Fortunately, they had brought in a new VP of Products named Emmett Fremaux, Jr. Emmett was kind of like Floyd Hall. He was a very smart guy and a maverick, and he wanted this service to work. He shot a video of himself introducing the digEplayer, which we loaded onto every unit. He was very happy about that, and I asked him to please package us in with the sleeper cars, which he thought was a good idea. However, instead of doing it on the whole system, which we really needed, they started with a beta test limited to *Coast Starlight*, the train between Seattle and Los Angeles. Even though it wasn't totally ideal, I was happy something strategic like this was happening.

Anybody in a sleeper car on the *Coast Starlight* was going to get a digEplayer for free. They would get the unit from us, and they'd fill out a voucher, which we would submit to Amtrak. Amtrak would then cut us a check. A much better model! This started to happen, and it increased the sales in Seattle and LA by 500% overnight.

We were cash-flowing, and things were growing, but still needed modest working capital each month. It wasn't anything that was going to make Brent poor, with the guy sitting on $250 million in cash. We had the Auto Train doing well, and now the *Coast Starlight* was flying, but we just didn't have enough sales yet in those other cities until Amtrak packaged the players in across the system. Emmett assured me that was only a matter of time.

Soon after, Brent's mood started to change on the whole thing. He was having a terrible time in a lawsuit with the firmware provider of the digEplayer, eDigital Corporation, who refused to make more players, and his 2nd generation player, his plan to get around them, was well behind schedule. At one point, they started to email that they needed players back from us for other airlines. It was clear to me the honeymoon was over. He demanded that I "reduce expenses now" while I was very busy growing revenue and doing what was needed to create enterprise sales with Amtrak. I didn't particularly care for the way he 180'd, especially since his eDigital problems were self-inflicted. This was a new business, and I had rolled out the entire country. I had spent weeks at a time away from my wife and children; we had new babies, and I was living on the road, eating at Waffle Houses. I spent endless hours riding on trains to save money, so we were with the customers in the field and could move players around for free.

Some of it was just unbelievable. One story, I was in Emeryville with Glenn, and we said we would bring 40 players to LA for the *Coast Starlight*. We rode down to Paso Robles, where the train stopped and broke down. There wasn't even an Amtrak station there, it was a bench outside of the post office where you sat waiting for the train to come.

There was only one train going through that whole town every day, and it was the *Coast Starlight* going north and going south. We got off, and I said, "Listen, let's just catch the other one going back because we're never going to get out of here. This train's finished. They're going to have to come tow it, and we're trapped."

We had no hotel and no rental car, literally in the middle of nowhere. Glenn suggested we should wait for Starlight, which was 5 hours late. They were just about to shut down the post office, bringing down the roll guard and everything.

It was already 6 p.m. and getting dark. We had been there for hours waiting for this train. The lady said to me, as she was leaving, that the train would be here soon. She then said, "There is also a bus out right now that is going back to Emeryville." I walked outside, where Glenn was sitting on the bench.

I said, "Grab the gear. We're getting on this bus." He said, "No, really? Why don't we wait for the train? It's so much better than that bus. The bus is horrible, and you can get us rooms on the train, Josh. *C'mon*."

I said, "Glenn, get on the bus."

We were tired and hungry. Once on the bus, Glenn passed out immediately. There was nice air conditioning on the ride, and while we had no food or water, I was quite comfortable. The next day, we found out that not only did our train break down, but the other train on the way, the one we were 'waiting for,' had derailed and never even made it to Paso Robles.

We continued submitting the voucher reports to Amtrak; however, we weren't getting paid in what could be construed as a very timely manner. As a public/governmental agency, it took almost eight weeks for them to process requests and send checks.

From a cash flow standpoint, it was very hard to wait eight weeks for a startup company. So, we would wait and then get an $85,000 check or something like that. It was substantial money, but it was still very late, and when you tied it into the money that was already being fronted by Wencor for the payroll and all the other expenses of the company, it was problematic. By the time the checks came in, I felt like Sonny Bono from "*I Got You Babe*", where "before it's earned, our money's all been spent."

Everything was do or die, as is always the case with startup companies, but I felt like we were months away from being packaged into more lines, which would rocket us past these early growing pains. *When the checks were $685,000 instead of $85,000, everything would be stellar.* In business, there are few problems strong profits can't deal with.

One particular manager of mine named Gregg, someone in way over his head, began talking behind our backs to people at Wencor about me and the Company, as disgruntled employees sometimes do. He always asked for raises, loans, and time off, which were often denied. We were not a bank. He would tell me, "Ask Wencor for it," to which I'd say, "No Gregg, I will not." They were my investor, my partner, and my employees worked for me. Yet Gregg had direct dialogue with Wencor about changing content and other things, I realized that communication existed. I couldn't prevent all of what he was doing, and since we were away so much, I didn't quite know the extent of it until later.

One day soon after, when we were home, my son told my wife and me that his heart was "beeping very fast." We were like, "What kid says that?" so we took him to his doctor to be checked out. When we arrived, his heart was beating 260 beats per minute, the doctor had to check three times to make sure his equipment wasn't faulty.

Brett's heart was in tachycardia. The doctor said to call an ambulance because "we didn't want him to die." 911 came, and my wife rode in the ambulance with Brett. I followed them in our car, and I was just hysterically crying. I didn't know if my son had died in the ambulance, if he had had a heart attack, or anything else. I was truly terrified, and I'm not much of a praying man but was asking God if he was listening to please watch over my son and give him a chance to live.

We arrived at the hospital, and Brett's heart was pounding at 265 beats a minute. It was going up, and they took him right into the ICU; they didn't know what was wrong with him. We didn't know whether he was going to make it through the night. I only told a couple of people in my company what was happening because I still didn't know what was going on. That evening, they transferred Brett via ambulance to Miami Children's Hospital in Coral Gables and had a cardiologist there waiting for him in their ICU. They put him on medication, and he was hooked up to all these wires. I was sitting in the room with him because my wife had gone home to be with our daughter, who was still only six months old and breastfeeding.

I spent the night in Brett's room at Miami Children's, and they had him on a whole slate of medications that they thought would help. I remember a doctor coming into the room at around 3 o'clock in the morning; he said to me, "You see, he's doing better." I looked, and he was still at 175 beats a minute down from the 265 that he was at when he came in. It was still supposed to be at 90 beats a minute or, maybe even 120 after a whole football game. He was still in tachycardia, but the medication was starting to help slow it down. Eventually, his heart rate came down to a point where it was back to a sinus rhythm. The doctors didn't know yet what was wrong with him.

Yes, I had a company I was leading. In Utah, I had a partner who was providing funding. We had made what appeared to be a miscalculation by opening up on the West Coast and the Midwest without Amtrak doing the bulk of the sales and us mainly the fulfillment. I couldn't pivot from that immediately, but I had convinced Amtrak to move to where the players were packaged in with Sleeper cars on one train, and we were getting guaranteed revenue. That was growing, and I could see big money within 12 months.

Because it was new, taking almost two months to get that money was also an issue. The manager Gregg, who was at this point engaged in buffoon-like 'sabotage,' I found out later, was extremely emotional, jealous, and greedy, just a horror show of a person. He immediately used my son's cardiac emergency as an opportunity to try to hurt me while he could.

I was in the hospital with specialists in the room with my son when my phone rang; it was Brent and his lawyer. Gregg had unscrupulously set them up too, to call and ambush me in the hospital as I met with the doctors, with my son sitting there with wires coming out of his chest.

I told Brent, who apologized profusely for Brett's condition, that it was ok and that I should have fired this silly person months ago. He had improperly taken probably 25-30 digEplayers home to his kids and friends. Jay and I looked once in his car, and five of them were on the floor strewn like they were junk. He was just taking them home, two at a time. I told him, "Please go down there and bring them up immediately, and tomorrow, bring back everyone you have." He looked at me obnoxiously, like they were his. When he brought up seven players from his car, the other employees were dumbfounded. Here we were, struggling for inventory, and this guy who was supposed to be a manager had seven players in the heat in his car. I should have fired him ten times over.

Nothing was more important than my son and his health. My wife and I were a complete mess trying to deal with it. We couldn't sleep at night and had a baby daughter who needed full-time attention as well. Most days, I'd be coming home from the hospital at 5 or 6 in the morning, and instead of going to sleep, I'd take Mia into the bathroom and give her a steamer.

It turned out Brett had a rare condition called Wolf Parkinson White Syndrome, which required two surgeries on his heart called catheter ablation. His doctor, Ming Young, had performed the procedure around the world and truly saved his life. Brett was healed at Dr. Young's hand, and we could finally rest.

During the long hours of waiting and hoping, and after attending an aviation conference in Miami where I met executives from Southwest Airlines, I created a major pivot for Railway Media. I called it SWA Movies. Southwest didn't offer any entertainment on their flights despite being one of the largest airlines in the country.

I sent them a business plan I made in one week with Growthink, showing the potential earnings and player distribution. The executive in charge of the deal, Angela Vargo, invited me to *Love Field* in Dallas to pitch the idea to

Southwest. They had a consultant helping them decide their next move with onboard entertainment, as they were planning to do something big; I wanted us to be their move. This was a chance to do so by proposing the migration of certain Railway Media infrastructure, assets, and personnel to key Southwest airport locations like Chicago, Orlando, Baltimore-Washington, and Las Vegas.

First, I proposed moving manpower and digEplayers from the Chicago Union Station store to O'Hare (*ORD*). In Vegas, I planned to deliver a nice kiosk to McCarran Airport. There were also big plans for Orlando and BWI, where we had existing infrastructure from the Auto Train we could deploy. I could set up something nearly immediately in all 4 markets.

I formulated a strategy to transition the necessary assets to Southwest Airlines. I brought in Bill Utset, a former Rockwell Collins executive who was experienced in aviation. He worked remotely for me while I paid him out of my own pocket. I advised him to wait until I had the Southwest contract before leaving his current job. I needed his expertise for planning and to show Southwest that I had strong aviation support.

I showcased my ability to quickly deploy resources to the critical Southwest cities using the infrastructure I already had in place. I believed I could make swift adjustments. These cities were key for Southwest's leisure flights, such as those between Orlando and Vegas, serving vacationers traveling from one leisure destination to another. I had this feeling; I was so fixated on this deal. It was like I finally saw a way to big-time, positive cash flow immediately by combining our efforts with Southwest and giving Amtrak time to grow the voucher program.

I felt this was a fantastic plan to right the company immediately. I went to Dallas to meet with Southwest Airlines at their incredible headquarters at Love Field and spent the night in a hotel. The next morning, I was ready to crush it.

The meeting with Southwest began extremely well. I explained our positioning and the presence of our team. The interest was genuine, and they asked insightful questions about pricing and rentals. I suggested that we could offer players for free to those who chose their premium seats in the first year, charging the airline only $5. They found this model valuable, and I felt a ton of positive momentum building. Then, their consultant, a British aviation expert, entered the room, altering the atmosphere. Despite being in Dallas, where people were typically friendly, his demeanor was quite the opposite.

And so, I found myself explaining the plan again to their consultant. I detailed how we would migrate assets from Railway Media to key Southwest airports, showcasing the players and presenting the concept. His response was a single question: "Are you with Wencor, eh?"

I replied affirmatively, saying, "Yes." He let out an obnoxious laugh, rolled his eyes, and that was it. The energy took a sharp turn. I quickly sensed that I wasn't the only one in the room who had heard about the global shortage and litigious situation preventing new digEplayers from being manufactured.

DigEplayer, as a going concern in the aviation space, was riddled with issues, and the consultant knew all about it. He knew they were entangled in a lawsuit they were badly losing with eDigital, the technology's original inventor, and digEplayer XT, the second-generation model, didn't function properly. They had rushed it to market without proper testing, which led to well-publicized problems. The initial digEplayer, the one Bill Boyer had developed for Alaska Airlines, worked perfectly. However, new production was frozen by the litigation.

My sources within Wencor, I had a lot of friends there, had already been indicating that within the whole digEplayer operation, things there were falling apart behind the scenes. So, after a promising start to my meeting with Southwest Airlines, everything changed when this consultant weighed in. His single derisive comment shifted the atmosphere, and I left the meeting with them, promising to get back to me.

As I sat at the airport, my phone rang. Angela was on the line, thanking me for everything we had done but informing me that they would be passing on the opportunity. They had decided to install Wi-Fi on their planes, allowing passengers to watch YouTube on their personal devices. I was incredulous, asking if people would prefer to have a choice to watch full-length movies as well. However, it was clear that the consultant held considerable influence within the bureaucratic structure, and the decision was beyond Angela's control.

The financial reality of the miss was harsh. While the Coast Starlight payments provided some relief, it was not enough to offset until we added more trains. I was also bothered by a betrayal within my team of someone I hired, trained, and paid, and I tried to deal with it amicably; we were involved in so many sensitive business development issues I thought to keep the status quo instead of terminating the person as I should have. The plan to bring Bill on board to facilitate the migration to Southwest had fallen apart.

But as life often does, things took a surprising turn. Sometimes, when you push positivity into the universe, it comes back to you in unexpected ways. Shortly after the disheartening Southwest encounter, a ray of light emerged.

The day I returned from Dallas, an email from The Hertz Corporation appeared in my inbox. The sender, Stephen Maughan, worked under Hertz CMO Frank Camacho. They had been impressed by a letter I had sent, hedging my bets in case Southwest didn't happen, and wanted to set up a meeting to hear my pitch. I responded, suggesting it take place the following Monday. I grappled with the fallout from the Southwest meeting and wanted to put it behind me immediately and capture this new positive energy.

Maughan, a guy almost the same age as me with a young family, was very intelligent and friendly. We scheduled for the following week, and though I was still carrying the weight of the Dallas disappointment, I was eager to see where this new opportunity would lead.

On the morning of the meeting with Hertz, I boarded a 5 a.m. flight, geared up in my best attire for this pivotal encounter. I arrived at Hertz's Park Ridge, NJ headquarters, appreciating the pleasant autumn ambiance. The environment was strikingly different from that of Amtrak. Here, it was a for-profit enterprise, intent on generating big-time revenue all day, every day. Maughan's responsibility was to enhance their offerings. Their "NeverLost" navigation system rented in large numbers, contributing a staggering $380 million in revenue in 2007.

I envisioned tapping into a fraction of that potential by offering movie rentals for families with kids. During our meeting at Hertz, Steve and I acknowledged the impact of backseat entertainment on children during travel. It was evident that this aspect held promise.

After our initial meeting, we took the time to greet Frank, who expressed his gratitude for my presence. He reassured me that I was in capable hands. I showcased the digEplayer to him, highlighting its features. I had even brought a custom backseat mount, a personal touch reflecting my family's reliance on such entertainment during travel.

Both Steve and I reiterated to Frank the positive influence backseat entertainment had on families. Frank expressed great interest and willingness to collaborate. Subsequently, Steve and I sat down in his office to discuss the way forward. He confirmed that the target audience was, indeed, families with children.

In our discussions, it was decided that we would begin with a trial run in one location before potentially expanding nationwide. The trial location would be Orlando. Looking back, I realized that being based in Miami, I might have suggested the Miami International Airport location instead. Yet, at the time, I was content with the arrangement they wanted. The Orlando Hertz location was convenient, as it was a destination my family and I frequently visited.

Around this time, Wencor initiated a recall of more players. They requested our team to return them, further diminishing our inventory when we needed them all and then some. Their digEplayer XT model was still wrought with technical issues and was now a total disaster. Additionally, the legal dispute with eDigital, the technology supplier of the model that worked, raged on. As a result, they were still unable to produce any new players.

The recall action struck badly, further eroding our revenue. Frustration began to boil within me, and I felt that this Hertz deal could be a turning point. To ensure a successful launch with Hertz, I recognized that I needed to engage a partner who could help me present this offering in the best light possible. Disney immediately came to mind.

I reached out to The Walt Disney Studios in Burbank through the non-theatrical department that had provided content for Amtrak. One of their Executives contacted me regarding the Hertz opportunity. This marked a significant step, as I was now dealing with individuals who held tremendous power and influence in the entertainment industry. Speaking to them was an experience that left no room for misdirection. They were absolutely brilliant and possessed a profound understanding of basically everything, often foreseeing things I hadn't even disclosed to them.

In our initial conversations, I soon realized that attempting to be evasive wouldn't serve me well. Rather, I opted for full transparency, openly sharing my plans and aspirations. They appreciated this candid approach, and it established a foundation of trust between us. In my conversation with Andy, the Disney Studio executive, he requested a package containing digEplayers, information about our company, our partnership with Hertz, and some details about Hertz itself. I compiled a comprehensive care package to demonstrate my commitment, ensuring it was shipped overnight to underscore my dedication.

The cost of overnight shipping, approximately $450, wasn't a concern. My focus had shifted to building a successful partnership with Hertz, and this opportunity seemed like a fresh start in comparison to the obstacles I had faced with Amtrak and Southwest Airlines.

The following day, Andy informed me that they had received the package and were in the process of reviewing it. A "go" or "no go" decision would determine the next steps. If the decision was favorable, a different conversation would unfold regarding doing this deal with The Walt Disney Studios. On the other hand, if it was a negative outcome, I would be informed promptly of the pass.

A few days later, Andy emailed me, requesting a conversation at 2 p.m., which corresponded to 11 a.m. in Burbank. I agreed and assembled a trusted team to join me in the conversation. Among those present were my brothers Kevin and Jason, individuals I intended to bring into the new company due to their loyalty and reliability.

When the call came from Disney, we were gathered in a different office I had taken up within the same building to maintain a degree of secrecy around my dealings with Southwest Airlines and Hertz. As I answered the call from Disney, I braced myself for whatever news lay ahead.

Having already been rejected by Southwest due to digEplayer's manufacturing issues, I was uncertain about the outcome this time.

To my wild elation, Disney informed me that they had reviewed everything, gathered feedback from their team, and decided to do the deal with us. My excitement was uncontainable. I held an immense affection for Disney, and their endorsement felt like a soaring victory. Despite the setbacks, this breakthrough with Hertz and a potential partnership with my beloved Disney was a turning point.

Filled with joy, I couldn't help but celebrate. My brother and team members were beside themselves, and I treated them to a celebratory lunch at Mango's. The party was nothing short of legendary. We indulged, consuming six bottles of Dom Pérignon among the four of us. It was a jubilant event, and our exuberance led to us accruing a bill of approximately $6,000, which I had comped. Although we were all worse for wear afterward, it was a memorable occasion that marked a significant shift from despair to elation.

Disney's endorsement signified a rebirth for me. The alignment of forces with Hertz and Disney gave me renewed purpose. However, the challenges were far from over. As we progressed with the deal, the intricacies became apparent. Despite my euphoria, I recognized that the details were paramount.

Disney's willingness to collaborate was amazing, and they expressed their congratulations. In response, I felt as if I had won the lottery. Despite the obstacles, I had Hertz and Disney in my corner, creating an amazingly powerful combination.

Upon further discussions, Disney continued to be excited about the deal. However, I anticipated some sort of content cost, given that Hertz was distributing to their cars and that we were supplying the players. Steve had informed me that Hertz would be renting out the players themselves, not relying on my team this time. This marked a departure from the previous business model. Hertz had an outdated point-of-sale system that couldn't accommodate the integration of our players. Instead, they had a line item for ski racks that was seldom used, mainly in places like Denver.

However, no other major airport utilized the ski rack, leaving it as a blank line. This tactic was used to register player rentals in the POS system. I explained this to Disney and discussed our intention to charge around $15 or $20 for each player per day. The plan was to create a comprehensive service branded with Disney's iconic characters, featuring Mickey Mouse, Donald Duck, and Goofy.

Disney suggested a royalty of 50% of the gross revenue, which struck me as very expensive. Despite expectations of negotiating room, Andy remained firm in his stance. I presented various structures and offers to accommodate a more balanced deal, such as sharing profits once a certain threshold was reached. However, Andy was resolved in his position. I wanted Disney more than anything, but I just couldn't make the numbers work or have another situation with too heavy a cost structure like what was still happening at Amtrak.

Looking at my own kids' preferences, I reached out to Nickelodeon as an alternative. Using LinkedIn, I contacted Nancy from Nickelodeon, explaining our preference for a more competitive offer. Nancy responded positively, expressing Nickelodeon's readiness to be accommodating.

While negotiations with Disney were ongoing, Hertz was ready to sign a national contract with us for the service. Meanwhile, we also initiated discussions with a player company that specialized in devices from the manufacturer Archos, so there would not be any player issues like we had suffered before. Nickelodeon and Disney were both in the running and while Disney was my deep desire, Nickelodeon's willingness to agree to a more competitive share for each party was favorable financially for my investors.

Ultimately, I decided to partner with Nickelodeon and informed Disney of the decision, and we parted as friends, as is the nature of business. I was heartbroken but also excited that the whole deal was moving forward.

We secured a deal with Nickelodeon, and they supplied their content to the Archos players. Branded as "Nick on the Go," the initiative began development in late 2007. The devices were fitted with bright neon orange covers bearing the Nickelodeon logo, reminiscent of the iconic slime image, and had over 40 hours of content.

Despite previous setbacks, I felt so confident in this new venture. Drawing from my experiences with Amtrak, a leaner cost structure and minimal field presence were advantageous. This time, it seemed like the pieces were falling into place. The initial rentals in Orlando soared during the summer, exceeding expectations.

We had around 700 players, which cost approximately $3 million to acquire all the necessary equipment and budget for rollout and implementation. Once we had successfully launched the initiative in Orlando, our entire team was confident that we were ready to expand further. With Steve's support, we began preparing to launch Nick on the Go in 45 different cities.

Each city required us to set up our infrastructure and equipment. This involved installing cable modems and incorporating RFID chips into our players.

Despite the challenges we faced, my determination remained strong. I had heard rumors that Gregg was planning to ambush me and 'take control' of my company. I laughed and just thought he was crazy at that point.

Wencor was displeased that I had deployed a competitor's players within Hertz, though they had taken back nearly every player we had for their stalled business. I firmly believed that I had the right to make decisions in a new company that would benefit us.

I took preemptive action, sending my trusted team members to various locations to retrieve all equipment before any confrontation would occur. In a well-coordinated effort, we collected the digEplayer devices, along with other assets purchased, and shipped them back to Utah. I also ensured that our employees were informed about the situation, providing them with their paychecks and additional severance. A startup isn't a large corporation with unlimited resources. I was a young entrepreneur striving to build a successful venture in a highly competitive industry, and business is business.

Wencor incidentally was happy to get the players back and use them for existing airline customers, and we called it a day. I always had tremendous respect for Brent, who has since passed away. His daughter had a child with special needs, and discovering there was no school for her to go to that was available, he built one for her, staffed it, and brought in teachers from around the country. He was a very tough businessman and a wonderful person and family man. I always appreciated our experience together.

By this time in 2008, my life was increasingly stressful due to the ongoing challenges. My children needed me, my wife needed me, and my dedication to the business meant I wasn't always present. Despite my efforts to provide financial security, I had to acknowledge the strain my absence placed on them.

In an attempt to justify my commitment, I questioned my wife whether my sacrifices could be equated to those of a doctor or lawyer, who often had to work 20-hour days too. However, I realized that the sacrifices I was making were taking their toll on my family.

Toops held my hand and just said, 'Look, this has been going on for so long. Where does it end?' It was late 2008, and Bear Stearns had failed earlier in the year. Our economy didn't seem to be doing well. I told her I needed to take action here because we had Nickelodeon, a brand the kids love, and we had Hertz. Kevin was here with me, and we had excellent people. I told her I loved her so much, and I was going to give it another shot, this time being older and wiser. So, we hit the road again.

We had successfully launched in Orlando, and we had 46 more cities to launch, with only four of us. Each person was responsible for 12 cities. We informed Hertz about the upcoming installations and had appointments set up with cable companies. The coordination and planning were remarkable, and I, along with my brother, Kevin, Bill Utset, and Jason, were on the road once again.

Each person had a designated region to cover. The travel schedule was intense, going to two cities per day. The process was smooth, as we would set up the equipment, train the Hertz staff on how to use it, and then move on. Everything was well organized.

During this time, we alerted Hertz Corporate that they now had the players. Our artwork for Nick on the Go was displayed alongside other Hertz offerings, including NeverLost, on their website, *Hertz.com*. It was an incredible achievement.

We returned after a week and a half with 46 Hertz airport locations rolled out successfully. All the players were in their hands. The devices just needed to be rented out and placed in the ski rack line of their POS, and the money would start rolling in.

Back at the office, we monitored the RFID data on screens, tracking the movement of players. We had no way to gauge the financial success yet, but we watched the players move in and out in rapid fashion.

Hertz ran a national TV commercial for Nick on the Go in the summer of 2008. Things picked up immediately, raising our expectations. However, around that time, the global economy literally collapsed. Lehman Brothers and other big banks failed, real estate values, credit markets, and all of Wall Street plummeted, leading to a massive decline in travel.

The Great Recession had hit hard, causing Hertz's stock price to plummet. The economic situation made it even more challenging for us. I had invested heavily in the venture, as had my father and others. They believed in the potential of Nick on the Go, and the combination of Nickelodeon and Hertz seemed like a winning formula. But now, everything in the US was just falling apart and quickly.

We were witnessing the promising partnership between Nickelodeon and Hertz fall victim to the devastating economic crisis. It was just heartbreaking. The dream I had been working so hard was unraveling before my eyes, and there was little I could do to prevent it.

Overnight, there was just no traffic. People were too scared to travel, and banks were drastically reducing credit limits, taking someone's $10,000 credit card line down to $500. It was a financial Armageddon, all happening during George Bush's final year as president. The Iraq War was ongoing, and the country was gripped by fear. In such a climate, my issues with thousands of dollars in sales monthly seemed trivial when compared to the massive fortune Hertz was losing.

The economic collapse of 2008-09 pulverized everyone everywhere. My home value plummeted, and I was underwater on my own mortgage. The housing market was a disaster, mirroring the general financial crisis. Through the support of my CTO, Adrian, I managed a short sale on my house. It was a relief to sell, and I dreamed of bringing peace to my wife and our relationship, which was strained due to the stress, lack of time together, and the challenges we faced.

During this period, I reached out to Swank Motion Pictures, the company that provided movie content for Railway Media. I managed to secure a deal where I worked to restore their relationship with Amtrak, which I did, and they paid me $4,000 per month. I leased a large new home in Aventura in a beautiful development called Golden Gate Estates. It was a gorgeous house, providing a fresh start for our family. Toops was so happy, as were the kids.

I was pushing for a deal where the players would be packaged in with minivans as was working at Amtrak. Hertz liked the idea, too, so much so, in fact that they inquired about acquiring Nick on the Go from us. Amazingly, we ended up making a deal to sell them the whole thing. The agreement provided a way for me to pay back my investors and put money in my pocket in 2009, when everything was as bad as I'd ever seen it.

With the acquisition money, I returned home to my family and took them on a trip to Disney World to reconnect after all the stress and challenges. We spent a week at the parks and in the pool with the kids, trying our best not to have a care in the world.

The sale of Nick on the Go to Hertz marked a turning point in my journey. As much as I wanted to clear my mind, I spent time contemplating the next steps, unsure of what the future held. While the deal allowed me to stabilize financially and repay investors, I was just uncertain about my path forward.

After the deal closed, I took a meeting in Miami Beach with a dear, trusted advisor, where I hoped to discuss my next move. For the first time in 10 years, I had no major career.

Richard Preston, my father's longtime CPA, who is also a business advisor and mentor to me, was blown away by what I had done with Hertz and the opportunity I had put together.

He asked me to another casual lunch with two of his wealthiest clients, Larry Grohl and Joel Newman. The lunch took place at the Rascal House, a classic spot in North Miami Beach. These individuals were tremendously rich, and their interest was piqued by what I had accomplished.

I explained my journey and showed them the impact of the experience. Particularly, Joel Newman was impressed by the strategic planning and goals I had achieved with Amtrak, Nickelodeon, and Hertz. He recognized the talent and hard work it took to establish partnerships with these groups and to deploy the devices across the country. He explained he was in the electronics business himself, which I immediately found fascinating.

The very next day, Joel reached out to me directly. He expressed an interest in meeting, and we agreed to connect. He gave me his address and asked me to meet him at his home the following day.

Chapter 4:
Life with Joel

As I drove through the picturesque streets of Aventura, the wind carrying a gentle sea breeze, I couldn't help but feel a mix of excitement and uncertainty. My destination was a strip known as Golden Beach, adorned with some of Miami's most opulent homes, nestled right alongside the ocean. Ocean Boulevard, a name that evoked images of grandeur and celebrity allure, was the famous road I drove along. This enclave held a fascinating factoid: Eric Clapton had recorded the hit album 461 Ocean Boulevard on the same block. In the midst of this realm of fame and luxury was an address I held on a scrap of paper, guiding me toward an encounter with Joel Newman.

The road ahead was both exhilarating and enigmatic. My recent sale of the company to Hertz and all the stories of the road had piqued Joel's interest, particularly the work with portable media players and my extensive contacts in Hollywood. The prospects of our meeting held a sense of intrigue for me, as for the first time in my adult life, I didn't know exactly what I was working on. With every passing mile, the anticipation grew, as did the question of what awaited me at Joel's home.

My thoughts wandered back to the journey that had led me to this juncture. Selling my company had been a monumental ending, and now I hoped to be on the precipice of something new, something potentially transformative, especially in the horrible US economy in early 2009. As the scenery transitioned from elegant houses to the lavish expanse of Golden Beach, I couldn't help but wonder about the stories these walls held and the lives they sheltered.

As I neared Joel's address, passing houses that expressed luxury and affluence, I felt a mixture of awe and anticipation. Suddenly, there it was, an ornate and imposing gate leading to an estate that seemed to stretch on forever. It was clearly the largest home in Golden Beach, and the address matched the one on the paper. I was momentarily taken aback. This was more than a home; it was an architectural masterpiece, a Mediterranean mansion gracing the beach directly on the Atlantic Ocean.

The gate opened, inviting me in, and I drove through; my heart raced with a blend of humility and curiosity. As I stepped out of the car, I couldn't help but marvel at the splendor of the mansion that loomed before me. It was a place that appeared straight out of dreams, a testament to boundless success. The housekeepers welcomed me with smiles and offered coffee, and I found myself surrounded by an air of graciousness.

Soon, I encountered Edith Newman, Joel's wife, a lovely lady and presence who greeted me warmly and guided me through the marvels of their home. The glass windows overlooked the expansive ocean, a vista that seemed like a living painting. I felt a sense of privilege to be in such a place; it was almost surreal.

With each step, I approached Joel's office, a room that radiated sophistication and accomplishment. And there he was, Joel Newman, sitting in his chair with a welcoming smile that defied any preconceived notions I might have had. Joel was a man of presence, a larger-than-life figure with an air of confidence that bespoke his successes and the warmth of a loving family member.

What struck me the most was his genuine interest in getting to know me. Instead of diving straight into business matters, Joel began with questions about my family, my passions, and my travels. It was a departure from the corporate world I had become accustomed to, a sincere desire to connect on a human level. His questions felt like a tapestry of curiosity, weaving the threads of our lives together into a meeting that transcended transactional intent.

As we delved into a conversation, I discovered Joel's journey from Cuban immigrant to nearly a billionaire. He kept a sealed cashier's check on his desk commemorating his first company's IPO in 1983, the day he was first minted a millionaire. That would happen many, many more times over. It was a tangible reminder of the culmination of hard work and visionary thinking. However, it wasn't the money that defined him; it was his humility and his willingness to share stories and listen intently that left a lasting impression on me.

Joel's tenure in the electronics industry, his legendary ventures into China in the late 1970s and 80s, and his ability to forge billion-dollar-plus deals with major retailers like Kmart and CVS left me in awe. His tale of success was interwoven with anecdotes of strategic decisions and unparalleled dedication. I marveled at the layers of business acumen he possessed, a testament to his ability to navigate the complex landscapes of entrepreneurship.

The conversation meandered to Elliot, Joel's son, and his company, which was in the toy industry. It was a world where licensing deals and innovative ideas converged, and Elliot's story painted a vivid picture of a family heritage marked by success. Joel's paternal pride was evident, showcasing his legacy as a nurturing figure, both in business and family.

In the middle of the luxurious setting of his office, I felt a sense of companionship with Joel, a shared passion for exploring opportunities and forging connections. His behavior, the way he leaned in to listen, and the warmth of his smile, all added up to an unforgettable experience. In the midst of his grand mansion, it was the authenticity of our conversation that resonated most deeply.

As our talk transitioned to the prospect of working together, Joel's demeanor remained one of collaboration rather than negotiation. His proposal was a challenge, an invitation to venture into uncharted territory. It was an opportunity to be part of something bigger than myself, a chance to contribute to a legacy that had already shaped industries. Then, he threw his changeup to see what would happen.

Our discussion had been warm and exploratory, and then Joel began to talk about his own companies, their history, the customers they had, and their operations in Hong Kong. "We've done a lot of big things for a small group," he said, "in our time, we've done some great deals and made," a dramatic pause where he looked at me, looked down, then looked at me again, "hundreds of millions of dollars."

Then, his eyes locked on me intensely without blinking once, looking for how I'd react to the statement. He knew all too well most people couldn't handle discussing anything of the sort, especially in any confident manner, and it was clear in a split second he was judging my reaction, my ability to adjust in a major meeting, and financial and business acumen all at once. I stared back at him confidently without changing expression, and he knew right away this wasn't my first rodeo. "Fantastic. Let's go do more," I answered. Joel smiled widely and shifted back to his relaxed nature. I felt like I had made good contact with his curveball.

Then, Joel spoke to me about joining Elliot in his company, emphasizing my capacity for strategic negotiations. He said he saw me as the ideal candidate to help bolster Elliot's business. I was offered the role of Executive Vice President; he told me to "March North and Conquer." I agreed to the position readily. Joel's conviction in my abilities bolstered my confidence.

I was curious about my compensation structure, naturally. Beyond a base salary, Joel proposed a percentage of sales beyond a certain threshold. Initially, the offer wasn't ideal, and I negotiated for a better package. Joel eventually agreed, granting me a percentage of sales from dollar one, a concession he claimed he'd never offered anyone before. This incentive structure made my potential earnings enticing, especially considering the success Joel and Elliot had enjoyed over the years.

Driving away from that incredible place on Ocean Boulevard, my mind was abuzz with thoughts and reflections. I had entered a world of extravagance and achievement, but what truly captivated me was the authenticity of Joel Newman, the man behind the mansion, the visionary behind the ventures. It was a journey into a glamorous world where success met humility and where the future held the promise of partnership and innovation.

With the deal set, I embarked on this new journey as Executive Vice President.

My first day at the office was a whirlwind of emotions. Walking into Joel and Elliot's headquarters, a warehouse in Miami Gardens, it was clear that this was a hub of activity. Electronics, samples, and goods lined the shelves of their display rooms.

This was the reality of selling merchandise and dealing with big retailers like Walmart, Target, and Best Buy. I had heard about Elliot and a deal he struck with a major retailer years before for Batman-themed electronics. The products didn't perform as well as expected, leading the merchant to ask for 'markdown money.' However, Elliot declined, and looking back, I couldn't blame him. He had made $50 million on the deal. The merchant was made very happy by a credit applied to the next purchase order.

A similar situation occurred with one of Elliot's product lines at another large retailer. They wanted markdown money, too, but Elliot stood his ground. He wasn't willing to take the hit; they had bought the merchandise but didn't display, market, and sell it properly, which wasn't his fault. It was a tough call, but Elliot had his principles, which always came first. Again, he made them happy too, with a credit against the next order, and continued a strong business relationship. I thought it was just brilliant.

These experiences gave me a glimpse into the cutthroat world of retail. I felt a rush of excitement as I delved into the strategy for our upcoming sales. However, the economic climate in 2009 was extremely challenging. The financial crisis had wreaked havoc on retail, leading to layoffs and organizational upheaval. Existing relationships had changed, and navigating this landscape wasn't going to be easy.

As I dove into my role, I realized that the industry was in distress. The stability and confidence that once permeated the sector had been replaced by uncertainty. Despite the gloomy outlook, one thing was clear – brick-and-mortar stores still relied heavily on merchandise to drive their sales, as in those days, e-commerce was in its infancy.

I remember meeting with Elliot to discuss our strategy. I was eager to collaborate and formulate a plan. I asked how we could connect with buyers and initiate sales appointments. His response was direct, "I don't know. That's *your* job." Vintage Elliot. While he maintained relationships with some buyers, the ever-changing landscape meant that he was, in many instances, as clueless as I was about who the new buyers and decision-makers were. He handed over the task of identifying buyers and securing appointments to me.

Armed with this directive, I set out to work, tapping into my internet research skills, which I had honed over the years, and embraced the growing platform of LinkedIn. Crafting my profile to reflect the new role, I began reaching out to potential contacts in the industry. My office became a hub of activity as I transformed it into a command center for the mission.

Despite the challenges, I found myself invigorated by the opportunity. The prospect of reshaping a corporate strategy within the changing landscape was exciting. My wife and children, enthusiastic about my new journey, eagerly interacted with the toys and merchandise I brought home, sparking joy and creativity. With more determination, I was committed to making a significant impact on this new chapter of my career. I worked regular hours and was home with them for the first time in years. We were very happy.

In the midst of getting up to speed there, I became increasingly aware of the familial traits that Joel and Elliot shared. They both possessed an innate charm that immediately put people at ease. Their laughter was infectious, and their shared humor bridged gaps and diffused tension. I remembered how a well-timed movie quote could disarm even the more stressful situations, especially with Elliot, who, no matter how mad he was about anything, could be brought to tears by my imitating 'Cousin Eddie' from *National Lampoon's Vacation* at any moment.

Yet, as the days unfolded, I began to sense the underlying pressure the industry faced. The weight of the Newman legacy, the expectations of the industry, and the 2009 economic turmoil all took a toll. My role was not just about strategy and sales; it was about navigating a complex ecosystem of relationships, decisions, and the ever-changing dynamics of retail.

And so, I embraced the new challenge, ready to march forward and shape the destiny of my role in the business. The road ahead was uncertain, the obstacles daunting, but I was determined to carve a path toward success in a landscape defined by change.

One thing I realized through the journey is the power of LinkedIn. I remember first receiving LinkedIn invites from people, including the Disney executives from the Hertz deal. I thought it was such a cool platform and decided to join. A well-crafted profile was crucial, as I knew that potential buyers would probably look me up.

I wanted to make sure whoever scanned my profile would see all of my credentials and experience. The world of retail is about relationships, and people want to know who they're talking to. At this point, it was a contact sport; the more people you contact, the better you'll do.

I started by making a list of the retailers that Elliot hadn't tapped into yet. I focused on both national and regional groups in the mass, specialty, and grocery sectors.

While I believed that I might not be landing multimillion-dollar accounts right away, perhaps these accounts were where I could start building my own client base.

It was clear that Elliot's primary customer was Canadian Tire, a mass merchant based in Toronto. I wanted to find my own contacts who were in a similar league. Hungry to make money, I believed that there was a market for what we had.

LinkedIn became the go-to tool for identifying buyers in the toy and electronics categories. I would search for relevant contacts using keywords like "Walgreens toy buyer" or "Kroger toy buyer." Some results were outdated, but that didn't deter me. I would then cross-reference those names with Google searches to confirm their roles and gather more information. Once I had a potential name, I would scour the web for their email address. This often meant getting creative and trying different combinations.

I followed the process of sending introductory emails with our presentation attached. If an email bounced back, I would cross that address off and move on to the next one. It was a trial-and-error process, but it worked. I realized that some companies had unconventional email formats, likely to deter salespeople like me. But I saw it as a challenge, a hunt to find the right contact. Sometimes, the most obscure email addresses were the ones that landed in the Buyer's inbox.

As I continued this approach, reply emails started coming in. Buyers were interested in what we had to offer. The initial interaction was critical, and it often led to the request for pricing and samples. This was my cue to propose an in-person meeting. Elliot had always emphasized the importance of being in the room with the Buyer, and I shared that mindset. A face-to-face interaction always has a different impact, allowing them to touch, feel, and experience our products.

In those early weeks, Elliot and I would have lunch together a few times. I'd show him my progress and how I used PowerPoint presentations to tease potential buyers. He smiled and nodded, and I could tell he approved. It wasn't about doing things exactly the same way everyone else did; it was about results. Elliot and Joel shared a similar philosophy: if you're putting meat on the table, your hunting method works.

As I refined my strategy, I also started organizing our materials more effectively. I categorized and labeled the emails and materials I received from Elliot and enlisted the help of a graphic designer friend to make our PowerPoint presentations more visually appealing. The resulting PPTs were polished and very professional, which I hoped would make a strong impression on buyers.

With each step, I was building our approach and refining my techniques, finding solid footing in this new role and adapting to the contact-heavy world of retail. The industry was changing, and I was hoping to be at the forefront, forging relationships that would drive our business forward. Despite my initial nervousness, I was committed to making my first sales meeting a success.

Kroger, the largest grocery chain in America, emailed me agreeing to a meeting, so I bore in, determined to make the most of the opportunity. Elliot showed his confidence in my ability by handing over the reins for the meeting, even though it was my first. He said, "You go." He'd given me a credit card to manage my travel, respecting my inclination to control my own schedule and arrangements.

However, as the Kroger meeting approached, anxiety gnawed at me. I was facing the challenge of shipping our samples across the country in time, the merchandise had to make it to Portland, Oregon, from Miami by Monday morning. There was no room for error or FedEx mishaps.

I meticulously packed the samples, attempting to optimize space within the boxes. I wasn't just shipping products; I was sending a piece of our hard work and enthusiasm. I tracked the FedEx shipment like a hawk, crossing my fingers that everything would fall into place.

The eve of my departure arrived, and I set off for the airport, laden with anticipation and ambition. Although the journey was tiring, traversing time zones and layovers, I couldn't help but feel excited about the opportunity ahead.

Portland's Best Western provided a momentary respite with its continental breakfast of weak coffee and half a banana. It was pouring rain there, as usual. In my pursuit of professionalism, I'd somehow neglected to bring the new suit I had just fitted. I brought my blue pinstripe instead, which I thought fit me extremely well. It had been my power suit.

The morning of the meeting dawned, and my nerves mounted. I eagerly waited in the lobby, mentally rehearsing the pitch and hoping our presentation would captivate the buyer. Just as I was about to lose my composure, as it was 15 minutes after I told myself I had to leave, the FedEx truck pulled up.

With the samples finally in hand, my spirits soared. However, life has a scary sense of humor sometimes. I was led to the meeting room at Kroger, and just as I was about to set up the samples, disaster. I leaned over to pick up a keyboard out of the box, and my pants gave in and split completely open, and I mean completely, to where the whole back and leg were dangling off.

Freaking out, I grabbed a Stapler and attempted a makeshift repair job, frantically trying to keep my dignity intact. It was a scene right out of a Chevy Chase movie. I stapled my makeshift pants back together and finished 15 seconds before the buyer came in.

Meeting the Kroger toy buyer was a blend of excitement, opportunity, and distraction. With the fear of the staples popping out and everything coming free, I managed to engage in a productive discussion about our products. Despite the internal struggle, the buyer didn't notice and was intrigued, and she invited me to see how my merchandise could fit into their store layout.

During our visit to a local Portland Kroger store, my attention was divided between my presentation and the precarious state of my pants. Navigating the aisles and shelves was a challenge, but I was determined not to let it show. It was insane. Back at the office, I bid my farewells to her and her assistant buyer, eager to hear their response.

A week passed, and I learned the patience that comes with the territory of sales. Joel and Elliot, with their understanding of the industry, reassured me that the process was just as important as the outcome. The next day, an email notification came through, bearing the promise of progress. It was clear that my efforts were not in vain. The email from 'procurement@kroger.com,' signaled a significant milestone in my sales journey; this must be a purchase order!

The Kroger meeting had been a mix of humor, excitement, and unexpected hurdles. As I opened the email, I knew I was venturing deeper into this unpredictable, exhilarating world. Even though it was a rite of passage for me, I felt it was appropriate to forward the email to Elliot. He did not reply to me right away.

I had left Kroger pricing, minimum order quantities, and other details at the meeting. Then, an hour later, Elliot buzzed and asked me to come to his office. His expression wasn't the happiest. So, I asked him, "What's going on? What did they say?"

"What?" he replied, "They gave us an order." I was taken aback, "Really? They actually did?" My very first sales meeting and I've landed an account. I couldn't believe it. And the order amount was what? $1 million? More? I was completely clueless about the details.

Elliot then revealed that the order they'd placed was for approximately $595,000. They were taking a chance on us, an unknown vendor to them. I was ecstatic that my first call had yielded a sale. Elliot had mentioned the hour delay was him calling the procurement department and confirming the order they sent.

"So, what did you tell them?" I inquired. "I told them everything we discussed," Elliot explained. "Our best pricing is FOB Hong Kong, and this is not FOB Hong Kong. They want us to deliver it to their distribution center in Cincinnati, Ohio. I quoted them accordingly for that option." He still seemed agitated. It was as if the order irked him, and I couldn't quite understand why. "Come with me," Elliot said as we walked down the hall.

We entered Joel's exquisite office, where Elliot handed the purchase order to his father. The name 'KROGER' was emblazoned across the top, and I was feeling very proud. Joel, with a knowing look, understood that this was a significant moment for us. He acknowledged the new customer with a nod, smile, and a wink at me, unbothered by Elliot's frustration.

"Dad, what is this order? Do they call this business?" Joel turned to his son and said, "Elliot, Look at the big picture. Josh has only been here a short while, and he's now opened an account with a large, untapped company you have never sold to or even called upon. Kroger is a very impressive customer, and half a million dollars is a nice order."

Joel's words resonated right away with Elliot; his anger seemed to dissipate as his father's wisdom took hold. It was a transformational shift in perception. The order was sizeable, and the potential for growth with a customer like Kroger was limitless. Joel's positivity was infectious, a unique light that radiated from within him. When he spoke, you couldn't help but believe.

This encounter was more than just a pat on the back; it was a turning point. Elliot realized that my achievement was significant, that securing a half-million-dollar order from a completely new company on your first meeting was no small feat. Joel's guidance altered Elliot's mindset, transforming his irritation into admiration, and his father commended me, "Great work."

Elliot added, "It's good work, not great work," more vintage Elliot. Joel got a kick out of the whole thing; it was all positive to him, and we left while he giggled about Elliot's 'good work' comment.

I was encouraged by the acknowledgment but didn't want to ruffle Elliot's feathers. I also aspired to reach larger clients, even while appreciating the accomplishments of the current ones. My focus expanded, and I continued employing LinkedIn to connect with toy buyers from other retailers like Aldi, Radio Shack, H-E-B, Best Buy, and Barnes & Noble, all untouched territories, according to Elliot. More purchase orders soon came from my efforts at Aldi and H-E-B, roughly the same size as Kroger.

I believed that giant corporations like Walmart were well worth pursuing; they gave you orders that could get up to 8 figures quickly. The key to them is persistence; everyone in the industry is trying to contact them. I sent email after email, casting lines into the vast sea of perceived opportunity. It felt like being a fisherman; you could bait all the hooks and cast all the lines you wanted, but ultimately, you had to wait for a bite that may or may never come.

In the midst of the waiting game, an unexpected email blinked into my inbox. It was from the Walmart buyer, finally, the one I had been emailing. It read that he would be gone for a month but could 'meet us tomorrow if we could make it.' The persistence paid off, and I excitedly informed Elliot of the meeting I'd confirmed.

Elliot's reaction was a mixture of surprise and concern. "Why tomorrow? Why not next week?" he exclaimed, worried about the lack of preparation time. I explained that the buyer was leaving town and could only meet the next day. Elliot relented, "Then I guess we're going tomorrow. Set it up." He entrusted me with arranging all the details.

The meeting was set for 2 p.m. the next day, giving us some time to spare if everything was on time. Our flight, however, would land around 11:30 a.m. With no time for a leisurely evening departure, I located a nearby FedEx drop-off open until 7 p.m., got our sample package there, and confirmed early morning flights. I booked us rooms at the Comfort Inn in Bentonville, Arkansas, right by Walmart's headquarters.

As we had sent our samples, brochures, and materials via FedEx, Elliot expressed the desire to leave very early for the airport the next morning. I agreed and picked him up before sunrise. The flights I managed to find to Bentonville took us through Charlotte, adding up to a long travel day.

At the airport in Charlotte, after some airport BBQ food, we caught our flight to Bentonville. As we waited to depart on the tarmac, I noticed Elliot's energy waning, and he laid back and went to sleep. He told me early morning starts were not his preferred mode of operation; he liked getting there the day before. Landing in Bentonville, he was hungry again, urging us to eat before checking into our hotel.

We went to a local BBQ joint everyone was raving about. They had a big wood oven, and we could smell the hickory burning when we walked in. I decided to go all in and ordered a two-meat special with brisket and chicken. Elliot, always the gourmet, got a three-meat plate with scalloped potatoes and mac and cheese.

We gorged ourselves silly; two guys taking down two full BBQ meals in just two hours. As we left for the car, a growing pressure in my stomach signaled trouble. Elliot looked at me and confessed, "I've got to take the biggest crap." I agreed. "Me too, jump in the car, let's go."

The hotel was situated in a remote area near Walmart, surrounded by cow fields. It was part of a row of three hotels, Best Western, Comfort Inn, and Hampton Inn, all full of salespeople there for meetings too. When we reached the hotel, I was more concerned about my impending disaster than if the FedEx boxes for our Walmart meeting had arrived yet.

I rushed inside, desperately seeking the men's room. The hotel clerk was oblivious. "Sorry, no restroom here." My panic intensified. I realized I was not going to make it. Luckily, the person in front of me finished checking in, and

I hastily got my room key. My room was on the second floor, and I hit the elevator, praying I wouldn't embarrass myself before the Walmart meeting.

I stepped out onto the second floor, wobbling like I had broken legs, barely making it to my room. I threw my bags into the hall and fell through the door, somehow managing to undo my belt and pants and barely avoid disaster in the nick of time. When I made it into the bathroom, it was the scene from 'Dumb and Dumber.'

I washed my hands and stepped back into the room, only to see the extensive boxes, luggage, clothes, and shoes of some other man's room I was in. The knucklehead at the desk gave me a key to someone else's room! I hastily exited, imagining what would've happened if the guy had walked in on me; how insane that would have been. I cracked up to myself as I imagined him on the phone with 911, pounding on the door of his bathroom with a stranger inside. Good Lord.

Back at the front desk, I returned the key and told the dimwit, "You gave me someone else's room." He said he was sorry and handed me another key. I finally opened the right door; my stuff was still strewn around the hotel's hallway, and when I was in my own room, I finally breathed easily. I called Elliot and told him the story and heard him fall off his bed laughing.

After this chaotic start, the Walmart meeting was a whole other experience. We arrived at their sprawling campus, feeling like we were entering a giant university. Inside, there was a waiting room filled with about 60 people, all there for potential multimillion-dollar deals. It was a zoo, people practicing speeches, nervously checking their samples.

We finally got in, but the outcome wasn't what we hoped for. The Walmart buyer, Scott, was polite but candid, "Come back when you have something more appealing or that I haven't seen six times already." We left empty-handed, with no deal or interest.

During the flights back, I talked with Elliot, discussing that some innovation was our way in with the big players. He was used to sourcing existing products, but we felt that wouldn't cut it with Walmart. We needed fresh ideas, so we jointly agreed it was a good idea to attend the Licensing Show in Las Vegas.

At the show, we found ourselves among the giants there. Disney, Hasbro, Mattel, and many others had massive booths, and we were trying to get noticed and see if there were any good license opportunities that would be a great fit for our products. After walking the floor for several hours, I stumbled upon Scholastic's booth, thinking about those book fairs from elementary school.

Gary from Scholastic was manning the booth, and after describing some of our learning-focused merchandise, he was intrigued. Elliot was not sold yet on the brand as a license, but when I mentioned Scholastic's presence in schools, his interest was piqued. Gary went on about the successful book fairs, and suddenly, we were on to something. Scholastic was a brand inside educational institutions where no other brand was. That was incredibly unique, unlike anything these other licenses could even compare to, especially the smaller ones like this, which were in our price range. Obviously, we weren't talking about Disney here, but Scholastic, in my mind, was great. The advantage they had, being in elementary schools and having that presence, was something we could pitch and leverage at Walmart.

The first Walmart meeting might not have gone as planned, but the encounter with Scholastic opened up a new avenue. It was a reminder that raw innovation and finding the right partner can sometimes make all the difference.

I suggested the idea of pitching Walmart and Sam's Club Scholastic, getting into kids' backpacks in schools with coupons and other incentives. Elliot, who was usually initially skeptical, right away thought the idea was good and sat down with Gary. They became so absorbed in the discussion that I left them alone to talk.

When I returned, Elliot and Gary were already deep into crafting a term sheet, working on a licensing deal. It was surprising, but I was so pleased to see him moving fast on it. He and Gary were negotiating back and forth, haggling intensely over the terms. Gary initially wanted a significant downstroke at license inception, maybe a $100,000, but ended up accepting $25,000. It was a huge compromise, showing Elliot's great skill at negotiating.

I wasn't the only one who knew how to make big deals; the name Newman means you know what you're doing at any moment.

Back in Miami, after negotiations and back-and-forth with Scholastic's lawyer, we signed the formal agreement and sent the check. Now, we were Scholastic's licensee. They wanted to hold a kickoff meeting to discuss our plans for a launch in 2011, which was a year and a half away. Elliot was initially surprised by the timeline and joked about whether I planned on eating or paying bills until then. He obviously had a point; in that industry, especially when competing with major players for accounts at mass retailers, speed was crucial. "Either they want the license, or they don't," was his position.

We discussed why they wanted us to wait until Black Friday 2011 to launch, suggesting we use the time for research and development and to create products to compete with Leapfrog. Elliot noted that business moves quickly, and we were not going to blow a year in development, especially when a new license had given us immediate advantages. The plan was to get into kids' backpacks in schools across all 50 states, totally unique and perhaps never discussed at mass retail.

We decided to call Walmart and Sam's Club again. I personally contacted both buyers, explaining that we had something groundbreaking, unlike anything they'd seen before. They agreed to meet us again. This time, we went to Bentonville to pitch the Scholastic brand concept without even bringing merchandise. It was an entirely different story; the buyers were genuinely interested in the new strategy. The prospect of infiltrating schools and putting their branding and coupons into kids' backpacks was tremendously intriguing to them.

We returned from Bentonville feeling positive and confident. I was hopeful this could be our breakthrough; Walmart and Sam's Club were interested in the pitch. This time, it seemed like we had a chance. However, there was some debate regarding the product itself. I believed we should invest in R&D for some new compelling products. Elliot mildly agreed but also had his people in Hong Kong looking for products that already existed. The idea was to work with existing molds of other manufacturers he dealt with, repurposing certain merchandise with our license. He knew a lot more about the business than I did, and I agreed we could have a breakthrough faster and with less risk and time his way. It was a tough call, but it was his to make.

We hit Vegas again, attending the Consumer Electronics Show (CES), where we explored various electronics innovations. There, Joel focused on electronics business deals from his display room at Caesar's Palace, and Michael, Joel's younger son who had joined the company, connected well with me. I loved hanging out with the two brothers; we had a blast every night. Michael was just as brilliant as Elliot, and he was well into the swing of things on the electronics side of their Company.

Later that week, we flew to Hong Kong to visit Elliot's office and see samples for Scholastic. I was in awe of being in Asia for the first time, though I was battling hideous jet lag. The first few days there, I didn't venture much beyond the hotel and our office due to exhaustion. I learned some cultural nuances, like how belching is socially acceptable. Everyone in his office burped openly as someone might cough or sneeze here, and I kept busting out laughing in the private office we were in, which made Elliot crack up too.

We went to the lavish Peninsula Hotel, where Elliot had arranged a Rolls Royce Phantom and Helicopter standing by; we had afternoon tea in the lobby next to Jean Claude Van Damme. He took the Canadian Tire toy buyer on the chopper for a night out in Macau.

Joel had described many times the lengths people in the industry go to cultivate good relationships with buyers. This was an essential part of the business, of building trust and rapport. Years before, he told me a Buyer canceled a deal on him for no reason, and he found out later a competitor had arranged an entire payoff of the Buyer's home mortgage. "Take care of your Buyer, and watch everyone else around you like a hawk," Joel told us, "There isn't much someone won't do for a $10 million order."

The day came to review the samples and packaging that Kathy, Elliot's Hong Kong manager, had made for Scholastic. We were extremely excited to ship them to the Sam's Club and Walmart buyers in Bentonville. I wasn't totally in love with the samples she sourced, which was my point the whole time, but we hoped the brand was strong enough for them to buy in. The packaging was beautiful, though, and Elliot said we would create some new merchandise in Year 2 if this worked.

Three weeks later, Walmart passed, but Sam's Club was still alive and contemplating a buy. We were still alive.

One week later, Sam's Club said they would place an order. Then, they too, passed.

Elliot dealt with the decisions with a shrug. He wasn't thrilled, and he seemed more open to other ideas. Other retailers of ours were buying the Scholastic merchandise in quantities, not the kind of order you'd get from Walmart, but it was still a financial success in getting the license.

We discussed the need for some additional innovation, and Elliot said he had reflected on what he was seeing, and it was clear that the Great Recession had indeed changed buying trends. We continued to brainstorm, as having a unique and compelling product was essential; Elliot had sold tens of millions of dollars or more in merchandise in his career, and he knew what it took to be on top.

Out of nowhere, I received a call that my father had been hospitalized with pain. Once admitted, an MRI found a large tumor in his back, and he needed surgery to remove it nearly immediately.

The surgery to remove the tumor, which turned out to be benign, went well but was invasive. It was clear his recovery was going to be several months. I had to make a difficult choice, but it was evident after going over there that Mango's needed me back full-time and right away. My decision was made; I knew I had to step away from my position with Joel and focus on my own family business.

I walked sadly into Craig Electronics the next day to deliver my resignation letter. It contained details of the deals I was working on, along with contact information of the Buyers involved. I wanted to ensure a smooth transition for Elliot to take over.

The Newmans were dismayed by my decision. Joel asked if there was a monetary amount that could change things. It was a good position to be in, but my mind was made up. I loved their family, but this was *my* family. I expressed my gratitude to Joel and his sons, giving them all a big hug before leaving.

Looking back, I was so grateful for the path I had taken, the people I had met, and the challenges we had overcome.

I later learned that the Newmans were surprised by my departure and thought of offering a significant package to keep me. But I had already set my course and officially returned to Mango's on Memorial Day Weekend 2010. It was a whirlwind transition, but I was ready to roll up my sleeves and energize the family business as my dad recovered.

The victories with Joel weren't just about business success but also tremendous lessons. They were about becoming a better leader who made thoughtful, careful decisions and approached challenges with optimism, balance, and reason. Joel's influence had helped mold me into a more composed person, someone who wasn't hasty and weighed each move with precision and detailed strategic planning.

That didn't mean taking five months to make a decision or even five days or five hours. Sometimes, you just need five minutes, possibly to call your advisors and trusted partners for a word on something, so you make sure to consider the primary issues and the whole picture. Just don't do something in 5 seconds, especially based on emotion, it rarely works out well.

Even after I left, Joel and I maintained a strong connection. He would call me four or five times a year simply to check in and see how I was doing. It was heartwarming to hear from him, to share my progress, and to know that he was still interested in my journey.

Tragically, Joel's unexpected passing in early 2022 left a void in the world. It was terribly sad; the world lost a truly remarkable individual. I will always cherish the time I spent with him and the lessons he taught us. He was not just a mentor and a boss but an angelic presence in my life, and his absence is deeply felt.

Chapter 5:
Ocean Drive to I-Drive:
Mango's and the Battle for Skyplex

It was from Ocean Drive to I Drive. That was the motto we used, the battle cry at the start of 2013 when we finally secured the International Drive site after a year and a half of pursuing the property.

Looking back to the first time I walked through it in June 2011, I had no idea that we would embark on a property acquisition marathon that would last three years and seven months, involving eight parcels sourced from eight different parties, none of which were for sale. The end result would be assembling nearly 18 acres right at the intersection of International Drive and Sand Lake Road and investing nearly $70 million in property alone.

It came from deep within, seeing the value and potential in what was significantly underutilized land at the corner of Main and Main. It became the cornerstone of my life as I began striving to get this accomplished.

We had been embroiled in negotiations for a Mango's on the Strip in Las Vegas, going back and forth with Caesars Entertainment for eight months regarding a specific site we thought was amazing. I was interacting with some top people at Caesars, including the president of the Flamingo at the time, Rick Mazer.

We believed we had a fantastic deal at the Imperial Palace, now known as the LINQ Hotel, right next to the Flamingo. At that time, they hadn't even announced the High Roller Ferris wheel or the major development that would become The LINQ complex. Everything was still very much within the Great Recession's grip. Having a distinctive Latin club opportunity, not just another EDM ultra lounge, was exciting for Caesars. They were enthusiastic about us, and I liked Rick and Paul Baker, his main executive vice president.

Paul, an MBA from Harvard Business School who was also a West Point grad, impressed me with his education and strong, confident leadership. We were dealing with a lot, including the design and presence on the Vegas Strip. My dad and I had disagreements, such as an insistence on balconies and other details he wouldn't compromise on, which caused ongoing debate.

Eventually, I decided to explore Orlando as an option for Mango's due to the convenience of managing it from Miami Beach, but primarily the ability to buy a building as opposed to leasing a space in Vegas. Travel between Vegas and Miami was challenging too, with limited, long flights. So, Orlando seemed like a more feasible choice.

I reached out to CBRE in Orlando and connected with a broker named Bobby Palta, who ended up becoming a dear friend. I told him I'd visit to scout locations for Mango's. He had visited our Miami Beach location multiple times, and his brother was a long-time customer. This made him excited about a significant user's interest during a severe recession. Flying to MCO, he picked me up in an old Toyota Landcruiser, and by the time we had finished a few things, Bobby had a new Range Rover.

As we drove from the airport toward International Drive, he discussed the day's tour and the locations we'd see. The first stop was a closed Houlihan's and Sizzler building. While it was close to the Orange County Convention Center, it didn't resonate with me due to low ceilings, limited space, and perceived parking issues. It just didn't feel right. We moved on to the second site, the one that clicked. There was no need for further stops.

The site was an old TGI Fridays Front Row building, the largest in the US, which was closed for nearly two years with a homeless man's clothes strewn about the patio and a crooked 'For Lease' sign dangling in the window. The potential was evident, and I took videos with my laptop's camera to show my dad. I became obsessed with the building, and it turned into a mission to acquire it. Owned by a group from NYC, the building's mortgage was in default, and the property clearly in distress.

Working with these Sellers, given the state of the site, seemed promising. The building was in pre-foreclosure chaos, which I knew was a great opportunity. Despite the lender complications, I insisted we should pursue it. If you can get a prime property at its worst and turn things around, that's precisely how you make money in real estate. I got my dad to come up and see it, and he was equally enthusiastic.

Previously, we had been considering trying to reopen our Miami Design District club, Power Studios. It had operated more than 12 years prior but shut down due to permit issues in 2000. Our idea was to sell Power Studios to fund the purchase of the Orlando building. We believed in the timeless concept of Mango's, unlike the trendy clubs that come and go.

We decided to pursue the contract for the Orlando building, and after some back-and-forth, they accepted a term sheet. We sent a contract, but the process got tangled with the seller's family drama, legal issues, and attempted price increases.

My dad was livid with their attempt to increase the purchase price after we agreed in the LOI, but I was happy to see the end of it due to the struggle I'd been through to get it under contract. Bobby and I even talked about writing a book about all the twists and turns of getting this deal; it had taken nearly a year and was just beyond crazy.

So, finally, it was under contract for $10.4 million. We began looking to sell Power Studios, which we owned for basically nothing. If we sold it, we'd face a huge tax bill—around 35%—unless we used a tax-deferred 1031 exchange, where the IRS permits you to defer capital gains tax by exchanging 'like-kind property' instead of withdrawing money from the US economy.

When you sell the subject property, the money needs to go to an intermediary and can't touch your bank account. That money stays with the intermediary in escrow, and when you close on the replacement property, the money goes from the intermediary account to the closing agent. If the IRS examines the transaction, there's no tax due—it's a good 1031 exchange. This was crucial as deals for Power Studios kept falling through. People looked to save the building, but it was just unsalvageable.

Our Orlando building was under contract, and it was clear we would need to close on it before we could sell Power Studios. After we completed the sale, we embarked on the rare *Reverse 1031 Exchange*, where the intermediary actually takes title to the property before the replacement property is sold. It was a big risk to buy first and then need to sell a commercial property under the 180-day deadline. Months passed, and seemingly out of nowhere, a deal came in for Power from Lyle Chariff, a Miami developer, and his partner, Shawn Chemtov. They planned to buy Power Studios, knock it down, and construct a retail building on the site with a tenant Lyle lured to his vision of the redeveloped property.

Thankfully, they were interested solely in the land, not saving the building, which was literally falling down. They offered $8 million cash, no contingencies. They wanted to ensure there was no hindrance to their development, which there wasn't, and Chariff and Chemtov closed the deal just 15 days before the required 180-day window of the Reverse 1031. The $8 million went right to the intermediary to pay down the initial mortgage on the Orlando building, and we soon got title to everything. The reverse 1031 exchange worked beautifully, but I told my wife it may have shaved a few years off my life.

With Mango's and Power Studios dealt with and an additional 4-acre land parcel Bobby and I arranged to buy for $3.1 million for parking across the intersection, it was time to announce Mango's Orlando. We put out a press release on December 12, 2012, and were overwhelmed by the excitement it brought. People were thrilled about our expansion in bringing Ocean Drive to I Drive. In the midst of the Great Recession, our deals seemingly inspired people around us and in our communities. The social media response was overwhelming.

I was asked to move to Orlando by my dad, which was a huge change for our family. Though it felt good to be on our way with the business after so long, my wife was shocked when I told her about the relocation. She had strong connections in Miami, we both did, and I tried to reason that it was important for my career and our family's future. At the time, I was 37 years old and believed it was the right step, and though there was a lot of unhappiness surrounding it, I plowed forward, self-absorbed with the career-defining deals.

Because we loved Disney World, we had gone up to Orlando for years and years, vacationing there primarily. My wife adored Disney and its Parks and Resorts, as did our kids. So, I thought that once we got up there, we could get annual passes, have friends over all the time, and just enjoy the new lifestyle. Also, Orlando was still reeling from the housing crisis, and I believed I could find a great home for us that would excite her.

We moved to Orlando on August 6, 2013. The kids started classes at Windermere Prep the following week and felt a good connection with the school. We began working with the designers for Mango's and hired an architecture firm recommended by members of the community called L2 Studios. I signed their contract and sent them a check immediately to get them onboard. My father is more of an artist, and I knew he needed a team to help with the sequencing and organizing aspects, which was crucial for a project like this.

With L2 onboard, we hired CBRE as the project manager. They assigned Rick Wilson, a fantastic guy who was with us throughout the project. We were now in the process of planning and designing Mango's Orlando. It was coming together in our minds and on paper. We owned the building and were actively working on the design and architecture through the first half of the year.

While doing all of this, I was seeking counsel from my father's first cousins, Bernard and Robert Friedman, who were extremely wealthy, experienced real estate developers in New York City. They provided valuable guidance through the 1031 exchange, real estate contracts, closings, and loan processes. They were instrumental in keeping my father calm and providing insights into these big business endeavors. Robert was particularly interested in our ventures in Orlando due to the excitement and potential he saw.

One day, my Orlando attorney, Trippe Cheek, informed me that Bill Kitchen, a well-known ride inventor from a company called U.S. Thrill Rides, contacted him about a roller coaster concept he had created called the Polercoaster. The attraction was a vertical coaster that fit on a small site and went straight up instead of horizontally. Kitchen saw the 4-acre parcel we purchased for Mango's parking on the Orange County Property Appraiser's website and thought it was a perfect site for this new attraction. I was intrigued when Trippe shared the email with me. I mean, how many calls do you get about an experimental rollercoaster no one has ever seen? Instead of dismissing it as madness, I shared the details with Robert.

Although most wild ideas don't get a second thought, I did like the concept of a vertical roller coaster, but that's where it ended. I had shared it with Robert, who I thought would never bring it up again. However, Robert discussed it with Bernie, contacted Bill Kitchen without mentioning it, and had meetings with him. I guess they liked what they heard.

One day in July 2013, my last week in Miami, Robert called me, saying he had something important he had to tell me. It ended up being one of those moments Bud Fox alluded to outside of Gordon Gekko's office.

"Josh, listen carefully," Robert said, "We've discussed it, and Bernie and I want to build the roller coaster."

I was so stunned, I stood dumbfounded. They had recently completed a hotel on 42nd Street in Times Square, so their interest in this project was remarkable.

I immediately called my father, who couldn't fathom it either. It was unbelievable, we were, out of nowhere, seemingly venturing into a whole new dimension. This wasn't just about a new nightclub anymore; were we really going to build an iconic 400 to 500-foot tower on a world-famous street? The thought of creating an icon like this with these guys was really too much.

I was ready to dive headfirst into this unbelievable development. We had already committed to Mango's, and while my family situation was tenuous and stressful with the move, we were now talking about an entirely different scale. The prospect of creating a massive tower was mind-blowing. I was also hoping that my wife's curiosity would grow beyond just not wanting to move to Orlando outright.

I told Robert, "Let's do it!" and given our existing commitments and the excitement of embarking on such an ambitious project, he knew I was already well positioned to be the Coaster development's boots on the ground.

As far as prospects of our outlook improving for this move to Orlando, this seemed extraordinary. Even more so, it reiterated to me at the time that what I was doing in Orlando was right, and I was hopeful that as things got bigger and more exciting, Toops would get more enthusiastic about the whole thing. I loved her so much, and to see her so upset about something I thought was so positive was devastating to me. In reality, I was too ambitious and selfish to consider her side and do what was needed for her contentment, as well as my own.

As we discussed the move, I tried to change her view on things. I said, "You know, we're doing the right thing. If President Obama was in this car with us right now, he would say, 'You guys are doing amazing things here. You're doing right for your community. You're creating jobs.'" And sometimes she'd consider that, and sometimes she said, "I just don't want us to go, can we stay?"

I said, "I'll be there alone. I'm going to live there without my family?" I implored her we had to go together and was trying to manage the situation. But now that Robert was talking about building the Polercoaster, things for me had taken on a whole different mindset. We also now had to figure out an alternative parking situation for Mango's because we weren't going to use those four acres for the Club any longer. I worked with that on a parallel path, eyeing the Walgreens store next door, rumor was it might be going up for sale. More on that later.

The plan now was to use the 4 acres of land for the Coaster site. The main issue was that the site itself was a back parcel and didn't have any frontage on International Drive. If we were going to build an entertainment complex for this mega rollercoaster, we had to have I Drive frontage. There were going to have to be some front parcels that were added.

We also continued our weekly meetings with the L2 architects as the design of Mango's went on. This is my father's wheelhouse. He takes three times longer than anybody else would to design sometimes, but nobody else could do anything like what he did (or does). It's a spectacular, one-of-a-kind venue. I wanted to let him continue to do his thing with the architects at L2 Studios as far as Mango's, as I focused intently on trying to increase the size of the roller coaster complex's site, which required tremendous focus and intensity.

Because I had been told by the Friedmans to try to add whatever frontage parcels we could, no matter what, to the 4 acres to give us a front entrance, I went into acquisition mode and hit the gas. Looking at Google Earth, which was the easiest way to really examine the site, I immediately identified there was a Burger King that we had to have, which was directly contiguous to the 4 acres and would provide much of the frontage we needed.

Looking at it on the Property Appraiser's website, it was an unusually large site, probably from old code in the 80s, and was very overparked. All these sites seemed overparked, with a lot of underutilized land. It was approximately two acres, which I found very big, and it only had a small Burger King on it with a parking lot. There was a road that went in and connected right into our 4 acres in the back—the key parcel, to be sure.

We absolutely had to have this Burger King if we were going to be doing anything with the project. At the time, we collectively had all been excited about the prospect of building the roller coaster, but we hadn't decided on how the ownership would work, what the corporation would look like, and who would own what.

But we knew, being family, we all thought we would just figure it out on a parallel path. After all, we were surfing on a lightning bolt. We thought we had something extraordinarily special, and we, the Wallacks, were the ones who had the land. The Friedmans were the ones that had to make the move to buy in.

They were handling getting the rollercoaster license from U.S. Thrill Rides, and I was figuring out how to acquire the parcels, none of which were for sale. The first thing was to identify the Burger King site's land owner, which ended up being a corporation in rural Kentucky.

This might scare off some people, who would say, "Some LLC in Kentucky owns this? How could we even approach them?" Not me. I went onto the Kentucky state website and discovered that the owner of the LLC was actually a resident of Central Florida. His name was Mark Lineberry, and he was the principal of a company called Lineberry Properties.

I could see from the portfolio on their website that they owned other Burger Kings and triple net leases around the country, brands like Pizza Hut and Taco Bell that pay rent like clockwork. This was the scope of their property business. I decided to reach out to Lineberry and see if he'd be interested in selling Burger King and, frankly, figure out what it would take to get it.

Knowing as much information as you can about who you're going to be dealing with is the best way to handle a situation like this. Knowledge is power. What do they do? Are they well-known? Are they involved in philanthropy? What college football team do they follow? Are they in any kind of financial or other trouble? Anything that can help you connect with a seller and achieve the objective is a good thing. That was the case with this situation, and I spent time doing research on Lineberry.

It didn't take me long to find a case number against him, which I looked up through a number of different clerks of courts. I then read a very damning indictment that the man I was meeting with at the time was under federal indictment for bank fraud in the state of Tennessee. Apparently, during the 2008 crisis, he had been building a hotel in Nashville and had a bank loan from a lender there that was supplying the construction funds.

The indictment alleged that he and a co-conspirator, who was his title agent, were falsifying construction progress documents. Then, the indictment read, they were submitted to the bank to show that work was being done on this hotel for draws on the loan, which, according to the charges, wasn't being done.

The prosecutors alleged he was taking the money and trying to cover his debts due to being overleveraged and exposed to the 2008 real estate crash. The bank sent in their own inspectors, and they claimed to have found that he was indeed not spending the money on the property. He was arrested and charged with fraud.

Lineberry was ultimately found not guilty and fully exonerated in court. However, in our time together, he was very much under indictment and facing perhaps decades in prison. I knew the guy could be sketched out by some new person contacting him out of the blue, so I planned to call politely and say, "Hi, I'm Josh Wallack from Mango's," basically telling him exactly who I was so he knew nothing was shady.

My plan was essentially to say to him I had just purchased the land next door to his and that I wanted to just say hello to my new neighbor. I alluded to the fact that I was interested in talking about a deal of some sort, but I didn't get into it to keep him positively intrigued.

After a brief breakfast meeting, I shared quietly and respectfully with Lineberry that I knew the legal trouble he was in, and that if I gave him a good number for the Burger King, it was a value he could potentially use toward restitution with federal prosecutors. Lineberry was very cool, a good guy, and he agreed. We closed at $4.15 million 3 weeks later, and Burger King was ours.

Now that we had the 4 acres and the Burger King, I was looking at other contiguous parcels for the site. There were three properties more that were key to putting together the whole thing in a way that would be something totally special. There was a 7-Eleven next to the Burger King, situated on an unusually small half-acre site. It was a very popular 7-Eleven, always very busy. Then, there was a Perkins restaurant, a huge, unique two-acre parcel on the hard corner of the intersection, a prime location that was absolutely incredible.

Adjacent to the original 4-acre parcel on the other side was a bowling alley and closed ice rink on four more acres owned by the legendary Dowdy family, prominent property owners in Orlando. I decided to pursue these three properties relentlessly.

With nobody aware of our Polercoaster plans, we were steadily closing in on the key parcels at the dynamic intersection. The challenge was securing the properties while ensuring that our project remained a total secret. We needed to negotiate and close without arousing suspicion about our ultimate plans. Acquiring the 7-Eleven, Perkins, and Dowdy parcels became a total obsession.

At the ICSC real estate conference in early 2014, a casual conversation with a broker I met named Blake Hunter led him to say, "I can assist you with 7-Eleven. I've dealt with them before, and they have a process for selling their sites. Many developers want to purchase parcels that might include a 7-Eleven store. It's a pretty common situation. Usually, if you make a reasonable offer, they'll respond in some way, even if it's a rejection. They won't just ignore you." It was very promising, so I hired him to investigate the move.

We decided to proceed and make offers on both the 7-Eleven and the Perkins properties. Unfortunately, the response from Perkins never came. The Perkins store was owned by G.E. Capital, a massive national REIT, and they didn't even acknowledge our offer. On the other hand, 7-Eleven did get back to us.

Their asking price for the property was a staggering $3.5 million. Considering that we had just spent $4.15 million on the adjacent site, which was nearly four times larger, this figure seemed quite steep. However, my partners, the Friedmans, were seasoned New York City real estate players; these numbers didn't intimidate them. We decided to go ahead with the offer and engaged 7-Eleven in the contract preparation process.

At the same time, we moved forward to meet with the Dowdys, who owned the large bowling alley property. It was quite a comical setting – we met at the bowling alley itself, at a folding table upstairs in their closed restaurant. I had brought Bobby along, who couldn't stop telling me this was totally a scene from 'The Big Lebowski.' Sitting there with the Dowdys, serious about our discussions, felt amusingly surreal. We agreed on a dynamic that I was '*The Dude*' and Bobby was '*Walter Sobchak.*' When in Rome.

Despite our enthusiasm and willingness to offer premium pricing, the Dowdys were savvy property owners. Their bowling alley had tremendous sentimental value as a family property. I put forward an offer of $6 million dollars for the bowling alley, only to find them unyielding. They declined the offer outright and told me that my number wasn't doing much for them. In a moment of brevity, I asked him what it would take to make a deal, and he told me, flashing that classic Ron Dowdy smile, "You need to come in here and knock my socks off."

However, our persistence continued to keep them interested. I increased the offer to $8 million, then $10 million. As I breached the eight-figure mark, it seemed Ron's children, Megan and R.J., recognized the potential of the deal and its importance for their family's future. Finally, they agreed to sell the bowling alley site to us for $12.5 million.

Even though this amount seemed significant, I rationalized it by dollar cost, averaging the acreage together and considering the potential value that the Polercoaster project could generate. With the notion of the amazing economics the world's tallest roller coaster and a thriving entertainment center would yield, paying a bit more for such an incredible site could someday prove to be a small expense.

By this point, I had engaged in intense negotiations with 7-Eleven, and after outplaying the determined franchisee who was entrenched in the store, successfully acquired the property for $3.7 million. At the same time, I was managing the intricacies of dealing with the Dowdys for the bowling alley. The process had tremendous twists and turns, including last-minute seller's remorse during the holiday season, which we had to overcome.

As I figured out the complexities of these acquisitions, we were making significant strides toward making the Coaster site a reality. Architectural vision plans were being developed by fantastic architects named Alan Helman and Mike Chatham and their firm HHCP, and we created an incredible name for the ride – The Skyscraper. The roller coaster was planned to stand at a staggering height of 570 feet, would be the world's tallest, and be located within an indoor entertainment complex named Skyplex.

With the site now under our control, a well-crafted presentation, vision, and enthusiasm in our hearts, we scheduled a press conference to unveil our ambitious project to the world. This was a dream come true for me, a chance to be associated with the iconic attractions that Orlando was world famous for. However, a leak to a seasoned news reporter, Greg Fox, led to an unexpected early reveal of our plans.

Fox broke the news of the Polercoaster on NBC WESH2 News on May 31, 2014, and reported we had secretly amassed these contiguous properties, masterminded a grand project, and the Coaster would be the world's tallest. The news spread like wildfire, and suddenly, we were thrust into the spotlight of Orlando's entertainment industry. As the story unfolded in the news, the realization hit me that our vision was becoming a reality.

Two days later, Fox followed up with another NBC exclusive story that delved into the specifics of our exact land acquisitions and the plans we had put together. It seemed as though we had been meticulously plotting this venture all along, quietly buying land through shell companies so no one would get wind, which was absolutely true. The community's anticipation was unbelievable, and the story made us the talk of the industry overnight.

Amidst the chaos of managing Mango's construction, change orders, delays, and juggling the Skyscraper project, the unexpected media frenzy added a layer of excitement and pressure. Our once-private endeavor was now the talk of the town, which was both exhilarating and daunting.

We found ourselves embarking on a great quest – the creation of the most monumental rollercoaster and awe-inspiring attraction Orlando had ever witnessed. With an uncanny knack for securing properties under the cover of night with a skill that no one could fathom, the media couldn't get enough, touting our feats as tactical brilliance.

The momentous day arrived, and on June 6th, 2014, we held a press conference, a moment that set the world ablaze about Skyplex. In an almost surreal whirlwind, news of our project cascaded across the globe. Major international newspapers, prestigious business publications, and esteemed TV networks like CNN, MSNBC, and Fox News all clamored to feature our story. Our triumph had transcended boundaries, reaching Canada, Mexico, England, Asia, and beyond. The spotlight was now firmly on us, and the exhilaration was unlike anything I'd ever known before. That afternoon, Skyplex and my name were both trending on Google's homepage and Twitter.

Mango's, a name already well celebrated in the nightlife scene, had given us recognition and respect in Miami Beach as community leaders. The Mango's Orlando project alone had been colossal. Yet, this was a completely different realm – suddenly, we were pivotal figures in the heart of Orlando. The transformation was leaving me astounded.

Returning home after the whirlwind press conference, the euphoria was strangely juxtaposed with a dark, empty house. My family was absent from the momentous occasion, having moved back to Miami a few weeks earlier when the kids finished their school year. The adrenaline that had coursed through me faded, and I felt a terrible emptiness. It was then that a vivid image of my young children Brett and Mia appeared, with them running happily together through the house with our dogs, laughing and calling for me to come and play with them, which lit up the world. The vision faded away as swiftly as it came, and everything went dark, leaving me sitting in the corner, unable to stop crying.

As I sat against the wall, in my mind's eye, I also saw my beautiful Toops cooking dinner in the kitchen, smiling at me. Her image then flickered and faded before disappearing completely. The grandest day of my professional life had brought me to a tearful breakdown, my emotions spiraling into a dark chasm. Alone in the house we had shared, I sat for hours on the cold floor, overwhelmed by a sense of desolation and longing to be with them.

My own emotions were foreign to me at that time. It was as though my ambition and immaturity had prevented me from comprehending the complex emotions that swirled within. My focus was on seizing opportunities and advancing my career, oblivious to the depths of emotional connection required from me. I believed that my wife should support my career and that her needs and desires could be met with some changes within our new life in Orlando.

In my selfish, self-absorbed state, I felt sadness instead of empathy and desire to connect, which gave way to feelings of resentment. Despite my deep understanding now, in those days, I was entangled in a web of emotions that clouded my judgment. I felt alone and hurt, left to navigate the journey myself while they returned to Miami. I missed them all so much. Well-intentioned voices offered their opinions, but who were they to comment on the intricacies of our family's dynamics?

My reaction ended up a maelstrom of emotions – sadness, regret, and a yearning for my family to be together. The magnitude of my career, building Mango's, acquiring the rollercoaster and Skyplex site, and everything else paled in comparison to the emptiness that pervaded my life. Despite the victories, I was shackled by solitude and a yearning for their presence each and every day.

Weeks passed, and on the Skyplex front, a glimmer of hope emerged from a friend's suggestion. Perkins had continued to elude us, and then, all of a sudden, there was a direction. I had been connected with Steve Borsewitch, an experienced real estate executive who possessed insight from his time working in house at GE Capital. He said he could come by and discuss, and our meeting took place at my house; to be honest, I was happy to have any visitors at the time. Amidst discussions in the living room, we laid out the complexities and potential strategies of this endeavor.

Steve revealed that the target Perkins site happened to be part of a single master lease that encompassed eight separate Perkins locations scattered across Florida. This intricate arrangement prompted the realization that our only path to securing the I-Drive corner was by acquiring all eight properties under the master lease. GE Capital would not go through the brain damage of trying to break off the one we wanted, so it was buy them all or walk. It was a moment of both revelation and daunting realization.

With this new knowledge, I approached our partners, Bernie and Robert, during a visit to Orlando. Seated at their hotel, I unveiled the intricate nature of the Perkins acquisition. Explaining that the entirety of the master lease needed to be purchased, I braced myself for their response to be "forget it." To my astonishment, Bernie's immediate reaction was, "Let's try to get it," showing a readiness to invest perhaps $30 million on the package. It was all I needed to hear, and Steve and I made contact and set up a meeting.

Negotiations with GE Capital commenced when we met with an asset manager from GE, Ken Heimlich, in their downtown Orlando offices. The gravity of the situation hung in the air – our project getting the hard corner hinged on the outcome of this meeting. Ken's professionalism and willingness to engage in a substantive discussion reassured us, and he suggested $32 Million as a purchase price.

Our in-person counter of $28 million was met with a sense of measured agreement from Ken. He recognized our seriousness and professionalism, traits that resonated with GE Capital's culture. They were used to dealing with buyers who showed a great sense of certainty.

Ken asked us to wait in his conference room as he conferred with his colleagues in their office and elsewhere. The afternoon was tense, yet it affirmed the significance of our proposal. I grew a little impatient, Steve and I being left alone for almost an hour. I hoped they'd return with an answer, and fortunately, they did re-enter the room, holding a document in their hands.

Ken explained that after considering our offer and consulting with his team, they were open to an arrangement. Typically, the seller covers broker fees, but in this case, they proposed that we cover the brokers' fees along with all closing costs, estimated at around $1 million. With these conditions, they were willing to finalize the deal at our suggested price, which, with the added costs, was now $29 million. I immediately sensed that the Friedmans might agree with this figure. So, I asked Ken for a moment, got Robert on the phone, and informed him about the new terms. His response was clear: "Make the deal." We shook hands with Ken, and it was clear a contract was imminent.

The exhilaration of making the monstrous $29 million deal was a bright spot amidst the challenges in my personal life. While my family situation was strained, I missed my wife and kids so much; this success brought a huge sense of accomplishment. Our efforts had paid off, and we had seemingly secured the premier piece of land for the roller coaster complex.

Once the agreement was drawn up and sent by their lawyers, we wasted no time in getting it back to them with minimal changes. Within days, we were officially under contract with a soft deposit of $1 million. The closing took place in December 2014, nearly a year before Mango's was set to open. Over the past 15 months, we had meticulously assembled the Skyplex site, and Mango's development was progressing steadily.

Construction was an artistic process, albeit with its fair share of stops and starts due to design intricacies. My father has a penchant for creativity over schedules and budgets. I handled the financial and administrative aspects while he brought his artistic touch and design to the project. Together, we had a strong partnership that contributed to our success.

The following months were a whirlwind of intense construction. As my family returned to Orlando, we settled into a great new neighborhood, and the countdown to Mango's opening began. The construction process was grueling, and the delays were frustrating, but we all attempted to persevere. I juggled community engagement, media appearances, and legal matters related to our projects. More than anything else, however, I had them back and was so relieved I could come home and find my family after more than a year.

The crucial step then came that was critical: to rezone the land we had acquired for Skyplex into a planned development (PD). To achieve this, I teamed up with Angel de la Portilla, our trusted political strategist. We engaged with the Planning and Zoning Board (P&Z), an advisory body to the Board of County Commissioners. However, we soon sensed resistance, and it became clear that a tremendously formidable opponent to Skyplex emerged, Comcast/ Universal Studios, who, to say the least, was not in favor of our project.

Universal's influence was extremely powerful and substantial, and they were using their connections to sway the P & Z board. Some who had initially supported us were changing their stance due to the pressure. The situation was disheartening; we lost 4-3 at the advisory board level. This was a non-binding vote; all that mattered was the Board of County Commissioners, but I was extremely angered by the move, and the Miami in me emerged.

On TV, I took a defiant stand against corporate bullying, publicly challenging Universal to face me and vowing not to compromise our vision. I refused to back down; if they wanted a fight, they had it. Orlando was my home now too. It was clear there would be a tremendous showdown at the actual zoning hearing in front of the Orange County Commission.

The response from the community was overwhelming. People resonated with our fight against corporate interference, Wall Street against Main Street. Universal launched a local campaign against us, sending out mailers to County residents. We countered with a highly strategic move, leveraging influential theme park bloggers to rally support through their extensive social media and YouTube networks. Orange County was flooded with tens of thousands of letters in favor of Skyplex, which caught Universal off guard.

The crucial day arrived on December 1, 2015, the hearing in front of the Board of County Commissioners for Skyplex's rezoning. Mango's stood just two weeks away from its grand opening. The world was watching a high-stakes battle of our family against Universal's dominance.

Thousands of people tuned in from around the world since the hearing was streamed live. It had been Universal versus Skyplex on the front page of newspapers for weeks, and all eyes were on how I would survive in this fierce level of combat with an Apex Predator. Most people thought we were swimming against a tidal wave and there was no chance for us at all. That propelled me harder, and I worked tirelessly on our presentation so our punches would have maximum impact.

With my attorney Hal Kantor, I presented our case to the commissioners, emphasizing our commitment to the project, what it meant to the community, and a bit about the hypocrisy of their opposition. The Chamber was overflowing; the momentous showdown was breaking news everywhere.

The battle between a corporate giant and a determined family captured hearts and attention everywhere. The outcome remained uncertain, but our resilience and determination were unwavering.

Filled with confidence, we believed our overall presentation was solid, and everyone seemingly wanted us to succeed. As I gazed out at the audience, my family was there: my wife, kids, dad, and aunt, all there to support us. Our new staff in Orlando and even the Mango's employees from South Beach came up. It was packed, standing room only, with media from all over in attendance. My son Brett coming up to the microphone and addressing the Commission was the highlight of the meeting for me.

After the 5-hour hearing, the Board voted 7-0 to approve Skyplex's PD. The victory resounded across the world; I received nearly 80,000 DMs from strangers on my personal social media accounts from people in 50 countries, and, again, Skyplex was trending on both Twitter and Google's homepage. We redefined land use on International Drive forever that day.

After that, we set out to begin the design of the facility, but more than anything, there was no time to rest with Mango's Orlando so close to opening. I needed a long vacation with the family, but that was not in the cards. Opening the nightclub that we had been building for years was the immediate future. It was truly a December to Remember.

Mango's opened 16 days later, on December 17, 2015, to total madness beyond our dreams. Thousands of people fought to get in; it took 3 hours just to get your car into the valet ramp. We had purchased the Walgreens next door and knocked it down as a surface lot, but it was clear we immediately needed to turn that into a parking garage as soon as we could.

I was beat up beyond belief and could barely make it through the nights, especially with the parking shortage that had been created. Sometimes, I was outside for hours, where the lot was like a warzone, trying to get people in.

As people continued pouring into Mango's, we set out to get the garage development going. We now had Skyplex rezoned; we had the site for the parking garage and believed building it could be a great preamble for the eventual Skyplex construction.

I was literally exhausted, physically, mentally, and spiritually, but now another project, building the garage in order to help Mango's become a complete development, took center stage. In the middle of it all, as much as I loved my wife, the immense stress was taking its toll. I was trying to stay on track, but the track itself was leading toward the edge of a cliff.

Chapter 6:
The Garage Mahal and the Depths of Abyss

On June 20, 2013, a connection through Bacardi opened the door to an extraordinary experience. Game 7 of the NBA Finals, the defending NBA Champion Miami Heat against the San Antonio Spurs, was the Series' deciding game. The Heat, having won the title the previous year, were now on the edge of being Champions again after a miraculous Game 6 win.

The atmosphere at the Arena was electrifying, the tension incredible. A constellation of stars graced the occasion, all eyes fixated on LeBron James, Dwayne Wade, and Chris Bosh as they stepped onto the court, favored to reclaim the championship.

In the middle of the fervor, in the early evening, my phone rang, a call from Orlando's preeminent developer, Chuck Whittall, who was building the 400' Orlando Eye Ferris Wheel on International Drive. Chuck was in Miami with Brenden O'Brien, a Walgreens real estate executive, and asked if I was at Mango's. Immediately, I felt an unexpected opportunity was at hand: the Walgreens next door to our Mango's Orlando location, a property we had to have, was rumored to soon be up for sale. Recognizing the potential to try and secure the deal through a monster night of fun, I asked Chuck and Brenden to meet me at Game 7.

With impeccable timing, I guided them to an accessible door in the Arena parking garage behind the VIP Suites and, aided by some borrowed Bacardi badges from my colleagues, got them both in. The tickets, likely valued at $5,000 per person, were a comp to the biggest sporting event in the world. Chuck, familiar with such lavish experiences, was happy as can be. Brenden, an Illinois native somewhat new to Miami's glamor, joined us in the Suite and was impressed by the glitterati around him and getting in for free. Bacardi's bountiful offerings ensured our enjoyment; we partied the whole game and were down on the court during the Heat's NBA championship victory celebration.

Together, we shared the ecstasy of winning the Title and the thrill of the NBA trophy presentation. Later, at Mango's, the party continued. Amidst the celebration, I seized the moment I had planned, leaning over to make sure Brenden was having the time of his life. Waiting hours for that single moment, I asked him to promise to sell me the Walgreens property adjacent to Mango's. His affirmation sealed the deal, "Of course, don't worry." Brenden was a buddy now, and I was fully convinced he'd make it happen.

The following weeks buzzed with tension. Brenden's nod of approval had indeed cleared the path. An email exchange from Walgreens' in-market broker, Dennis Sargeant, marked the journey forward. Their internal discussions swirled around pricing, while some at the brokerage suggested leasing the property and then selling it for a higher value. Sensing the stakes, Dennis consulted Brenden at my asking, who reaffirmed Walgreen's intent to sell 'as is.' The deal awaited, the culmination of 2 months of coordination. As we hosted friends one evening, I received a call from Walgreens Corporate and retreated to a closet in my children's playroom, holding my breath.

I braced myself, and Brenden's voice revealed their ask was $5.3 million. I was pleased with their pricing. Clearly, they weren't greatly overvaluing the site and wanted to make a deal. My initial impulse to always negotiate a first offer tugged at me, but the stakes were way too high for any uncertainty. Even a $100,000 counter would trigger a complex reroute up the ladder of bureaucracy for approval, and who knows what could happen, how long it would take, or if the entire situation would change completely. Some new Executive could have gotten involved who had different ideas, and all of a sudden, my deal could've been cast to the wind. To me, it was a risk not worth taking at all.

I decided to make a deal with them right then and there. When Brenden and his colleagues quoted the price, I asked them to hold on and counted to fifteen, taking time to show them I was contemplating the number and not impulsive.

Multiple executives were on the call, and with a company like Walgreens, it was crucial to show a very professional demeanor and a great level of certainty to give them confidence in us as a Buyer.

Then, resolute and calculated, I affirmed calmly, "You have a deal." The next day, a term sheet arrived from Dennis, which I quickly signed as our commitment cemented. Brenden, with his unique vantage point within Walgreens, assured us of a forthcoming purchase and sale agreement.

Our stride toward Mango's development took a twist. The Walgreens property beside us became the key parking lot instead of the originally planned 4 acres across the street now slated for Skyplex. The Walgreens site also offered an exclusive 90 parking spaces, crucial for the Mango's building permit we sought. Walgreens' cooperation extended to penning a letter to Orange County, formally assigning their parking spaces to our venture, and expressing persistent confidence in our deal closing.

Yet, the passage of time found us waiting for the purchase and sale agreement to materialize. It was really just that their legal department was backlogged. Tensions escalated, and my father's patience weakened. Comparing the process to dealing with an institution rather than an individual, I told him, "Walgreens is like dealing with the Church, Dad. When they make a commitment, it stays." I emphasized even emails exchanged with a public, corporate entity hold steadfast, devoid of the impulsiveness that may exist when doing a deal with some regular person. If no one made a mistake or changed terms, nothing would get off track.

Despite this assurance, an unexpected source of resistance arose. Another neighbor in our plaza, Orlando businessman Eric Holm, the nation's top Golden Corral franchisee, cast a shadow over our plans. Unacquainted with him prior to my move to Orlando and acquisitions in the Plaza, Eric enjoyed unending success from his prime location and didn't want a disruption in the operation.

Our ambitions, however, raised his eyebrows. Transforming Mango's into a sprawling entity and repurposing the Walgreens lot as a parking garage unsettled him. Why mess up a good thing was his point. Perhaps viewing me as an outsider, a carpet bagger from Miami, Eric's actions demonstrated his intention to safeguard his interest.

In retrospect, Eric's feelings were justifiable, and his concerns grounded. Our relationship has since blossomed into one of great friendship and mutual respect. A man of faith, family, and deep values, Eric revealed his true character over time. Yet, in those early days, suspicion colored his perception of me and my intentions. It's a testament to the complexity of human interactions and the difficulties of venturing on transformative journeys.

In the midst of this unfolding saga, Holm appeared as an unexpected obstacle, driven to prove that outsiders couldn't simply impose their will on a neighboring business that was established. It became apparent that lobbying efforts were at play, complicating my interactions at Orange County with regard to the garage. At the time, Tiffany Moore Russell, in her eighth year as county commissioner, felt the sway of these lobbying efforts, as Eric had retained a law school chum of hers who was a top lobbyist working on her at his behest. Meeting with Tiffany after, I sensed a shift, a hint of hesitation that wasn't present before.

Recognizing the need for political support to counter the pressure, I reached out to Harris Rosen, the renowned hotelier on International Drive. Through Harris, I was introduced to Angel de la Portilla, a top political strategist. Enlisting Angel's expertise marked a key move for us, and little did I know he would evolve into both a confidant and an extremely close friend.

Mango's construction was in full swing as we guided the complexities of closing on the Walgreens property. The Friedmans, our Skyplex partners, pursued a reverse 1031 exchange for their share while we secured our portion of the deal with cash. The timing, however, was not without its challenges, as some delays with their 1031 closing slightly delayed Friedman's transaction. Yet, Walgreens demonstrated exceptional flexibility, extending our closing date with understanding.

After the acquisition closed at $5.3 million, we demolished the Walgreens building and built a temporary gravel lot on the site, supplementing Mango's parking needs for its permits. Our focus shifted toward a planned parking garage on the parcel. Originally imagined as a modest structure with some fronted retail space, the garage design underwent a significant transformation as we considered a rooftop restaurant and additional parking spaces. Conversations with architects and precast concrete experts revealed the potential capability to expand the garage plan.

With the new design taking shape, we encountered the need for a zoning variance due to, at the time, archaic height restrictions in the area. During this process, Holm's legal representation reached out for a meeting. This was an opening to the impending struggle, a conversation loaded with an undertone of impending conflict. The message about talking 'before the war starts' was cryptic but clear, and despite our unfamiliarity, my response was one of stoic resolve. I never backed down from a fight.

The variance filing process was underway, and Eric mobilized his legal team, employing the services of skilled litigator Scott Glass. This added a layer of complexity to our variance hearing, which would have proceeded without a hitch in normal circumstances. However, Glass's extensive opposition clouded the proceedings.

Between Gunster Law's Derek Bruce as Holm's lobbyist and Scott Glass as his litigating attorney, Eric had a formidable legal team against the project.

Attempting to bridge the divide, I visited Eric at his incredible Winter Park mansion, seeking common ground. I strived for a more calming tone, expressing my intent to collaborate on a solution. Yet still, in those early days, the conversation bore no fruit, leaving us at an unfortunate impasse.

The upcoming variance hearing unfolded in a climate of tension and conflict. It was evident that Tiffany's stance was aligned against us, and prospects looked rough at the Board level. Faced with a real possibility of a potential loss, I made the decision to withdraw the variance motion. We took the opportunity to speak once more before the Board, during which Mayor Teresa Jacobs suggested an alternative path, rezoning to a Planned Development (PD) designation for the single Walgreens site.

Though a good solution, this shift underscored the outdated zoning regulations of the time. The fact that the bustling International Drive strip, the most intense land use area in the County, had a ridiculous height limit of only 50 feet highlighted the shortcomings of the antiquated zoning regulations. The clunky process, compounded by the potential for lawsuits, spotlighted how bureaucracy could slow business growth and make it a bad bet for new investors.

Adapting to this strategy, we pursued rezoning as a PD. Sensing our determination, Eric escalated his efforts, leveraging his litigation tactics. Glass filed a lawsuit against the Hollywood Plaza Property Owners Association and Mango's. The heart of their argument revolved around Golden Corral's perceived liability due to our intense development plans, accusing us of overburdening easements and unsuitably altering the area.

Litigation is often wielded as a tool of negotiation, a means to push adversaries into unfavorable positions and force compromise under duress. Eric's actions mirrored this approach, influenced by his high-level business acumen. While I empathized with his desire to safeguard his business, there was no denying that Eric was playing hardball. I believed that a resolution could be reached without resorting to more hostility.

Simultaneously, I delved into the political arena more thoroughly, recognizing the importance of having a friend in the office. Tiffany's term had concluded, leaving the District 6 seat open. With Angel's assistance, we assessed the candidates and gravitated toward Victoria Siplin, a dynamic attorney married to former Senator Gary Siplin. Her intellect, charisma, and charm captured our attention. We threw our support behind her, contributing both financially and morally to her campaign. As election night unfolded, our intuition was right, and Victoria emerged as the victor and the new commissioner elect.

With a newfound political ally in power, the tide began to turn. Derek Bruce's sway over the office had ended, ushering in a period of advocacy that aligned with our interests.

The situation escalated at the scheduled hearing for our PD rezoning at the County building. This time, we didn't enter peacefully; we braced ourselves for a formidable confrontation, recognizing the battle that would take place that day. Expecting conflict before the Board of County Commissioners, we came extremely prepared, and our proposal secured unanimous approval. The PD reignited our hope for the parking garage's construction.

However, Eric's determination remained unyielding. Recognizing we had our zoning; he instructed his attorneys to pursue legal avenues to stop us. Filing a lawsuit against Orange County blocked our ability to get a building permit; the move memorialized an environment of more uncertainty. We pursued mediation, hoping to reach a settlement that could facilitate progress, especially considering Mango's close opening soon after.

The pressures on me mounted, especially by my intense involvement with Skyplex and the challenges posed to it by Universal Studios. As time progressed, the tide seemed to shift. Our efforts in the face of Universal's opposition, I believe now, earned Eric's hard-fought respect. In a surprising turn of events, a cordial email from him arrived in November 2015, just weeks before the powerful showdown with Universal. Amid the upcoming clash, he seemed to recognize the mutual value our ventures brought to the area. An unlikely friendship emerged, prompting Eric to suggest a meeting to find common ground.

We arranged and drafted a settlement agreement wherein we agreed to offer him a more sovereign parking area around Golden Corral. This marked a turning point; what was once a powerful competition transformed into a collaborative effort for mutual benefit and friendship. I was told later that one of the most important, impactful letters of support for Skyplex and our family to Orange County came from Eric Holm.

With our legal dispute finally put to rest, we shifted our focus to constructive endeavors. Armed with a building permit, we could finally proceed with building the parking garage. The original vision had dramatically expanded to include a rooftop restaurant, resulting in a unique structural composition that added a steel package to the building's framework, a critical element for what was to come. The building plan was so grand we began referring to it as 'The Garage Mahal'.

With the key obstacles removed from zoning and permitting, attention turned to the financial aspect. The Friedmans, our partners, we believed held the key to unlocking the construction loan. A financing of approximately $16 million was needed to start the garage's development. Permitting efforts were already underway.

When we began site work on the Walgreens land, it made it impossible to park on it anymore. Mango's, which had been operational for a year, suffered a huge blow as it lost its only parking spaces on the side. The vision of having the Garage Mahal became our lifeline, a solution to the parking shortage that was now compounded. However, even as we ventured on this journey, the challenges continued.

The devastating Pulse terror attack in Downtown Orlando had frozen the city's nightlife, resulting in a four-month period of stagnation and hardship for Mango's and nearly everyone else. One of our best dancers, Anthony Laureano, was among the 49 killed, and 2 more of our staff were wounded on that terrible night.

Despite these intense issues, after the Pulse shock and funerals were behind us all, my focus turned to tunnel vision on bringing the garage to fruition. Even though I was heavily involved in the Skyplex project, the Garage Mahal held a sense of urgency as it had an immediate impact on Mango's operations.

Bernie initiated construction on the garage, beginning with site work, foundations, and necessary mechanical, electrical, and plumbing trenches. My hope was that the garage could be up and running within 14-

16 months, providing much-needed relief to Mango's parking challenges.

Unfortunately, progress encountered a serious roadblock. Our project initially faced difficulties securing a construction loan. Unlike refinancing or obtaining a mortgage for an existing property, securing a loan for a new construction job, without leases or a proven track record, was a different challenge altogether. Out-of-state banks, unfamiliar with the Florida landscape, compounded the problem.

The situation became incredibly stressful. The once-functioning parking lot lay unusable, dug up for construction. The Walgreens surface lot, which at one point accommodated around 150 cars, was off the table.

As we waited and attempted negotiations with various lenders, we thought we had made progress with a bank from New York. They sent an appraiser and held some meetings, but then nothing materialized, no term sheet, no deal. The process was marked by frustrating waiting periods where construction ceased, and workers demobilized, stopping everything in its tracks. I realized that a new, proactive approach was immediately necessary.

Taking matters into my own hands, I turned to City National Bank, the financial institution that had previously helped us refinance both of Mango's locations. Despite my hope that things could be expedited, the path ahead remained complex. Since they had provided a $35 million package and had a mortgage interest in the real estate, I emphasized the need for a parking garage at Mango's Orlando.

We commenced discussions with City National, presenting the details of the garage project. Armed with a solid proforma rent roll and parking income figures, I managed to get approval from their underwriting team. City National stepped up and offered a $17.5 million loan for the construction of the Hollywood Plaza garage, which the Friedmans and Wallacks closed on together.

However, this financing came very late to the party. Mango's had been grappling with parking issues since its opening, with the loss of around 50 to 60 percent of the already limited parking due to pre-construction and then delay on the Walgreens site. The prosperity of Mango's hung in the balance, dependent on the successful construction; the urgency was real.

It became an all-consuming work, a near-religious pursuit. Having already guided the challenges of building Mango's and rezoning Skyplex, I found myself, again, totally engaged in this new venture. After surviving a lawsuit just to secure zoning, the project became the final hurdle before Mango's could truly thrive.

While others were opening small restaurants and seeing customers stream in from adjacent surface lots, we were now mired in a years-long effort to construct another essential building. The Walgreens site, surrounded by a construction fence, stood as a witness to the financing delays that had stalled our progress. By the time we received a term sheet from City National for the loan, parts of the site were overgrown with five-foot weeds, highlighting the lengthy setback.

City National's loan closure, finalized in late 2017, provided us with a fresh start. The loan funds could empower Bernie to kick-start the construction process. However, time had passed, and many subcontractors had moved on, necessitating a fresh mobilization effort just to get the schedule back on track.

Bernie offered to take on the role of general contractor himself, which at the time made sense, given our collaboration on Skyplex. With the financing now secured, we were to put the wheels of progress back in motion and forge ahead with the construction of the Garage Mahal.

As the job progressed, it was relieving to witness the precast concrete structure taking shape. The building shell seemed to rise at an impressive pace, with each piece being secured into place by welders. I often found myself bringing visitors to the top of the structure on a golf cart and sharing my excitement and the incredible views from the top. The prospect of the Garage Mahal's completion meant Mango's would finally have the catalyst it needed for tremendous, unending success.

However, amid this excitement, I was grappling with mounting stress, frustration, and anger. Every day seemed to bring new challenges, and the situation was even made far worse by events in Miami Beach. The mayor of that time, who owned land across the city, had initiated a referendum to close Ocean Drive businesses at 2 a.m. through a binding public vote. This unjust measure required our full attention, alongside the garage construction and everything else. With pressure packed, 24/7 work, we crushed the boneheaded attempt via a supermajority win with 65% of the vote.

The end of 2017 marked a period when the erection of the garage coincided with the urgent need, day after day, to address the Miami Beach voter referendum. Balancing these demands led to an overwhelming level of stress. While I cherished my family, my emotional management was faltering. I was financially providing, but my presence and emotional availability were lacking. My wife shared her concerns, but I didn't fully understand her words as I should have, not even close. I was just so frustrated by the intense, tremendous challenges at work, and it compounded the tension at home.

This involved a larger issue, not just in my life but across the world. Loved ones usually offer advice out of care, not to criticize, yet many sense it negatively. I fell headfirst into this trap, responding with resentment rather than understanding, deepening the divide. In hindsight, I can clearly see reciprocating love and understanding is required in such situations. It's never a one-way street; one must give to receive.

Coming home, during dinner and family time, my mind was consumed by the Rollercoaster, parking garage, financial matters, referendum issues, and Mango's operations day to day, among other things. This isolation escalated, distancing me from them as I went further into a silo of unmanaged stress. While we went to parks on weekends, the emotional issues endured, and my gnawing anxiety resulted in a commitment to not work on Sundays at all. I aimed to spend this day with my family, totally and completely. However, the stress continued to rip me apart.

By 2019, my wife and I reached a critical point in our marriage. Selfishly, I believed that my sacrifices warranted greater understanding from her regarding the immense career pressure on me. The mindset was self-absorbed, misguided, and wrong. While it was true, I was financially responsible for our family, I became blind to the broader picture.

Looking back to that time, I know more deeply than one can imagine that merely providing financial support doesn't correlate to being a good husband and father. Any ex-spouse who barely or never sees his kids can fulfill some financial obligation by sending a check somewhere. It doesn't make them any less of an asshole.

The idea that just providing monetary support is good enough is simply ignorant and dangerous. Money can cover groceries, car payments, clothing, and dance lessons, but it's far from what any genuine person should offer. I can deeply assure you that it's not any advice to heed, and any person who tells you so is a fool who is likely alone, crying himself to sleep at night.

During this time, the focus on the Skyplex project in Orlando had waned. Although the project had been zoned in late 2015, it faced many challenges, much like the garage had. Despite overcoming huge odds, such as acquiring impossible land and brutal rezoning, the project struggled to get construction underway. The setback further frustrated me, given the significant promises I had made to my family and the world about the Coaster.

Nonetheless, the Garage Mahal was progressing. I had even managed to generate interest from The Walt Disney Company and Hulk Hogan as potential tenants, trying to still make big moves despite the Skyplex delays. I placed The Hulkster in the 7-Eleven across the street instead, and he opened his successful attraction, Hulk Hogan's Wrestling Shop, the weekend before WrestleMania 33 in Orlando.

My attention remained painfully divided between Skyplex and the prolonged garage construction. These complex issues, Mango's operations in Orlando and South Beach, and many other matters kept me totally preoccupied.

As the construction continued into mid-2019, it encountered multiple setbacks, particularly with the electrical system. An out-of-state subcontractor did a workaround he thought was ok, but it didn't follow the exact plans as needed. The result was months more of delay, reworking of their mistakes, and substantial costs. The obstacles compounded the challenges Mango's faced due to the ongoing construction, as the parking shortage persisted, years in.

Amid this madness, I struggled with maintaining any kind of balanced presence. My frustration and anger from work was destroying me. Though I aimed to be sweet at home, my absence and emotional detachment due to my work obsession created distance. My mind was consumed by business-related concerns, obsessed with projects and the future. This type of extreme dedication, while often necessary for an entrepreneur at certain key junctures in short bursts, is not always for and will lead to family losses if not tempered and controlled. You can't redline indefinitely; something in the engine will blow up.

The Garage Mahal's slow pace of construction remained a source of exasperation. The delays and mounting issues took a toll, affecting not just the financial bottom line but also the emotional well-being of those involved. I wrestled with the realization that my relentless pace had unintentionally created a depth between me and my loved ones.

The temptation for money and success subsides when you are alone in the world. If you're content with solitude and your kids' resentment, then working religiously around the clock might suit you. But remember, you'll become the 'Cats in the Cradle' guy, alienated from your grown children who won't want to know you. It's a lesson that is crystal clear for all who open their hearts to understand that very real truth.

Things were winding down to a terrible point. I was losing my sanity at home and even considered not being there anymore. Unknown to me, due to my own loss of balance after years of breakneck pace, I was single-handedly causing this unrest. Blind to my behavior and its impact, I pushed away my wife, daughter, and son, who were happily living their lives together.

My daughter and wife found solace in dance, sharing intimate and endless conversations about it. But my detachment and frustration persisted, leaving them feeling emotionally abandoned. This self-sabotaging perspective, where I continued erroneously believing financial support was enough, was just so deeply flawed. It led me to resent an apparent lack of interest in them spending time with me, all the while failing to acknowledge that my absence and behavior had completely pushed them away.

As the winter of 2019 arrived, I descended to the very lowest point in my life. The Garage Mahal was approaching completion, with a certificate of occupancy on the horizon, likely a few months away. Yet, I was still engaged in the severe emotional pain I was causing my family and myself. Our marriage was strained, and I reached a level of true derangement in my thoughts.

At my wit's end, I placed a deposit on a three-bedroom rental apartment, contemplating a separation. I was wrestling with emotions that seemed completely foreign, asinine, and illogical to me now. The version of me of that time was an entirely different person, a crazed individual who needed a wake-up call or a fool who needed his lights punched out, likely both.

The end of October 2019 marked the onset of the darkest, awful, most painful period ever experienced. Focusing on the Garage Mahal, I hired an economist to conduct an economic impact study, hoping to demonstrate the benefits of parking for Mango's and attract tenants to the garage.

Then came a glimmer of hope: a smaller Hollywood movie studio with an experimental VR theme park in China. My dad and I proposed exploring it as a potential avenue to reinvigorate the Skyplex project, and the Friedmans saw merit in the idea. We were deeply invested and still pursuing financing, and the project could easily be revitalized with such a big development. This vision of Skyplex was the most exciting and compelling since the inception of the project.

While I believed I was making the right moves, nobody at home seemed to care about my endeavors. I had made sure of that.

Despite the achievements and grand plans, my family's indifference remained. My absence had caused them to close off, their worlds turning inward while I remained rooted in my work. The lesson, too late, was that no amount of business success could replace the emotional presence and understanding required in a happy family.

My brain was a tangled mess, unable to let go of its garbage. I felt like I had stage 4 cancer of the mind, consumed by twisted thoughts. I craved solitude, away from the harmful vibes and the confrontation of my misguided actions. My mental state was declining sharply, leaving me to hold tightly onto business matters and the possibility of a brighter future.

It was as if I'd lost touch with reality, longing for isolation to escape the madness I'd created. My priorities were skewed, and I desperately needed psychological counseling and a peaceful retreat with my wife. I believed that a long tropical getaway could mend our relationship, but we were well past that point then.

Returning from a three-day trip to review specifications for the new Skyplex, which was now set to include a full Resort Hotel, I found no interest from my family about my experience. The gap between us had grown so wide, my insanity reached a breaking point. In a fit of emptiness and self-made hysteria, I moved to the apartment complex in a thoughtless attempt to make safe distance from the emotional pain that had consumed us.

I was in a foreign place, feeling nothing, neither better nor worse. It was as if I'd emptied myself of emotions. Plowing ahead, I focused on work, hoping that the opening of the Garage Mahal and the progress of Skyplex would fill any void and provide any meaning. It didn't.

I missed our Thanksgiving dinner for the first time in the kids' lives. Instead, I sat in Mango's South Beach with my father and Boris, eating at the staff buffet. I became emotionally distant, driven at work like a machine while battling the unbearable emptiness that had corroded my mind and soul.

In November and December of 2019, when COVID-19 was starting to surface in the world, my personal turmoil and breakdown coincided with what would become the darkest and most despicable periods in history. During this time, we saw other people. I fell ill and experienced symptoms of ED for the first time in my entire life. My dreams were filled with fantasies of my wife's affection, highlighting the depth of my emotional emptiness. My nightmares were intense, sweating through the bed.

I had reached the edge of despair and fell headfirst into the abyss. There was no other side to make it to, just a continuous fall, lower and lower.

The Garage Mahal received its certificate of occupancy in December 2019, marking its opening at last, but I felt nothing. I had long promised myself that I'd celebrate this moment by having my favorite childhood meal at McDonald's, but when I picked it up, it had no taste, and I didn't feel a thing, just the hollowness within me.

The holidays passed, and while I sent Christmas presents to my family, I spent the holiday alone for the first time in their lives. I visited my mom and stepdad in Naples on Christmas Day, laying in the fetal position on their couch all day and sweating through the bed at night. Despite their company, I remained withdrawn, limited to lying down and sharing the torment of my life with my mom.

The Rollercoaster, the garage, Mango's, none of it mattered anymore. All anyone saw was this mess of a person, a broken man.

Then, at the depths of the abyss, something remarkable happened. On January 10th, 2020, only days into the new decade, about eight weeks after our separation, I was at Mango's, trying to make it through another night, when I received a text from my Toops. Her words struck me like thunder, "I'm at Eddie V's, come and give me a hug."

My heart leaped with joy; I ran to my car and raced to Eddie V's in my Shelby Cobra, leaving fire tracks from the Mango's parking lot. I honestly put my life and the lives of other drivers around me at risk the way I flew there.

As I walked into the restaurant, I spotted her at the bar. My wife, more beautiful and incredible than ever, started walking toward me. She was riveting, so unbelievable, so amazing. Without hesitation, I took her hand, and we walked outside. "What are we doing?" she asked. "I'm here for my wife," I told her without a second thought.

Her arms wrapped around me, and we found ourselves at the edge of a lake, inside a wooden tiki hut decorated with torches. We sat together at the water's edge, the setting so romantic, and began to kiss. Our kissing was as passionate as it was the first time, 22 years before, and at that moment, my heart felt free and pure like it never had before.

I led her to my car, and our kissing continued, our emotions running wild. The incredulity of the situation washed over me; I couldn't believe that this was happening. In that instant, we were blissfully happy, just the two of us; she was the love of my life forever. I had been utterly, gravely wrong about everything, and she had remained steadfast, despite everything. I felt a tidal wave of regret for my behavior, our problems, how I had hurt her, everything. Nothing meant anything without this remarkable woman, my children, our loving home, and being together in the way we once were.

That night, we were reborn and reconnected as our hearts came together as perfectly as they could. We had been saved by our love.

The next morning, I headed to Walgreens for a simple cold drink, as there was nothing in the apartment I had existed in. Psychosomatically, since I didn't want to be there, I didn't have food, beverages, or anything of comfort at all in the place. It was a manifestation of how much I had lost, how far I had wandered from what truly mattered, and how much I absolutely hated myself and my life. I wasn't even worth having a bottle of water around.

A trip to Walgreens usually reflected the madness I was going through. I had been stopping there or at a grocery store, meal for meal, drink for drink, mirroring the haze I was in. Now, I was just floating on a cloud.

From my car, I decided to call her on FaceTime. She picked up from our bedroom, then slipped into her closet for privacy. Across the screen, we bared our souls, saying everything that needed to be said. I felt as though the previous, incredible evening was continuing to unfold. My love for this amazing woman, whom I had thought I lost forever, swelled enormously. I was completely aware of how much she loved me, and nothing else mattered at all.

Amidst the important legal preparations for a zoning hearing on dynamic digital art two days away, where we needed to support changes to the county ordinance, all I could think about was seeing my wife. I was consumed by the urge to hold her, to be with her. Unsure of how my kids would react if I showed up at the house unannounced, I booked a room at the Four Seasons that very night.

I texted, confessing my thoughts about her and my inability to stop. I asked if she would meet me at the Four Seasons that night. She responded with a vibrant 'yes,' and I assured her I would come straight from where I was. As our meeting ended and Hal was satisfied with our readiness to face the Board of County Commissioners the following day, I was breathless, counting down the moments until I could see her.

She had checked into the hotel before me, and while I tried my best to give Hal attention, I could barely manage. I was lost in happiness; my pain had disappeared completely. Less than an hour separated me from the love of my life, and the mere thought of holding her overwhelmed my senses. I could hardly think straight. Hal's voice pulled me back, declaring that we were prepared. I thanked him, sprinted from his downtown Orlando office to my car, and sped down I-4 at more than 90 miles an hour to the hotel.

With only a room number, I walked down the corridor with a deep belief that my future lay just beyond that door. I knocked, and the door opened, revealing a beautiful, dimly lit room decorated with sparkling candles. She was there, sipping wine. Swiftly, I changed into the same clothes, or lack thereof, that she was wearing. Our night together unfolded in intense passion, punctuated by moments of deep conversation, laughter, kissing, and loving. I was breathlessly exhilarated, fascinated by everything that rushed between us.

She was blowing my mind with the depth of emotions we were sharing. In a single night, we didn't just find ourselves in love or lust; we became irrevocably, unquestionably, and completely bound to each other, as if we were married all over again. I desired to understand every aspect of her life, everything she was feeling, and to hold her forever.

As she looked into my eyes, a deep change occurred within me. It was not a gradual transformation; it was instantaneous. The person I had become over the last year, or perhaps even longer, was someone I couldn't stand, a sad son-of-a-bitch, a pitiful man. But now, my heart and soul overflowed with love, and we marveled at the joy we felt together.

The next morning, waking up together in our beautiful room at the Four Seasons, I kissed my incredible wife, held her close, and shared my plan. I was going to the Board of County Commissioners to win the dynamic art law, and then I was coming home, forever. She said she'd be waiting for me.

As I set off on that morning, the joy in my heart carried me into the sky. I knew I was headed home to my children, to my wife, to our beautiful life together. I was going to make her and their lives more wonderful than ever before.

I never wanted to experience anything like the darkness I had lived through; no one should. I wouldn't wish it on my worst enemy. The dynamic art hearing, accompanied by Hal, went very well. Afterward, I thanked Hal with a heartfelt hug, to which he responded, "You don't need to thank me; you're my favorite client."

Those words echoed with me that morning. Though I was paying him substantial fees, I just appreciated him so much that day and realized I appreciated everything around me so much, like I had woken from a long coma or was cured of blindness. As I drove back for the last time to the makeshift living situation that I had suffered in for eight weeks, I hurriedly gathered belongings that fit in one carload.

I told my cousin, who needed furnishings, decor, and anything else that he was welcome to take the furniture and whatever he wanted from the place; it was all his, and I didn't care. I was never, ever going back there. I left the keys behind, symbolizing the finality of it all.

My focus was solely on driving back home to my family immediately. Creeping up the rope that little did I know was wrapped around my waist, I arose from the deep abyss that had all but consumed me. As I pulled myself over the edge, the past fell behind.

Walking through the front door, Brett smiled so brightly, my beautiful Mia hugged me with incredibly emotional happiness, and my wife's amazing smile floored me. We shared dinner as a family for the first time in 8 weeks, but for the first time in ages, we felt whole again. I informed the kids that we were going on a trip, and I couldn't wait to connect, have fun, and play together. I was aware that I had caused them terrible hurt, confusion, and pain. While I couldn't erase the past, I knew that, starting from that day, everything had changed forever.

Our life together was beginning anew in the 2020s. Reflecting on that time, the terrible pain leading up to our separation fades immediately in comparison to the images of coming together, the romance at Eddie V's, the unforgettable night at the Four Seasons, and rekindling our beautiful love at home. Those moments hold the most profound meaning for me.

We all make mistakes, sometimes terrible ones, but we can grow, change, and evolve. We don't have to remain in darkness; we have the power to align, transform, and move forward together. The most important thing in my life, what I learned through the worst pain one could imagine, and my hope for what is taken from this is a single truth:

REGARDING VICTORY: ADVENTURES IN ENTREPRENEURSHIP LED BACK TO LOVE

'No matter what level of success, wealth, or achievement you may attain, none of it matters at all if you don't bring it home to a house full of people you love and who love you.'

Chapter 7:
The Deal with Disney

Mr. De Valk, my 11th-grade chemistry teacher, had a saying: *"When all else fails, draw a picture."* His advice applied primarily to solving organic chemistry problems, but I later discovered its relevance in various other contexts.

Many (really most) individuals lack vision and the ability to grasp concepts, even after detailed explanations. However, if you present them with a visual representation, an image, or even a simple one, it instantly conveys the whole idea. A picture is indeed worth a thousand words. I found this truth reflected in one of the most significant deals of my life, which began to unfold in Orlando in late 2017.

Mango's had been open for a year when the adjacent retail space in our building became available. Given my active participation in the tourism community, I offered the space to *Visit Orlando* as their CEO, George Aguel, was a close friend and a former Disney senior vice president. Visit Orlando had operated an 'Official Welcome Center' on International Drive for two decades, but the location was subpar, and they were now on a month-to-month lease. I knew George couldn't stand the Welcome Center he had, and I invited him and his COO, Larry Hendrichs, to see the location with the hope of convincing them to lease it to really upgrade the facility. George was an amazing CEO, and the organization deserved the best.

A single tour was enough for them to recognize the potential. The high ceilings and grandeur of the space ignited their excitement, which led right to a lease draft. Despite the usual challenges of mixing friendship and business, the negotiation process between George and me was remarkably smooth. Once we were close enough, we decided jointly to sit down at his lawyer's office, order pizza, and not get up from the conference table until there was a signed and fully executed lease.

Visit Orlando subsequently moved into the retail space, subleasing sections to Walt Disney World, Universal Studios, and SeaWorld. Additionally, they dedicated an area to other attractions on International Drive, Gatorland, and Legoland. While overseeing the construction, I maintained regular visits to the site due to my familiarity with the team from the buildout of Mango's. This gave me some insight into what Disney was creating for their section of the Welcome Center. Ambitious displays included LED screens, projecting vibrant fireworks above and a scale model of Pandora, the land from Avatar in Disney's Animal Kingdom, among other features.

During the visioning phase for the *I Drive 2040* zoning overlay district, which was born of the mayor's desire to permanently fix the complicated processes following the contentious rezoning of the Hollywood Plaza parking garage and the Skyplex PD, the concept of *dynamic digital art* emerged. It involved using large screens or projectors to create visually appealing digital art in public spaces, a common practice in great cities around the world. This concept was especially relevant to the International Drive corridor, catering to the convention and tourist market, creating an environment that transported people to special places.

The code for I Drive 2040 included visual imagery of a building with dynamic digital art on its facade, as well as an inner courtyard with a video screen extending from the building. However, though it was contemplated in the vision plan, no specific ordinance had been established for the concept yet. Our involvement in the creation of the zoning code aimed to ensure practicality and feasibility for developers, which often wasn't the case in other municipalities. Orange County is the real deal, however, and we were working to move the area to the future.

I took the opportunity to discuss this innovation with Disney officials while they toured their new installation at Visit Orlando. Claire Bilby and Jodi Bainter, both seasoned, high-ranking Disney executives, were intrigued by the possibility of incorporating dynamic digital art to promote the Walt Disney World Resort along I Drive. I shared the code page with the images of the proposed dynamic art and showcased how it could be implemented on a prominent wall of the garage facing I Drive.

Disney's interest in the new concept was notable since they don't entertain unsolicited ideas. However, our connection as landlord and tenant in Visit Orlando paved the way for them to consider the unique opportunity. This moment marked the beginning of an exciting chapter, where the fusion of creativity, business acumen, and vision brought together two powerhouse entities.

I wasn't following the usual channels but speaking directly to decision-makers. They expressed interest and told me they'd return with more senior officials the following week to discuss it further. This was an encouraging sign. Busy individuals like them rarely spare a moment, and the fact that they wanted another meeting was promising. I marked the appointment in my calendar and awaited the day.

On that scheduled morning, they texted me to confirm, further demonstrating their engagement. When the team arrived, they toured Visit Orlando's setup and then proceeded to the parking garage. I showed them the view from atop the structure—an unparalleled vantage point overlooking the bustling crossroads of I Drive, Sand Lake Road, and I-4. It was clear that the location's potential impressed them.

I delved into the concept of dynamic digital art, explaining its flexibility and how it could be tailored to their needs. As we explored the idea, I realized that different facets of the Walt Disney Company would be involved in this discussion, spanning Burbank, Glendale, New York City, and Celebration, Florida. However, these segments operated relatively independently, which both facilitated and complicated matters.

Despite the intricate structure, their interest remained high. They conveyed that they had been seeking an opportunity along International Drive for two decades, desiring a landmark rather than a destination. I suggested that we could make the garage itself a distinctive Disney landmark, a notion that resonated with them.

The conversation was promising but guarded, as such conversations often are at the precipice of innovation. Their curiosity was piqued, but the next steps were uncertain. What transpired over the next few days was a testament to the potential for a genuine partnership.

A request for a written summary of the concept arrived from The House of Mouse, and I responded by drafting a comprehensive memorandum of understanding (*MOU*) for them. Crafted with meticulous detail, the *MOU* outlined the roles, responsibilities, and possibilities of this collaboration. Disney was intrigued; their curiosity had seemingly progressed to an exploratory stage, and I was excited to get their feedback once they had reviewed it.

The *MOU* was submitted, which outlined a mutually beneficial collaboration. This was atypical for Disney, a company accustomed to exercising significant autonomy in its developments. However, the prospect of a vibrant, captivating digital installation in this strategic location and on a grand scale intrigued them.

Weeks went by without much progress. Disney's propensity for meticulous analysis was evident in their cautious approach, but I held onto the belief that the spark we had ignited would continue to grow.

Unexpectedly, an email arrived from Chris Santoro, a Disney Global Real Estate executive in New York City. He expressed their deep interest in the proposal and their intention to explore it further. It was a moment that confirmed the resonance of the idea and the genuine momentum we had achieved.

The notion of dynamic digital art, once a theoretical vision, was now on the cusp of perhaps a real transformation. It was akin to a fire that had been kindled, a fire that we were nurturing, coaxing to life. As the embers of creativity continued to glow, we were poised to embark on an exciting journey that could redefine how we experience visual art in public spaces.

Santoro said another group would come and take a look; this time, I didn't need to join them. It was fascinating to witness the array of people converging on the Garage. They were, in essence, a microcosm of Disney's intricate ecosystem. Some were excited and optimistic, others cautiously curious, and then there were the pragmatists who brought with them a host of skeptical questions.

This was a testament to the massive scope of Disney's operations and their commitment to exploring new opportunities, even though coordinating all these voices could be as challenging as it was rewarding. The enormity of Disney's influence and innovation was tremendous, but so was the inevitable bureaucracy.

Nonetheless, the momentum continued. The idea wasn't just a spark anymore; it was a flame, albeit still a small one. The decision to bring in Todd Rimmer, a Disney Imagineer, was a pivotal indicator that they were not only interested but now invested in a plan formation. It was also a reflection of their entrepreneurial spirit, always looking to be the pioneers, the first to conquer uncharted territory.

The day arrived when their team again visited the site to meet with me. I was so happy to see familiar faces: Jodi, Claire, and other executives joined this time by the creative minds behind Disney's remarkable designs, the Imagineers. They were the architects of Disney's magic, the ones who gave life to dreams and made fantasies real. Rimmer happened to be one of the top Imagineers.

After the tour, we went up to my office, where I had set up a meeting table with refreshments. The atmosphere was relaxed, fostering open dialogue.

The meeting commenced with an array of questions – feasibility, logistics, and the regulatory landscape. Their inquiries were valid, reflecting the due diligence required for such a groundbreaking project. This wasn't just about creating a captivating visual installation; it was about orchestrating a harmonious convergence of creativity, technology, and regulation.

This marked the third meeting in our progression, and the presence of a top Imagineer driving the discussion underscored the gravity of the situation. Rimmer's questions were direct, unvarnished, and centered on the viability of the project. Could we truly make it happen? My response was an unwavering affirmation.

While the executives remained optimistic, an engineer like Rimmer's skepticism was natural, yet within it was a glimmer of genuine interest and hope this could happen. The discussions echoed a recurrent theme – the balance between Disney's visionary ethos and the practical reality of executing a project of this scale. Could the vision be translated into a tangible reality within the confines of Orange County regulations that had not even been created yet? Fair questions, but I radiated confidence about my ability to get it done.

I showed them the proposed ordinance code, urging them to embrace this opportunity and lead the way. Often, grand promises fall flat, but my track record with ventures in Orlando spoke volumes, was well known to them, and bolstered their belief in my confidence.

Following this meeting, my next step was to loop in Alberto Vargas, the visionary Orange County Planner. Alberto was an advocate for progress and urbanization, aligning with the vision for dynamic digital art. We had collaborated previously on projects, and he had been instrumental in making I-Drive 2040 into law.

I reached out to Alberto, knowing that his passion for progress and keen insights into the development landscape would be invaluable. I explained the essence of the Disney proposal, the first-ever dynamic digital art installation that could redefine the perception of International Drive. Alberto understood the significance of the project immediately, not just as a potential development but as a beacon of innovation within his vision for the area.

We organized a meeting at Mango's, and the attendees included executives from Disney, the Imagineers, and Alberto. Through our previous meetings, the Disney folks were well-acquainted with the nuances of both their aspirations for the project and how I had opined on the County's development dynamics. It was an opportunity for all parties to come together and discuss the concept in the context of regulations, feasibility, and vision.

This meeting was a convergence of expertise, where Disney's global influence, the Imagineers' creative prowess, and Alberto's strategic insights intersected to deliberate the prospect of dynamic digital art. However, this new territory was uncharted for Disney. Alberto, recognizing the significance of being a pioneer in this development, was willing to offer his best advice, as he usually does in any pre-app meeting.

This one was unique, though, and he and I shared a realization that someone had to take the first step and that someone needed both the financial depth and determination to see it through. The venture required significant capital, persistence, and the willingness to navigate uncharted waters, which meant risk. Someone also had to have tremendous vision and courage that everything would fall into place, and no one in the world fit the bill like Disney. Needing a driving force to bring it all together, Disney executives placed tremendous responsibility on me to make it happen.

I emphasized to Alberto the synergy between Disney's legacy of innovation and the visionary approach behind the dynamic art concept. I stressed to him they were the premiere art company in the world. They had invented and reinvented modern animation time and again.

Alberto understood the rationale and recognized that Disney possessed the elements needed to forge ahead. They were no strangers to embracing new challenges, turning

219

dreams into reality, and setting the precedent for what was possible. This was an opportunity to leverage their expertise in a new arena that aligned perfectly with their creative DNA.

A few weeks later, the Disney officials and the Imagineers had a second pre-app meeting with Alberto, which proved to be a turning point. It was clear that this venture was poised to transcend ordinary boundaries. Disney brought several renderings and a video representation of the envisioned dynamic art installation to the meeting. As I witnessed the awe-inspiring video showcasing a mesmerizing ribbon of LED screens, I was astounded by the magnitude of their creative vision. I was literally blown away and hoped Alberto shared my enthusiasm.

While Alberto viewed Disney's video rendering, my anxiety was palpable. His direction was indispensable for advancing. Alberto's words, 'This looks very, very compelling,' were met with a sigh of relief and excitement. Disney's executives and Imagineers were equally relieved, glad to have received positivity from the County in the pre-app stage.

However, there was much more to be done; the interaction between Disney and Orange County had only just begun. In subsequent meetings, we continued to refine the concept, focusing on the intricate details that would bring this project to life. Disney was now on a trajectory to proceed, yet the road ahead was paved with regulatory considerations.

Disney's ability to submit an application for the dynamic art installation rested on the draft ordinance created by Alberto and Staff becoming law. It was a complex document that had to harmonize Disney's creative aspirations with Orange County's regulatory framework. When it was being circulated, our legal counsel reviewed the draft and suggested modifications to ensure compliance without diluting the artistic vision.

Watching Disney and the County work in tandem was exhilarating, a sight to behold. These titans of industry, each accustomed to leading, converged with synergy and innovation as their common goal. I observed, sometimes speaking only when required, wanting their direct collaboration to gain traction and momentum.

Shortly thereafter, Alberto conveyed the completion of the draft, and the ordinance was handed to the County Attorney's office.

As the ordinance underwent reviews and readings, an unexpected complication emerged. During the second reading, discussions arose regarding the permissible text on the display, which was critical to any art sponsor. The existing language proved ambiguous, causing some apprehension for Disney. The urgency was real as we pressed for precise language that would satisfy all parties.

A pivotal moment unfolded during the meeting. The County Attorney left his seat on the dais and joined us in the audience to discuss the final language on the spot with Trippe Cheek, which we believed would work.

The ordinance passed its final reading and was celebrated as a significant milestone. Yet our elation was short-lived, as Disney's legal team conveyed their discontent with the final language. Their outside counsel, Orlando Evora of Greenberg Traurig, and Disney's in-house attorney, Carlos Brackey, articulated their reservations about the ambiguity of certain language. The ordinance just didn't work for them as it was.

Engaging in a series of discussions, I attempted to address Disney's concerns. My interpretation of the code's intent clashed with their apprehensions, creating some tension, and Disney's lawyers were unyielding, adhering to a black-and-white stance, leaving little room for compromise. The setback was profound; they were meticulous, but they were the ones that had to be satisfied.

A renewed effort commenced as we awaited a new hearing. Armed with newfound insight into precisely what they needed, we approached the proceedings with heightened preparation. The matter was brought before the Board once more where we could make our case. The mayor had graciously provided an opportunity to address the concerns.

We planned to advocate for a balanced resolution. The objective was clear: attempt to amend the ordinance language to accommodate both the County's dynamic art intent and this (or any future) art sponsor's reservations.

Enter Hal Kantor. Though my attorney Trippe had held reservations, we accepted a language compromise during that initial meeting with the County Attorney. This setback was solely mine to bear, but the entire team faced it. I prioritized the larger picture – a resolution that would appease all parties involved. This was now all-or-nothing, and I wanted Kantor at my side along with Trippe and Angel for the proceeding.

Our return to the Board would mark the culmination of our efforts. The revised language was the product of extensive back-and-forth aimed at bridging divergent perspectives. Our presentation emphasized the need for realistic flexibility with the art sponsor while maintaining the integrity of the code.

Subsequently, our strategy sessions shifted to Hal's office. We gathered to bring him up to speed on the intricacies, nuances, and historical context of the situation.

Concurrently, we engaged in negotiations with Disney for a lease agreement. The plan was to lease the outer walls for dynamic art and a store within Hollywood

Plaza, so a prime retail location was offered to Disney within the garage.

Against the backdrop of these negotiations, my life underwent a profound transformation. The night before the final meeting with the County Commission, my wife and I experienced an incredible reconciliation that completely saved my life, our marriage, and our family. Emerging from the worst period ever experienced, our love infused me with profound happiness and a renewed sense of purpose. On January 14, 2020, a day of crucial significance in so many ways, I stood before the Board of County Commissioners alongside Hal, Trippe, and Angel with a heart brimming with love and passion.

As I addressed the Board, I emphasized the essence of dynamic art installations, articulating the symbiotic relationship between sponsorship and art visibility. The ordinance should allow an associated sponsor with the capacity for text within the dynamic art in some reasonable manner, or why sponsor it at all? County Staff agreed and supported the position by proposing a compromise where no more than 10% of the total screen area could contain text. This was substantial enough for Disney's approval.

The County Commissioners, after listening to our case, undertook deliberations. Our district commissioner put forth a motion, and a unanimous 7-0 vote ratified the amended ordinance. The elation was profound as we exited the hearing. Disney, who had keenly followed the proceedings online, conveyed their jubilation at the outcome. Their executives, long pushing for the project, were thrilled.

After securing the ordinance, a new hurdle emerged. Disney's planned location for the dynamic digital art on the north and west sides of the building meant it would be visible from Interstate 4 (I-4). This positioning raised concerns as to Chapter 479 of the Florida Department of Transportation (FDOT) code, which governs billboard permitting.

Until then, my focus had primarily been on navigating the local landscape and securing approvals from Orange County. However, the realization that FDOT regulations came into play added a new layer of complexity to the situation at the State level. This challenge required an entirely different level of expertise and engagement.

Recognizing the need for highly specialized assistance, I carefully researched the matter and discovered Thornton Williams, an attorney in Tallahassee. Thornton's legal focus was FDOT, and Chapter 479 issues were a big part of his practice. His unique expertise in this area seemed to make him the clear choice to guide us through the State-level regulatory labyrinth.

Intrigued by his background, I decided to hire him no matter what. It was late in the day, past 5 p.m., but I knew that time was of the essence. I called Thornton's office, and to my pleasant surprise, he answered. Our discussion quickly confirmed my initial impression – he was the person we needed. With his guidance, we would chart a course through the challenging FDOT regulations and secure the necessary exemption.

His credentials, mainly as the former general counsel for FDOT, solidified my belief in his capability. I explained the intricacies of our situation, and Thornton's comprehensive understanding of Chapter 479 was obvious.

Engaging his services was immediate; he was the specialist required. His recommendation was clear: We needed a *Chapter 479 exemption*. This exemption would completely distinguish dynamic digital art from a traditional roadside billboard.

Thornton's approach was methodical, and his deep understanding of FDOT's inner workings was evident. As we embarked on this new phase of the journey, I was reminded again of the importance of always having the right guide in uncharted territory, and sometimes, only by aligning with the right legal mind could you possibly achieve victory.

Thornton's words echoed in my mind, "Let me ask you something, Josh," He questioned me whether Disney had a retail space planned for the garage. I affirmed that they were indeed setting up a magnificent retail store. His response was pivotal, "That's the key right there."

Thornton's insight was the missing piece of the puzzle. He explained that to qualify for the 479 exemption, the dynamic digital art display would be an on-premise sign for their retail store. The revelation was a game-changer to make everything work seamlessly within the legal and regulatory framework. The timing was impeccable. We hadn't yet finalized the lease, and this fresh perspective from Thornton offered the appropriate solution.

My next move was to convene a meeting at Greenberg Traurig's offices, where we could introduce Thornton to Disney's team and discuss the next steps. As we sat around the conference table, two things were abundantly clear: Thornton had their trust immediately, and I had found the right guy for the assignment. We already had the local ordinance completed, and with Thornton's counsel, I felt like we would qualify for the exemption. The deal with Disney was certainly worth the risk, as it had already been more than two years of work, and we were right there, together.

The key meeting day arrived in late January 2020, and Trippe and I drove out to the state capital from Orlando. Little did we know that in only four weeks, COVID-19 would shut down America. We met Thornton at Krispy Kreme near *Florida State University* to align roles and procedures. Who would do what, the key points to make, and where boundaries were. Within minutes, our dynamic was set. We had already worked together for a few months, so there was great synergy between us, but Tallahassee was another animal. Trippe and I agreed to the strategy Thornton prescribed.

Walking into FDOT's building was both exciting and humbling. They controlled the State's roads from the tip of Key West to the border with Georgia. Our meeting would be with the Secretary of Transportation, the top transportation official in Florida. Thornton presented his PowerPoint to The Secretary and other FDOT officials in the meeting. Our careful preparation was key, and the presentation was received positively. Although no immediate verdict was given, the vibe afterward during goodbyes suggested we had navigated this critical meeting effectively.

Within weeks, as the world grappled with the unprecedented impact of the COVID-19 pandemic, we continued to discuss how incredible our timing ended up being in obtaining the meeting when we did. FDOT had shut down offices, and there was zero chance of any such gathering indefinitely.

Nearly two months passed, which felt like no other time in our lives, as by the end of March 2020, America was on lockdown. I thought not to push for any update, hoping that there would be some word from the meeting at the right time. There was.

On March 27, 2020, FDOT sent an official letter that concluded the Art Display was not subject to permitting regulations under Chapter 479. Thornton's work shone through, and we secured the 479 exemption despite the unbelievable circumstances.

With the exemption now in hand, we were inching closer to turning this ambitious vision into reality. The pandemic had created extreme uncertainty, yet even amidst the chaos, we managed to achieve our final objective. Disney's legal team embraced the exemption, and together with the approved Orange County dynamic art ordinance, we obtained the full zoning for their permit application. What was impossible years before was now our collective reality.

In March 2020, as everyone did in America (both companies and citizens alike), Walt Disney World faced unprecedented challenges due to COVID-19. The pandemic closed the Resort for the first time in 50 years, shifted priorities, and introduced new uncertainties. But in the haze of the pandemic's onset, the dynamic art project retained its significance. They reshuffled a lot of things, but this development remained on a fast track due to its rare nature and overcoming the overwhelming regulatory complexities it did. A fully executed lease from Disney finally arrived in May 2020, a symbol of the resilience and determination the Company had as it prepared to reopen Walt Disney World.

Now, with a location theirs, Disney was poised to enter the next stage, the stage they most preferred: Creation. Designing the dynamic digital art installation itself, a collaboration with Mitsubishi and AOA, Disney's Imagineers set to work translating this extraordinary concept into a tangible reality.

The journey had been marked by relentless perseverance, strategic insights, and the invaluable role of the right people in the right positions. As the months passed, progress on the project steadily continued. The reopening of Walt Disney World during the summer of 2020 signaled a slight return to normalcy. The gears were turning once again, and I felt a sense of assurance that things were moving along as planned.

Amidst this activity, Disney worked tirelessly to compile the specifications required for their application. The project remained a well-guarded secret throughout this process, with only vague information circulating about Mango's pursuit of dynamic digital art. In February of 2021, Disney finally submitted their comprehensive 56-page application for the permit.

The tension was off the charts as we awaited the outcome. The complexity of the application process, combined with the unique nature of the development, meant more oversight, and all we could do was hope for the best. In June 2021, strolling through a mall in Coral Gables with my wife and children, my phone rang, and I saw that it was Alberto. The unexpected call carried a mix of anticipation and uncertainty; it was almost too much.

When I answered, Alberto delivered the exhilarating news very calmly, appropriately, and matter-of-factly: Disney's permit application for the dynamic digital art had been approved. We had done it.

The enormity of this achievement was not lost on me. The deck had been stacked heavily against us from the very beginning; it took more than three years, with countless obstacles and challenges along the way. Yet, against all odds, we had achieved what seemed nearly impossible. My wife's smile was beaming, and the kids kept asking if this meant we could get on the rides faster now.

Racing to share the news, I called my Disney contact, and they too, had just received the same call from the County. The Disney executives were absolutely beside themselves, and the leadership in Burbank greenlit the development that very day.

Because it was public record that a permit had been issued, the media soon caught wind. On June 24, 2021, news broke that a monumental digital art display created by Disney was to grace International Drive. The town exploded in awe as Disney had never done anything like this outside of their property in their 55 years in Central Florida. Immediately, the deal became a symbol of the synergy between Disney and Orange County and one of the most significant developments in the tourism corridor's history.

Construction commenced later that year, a testament to the collaborative efforts that had brought us this far. Theme Park bloggers followed the in-plain-sight erection of the project, 100 feet in the air. The unveiling, a momentous occasion for everyone, arrived on Memorial Day Weekend 2022, aligning perfectly with the 50th-anniversary celebration of Walt Disney World. This was the culmination of a dream years in the making. As Walt Disney said, a mantra in their Company, *"If You Can Dream It, You Can Do It."*

With the gentle hum of anticipation in the air, *the 337', 150-ton dynamic art installation* debuted atop the Hollywood Plaza Garage, simultaneously with the opening of the first-ever *Walt Disney World Store.* The synchronicity of these events was almost poetic, a fitting climax to an incredible journey.

The dynamic art was more than anything I had imagined, truly beyond my dreams. It was a vivid tapestry of light, color, and motion, an awe-inspiring testament to the creative process and talent of Disney. The world-renowned company had gone above anyone's highest expectations, delivering a *masterpiece that captured the essence of Disney magic* and the awe of Orlando. They proved to everyone, again, that they truly are the premier art company in the world, pioneering visionaries first and foremost.

As I reflect on this journey, what stands out most in my memory is not just the monumental victory achieved through the endeavor but the profound joy that illuminated my heart. The triumph was about more than the achievement itself; it was about experiencing it with my amazing wife by my side and reuniting with my family after the darkest of times.

This project, more than any other, became a symbol of renewal and rebirth. It was a testament to the strength of relationships, resilience, and the light that emerges from the darkness when your heart is full of love. Through every challenge and triumph, this journey brought us closer, and it was the unity within my family that made this victory truly exceptional.

The Disney dynamic digital art project will forever be etched in my memory as a testament to determination, partnership, and the power of hope. It wasn't just a magnificent business deal; it was a journey of the heart, one that encapsulated the essence of what truly matters in life.

Chapter 8:
Survival Stories: Small Business, Big Mission

(March 22, 2020) In this weekly series, dubbed Survival Stories: Small Business - Big Mission, *Orlando Business Journal* will revisit small business executives in various industries to discuss how they are grappling with the impossible decisions caused by the coronavirus. This series features Joshua Wallack, COO of Wallack Holdings and owner/operator of Mango's Tropical Cafe Orlando.

Survival stories: Mango's tries to fight off small biz 'extinction-level event'

Printed April 2, 2020

On March 14, drinks were being poured, music was blaring and dancers were creating smiles on guests' faces: Another perfect weekend for Joshua Wallack and his business, Mango's Tropical Cafe Orlando. But something devastating loomed ahead.

Wallack's entertainment venue at the corner of International Drive and Sand Lake Road was ending another weekend of fun and fast entertainment — which is what Orlando's tourism nightlife is all about — but it was the last time in quite a while he would hear that music, laughter and constant ringing from the registers. The threat of coronavirus was forcing him, and many other bars and nightclubs across the state, to shut down.

"Two weeks ago was our last day of operations. I was at Mango's and I knew it was our last day as we started working with counsel on how to handle this," he told Orlando Business Journal, in an exclusive one-on-one earlier this week.

It was a situation like none other for the 44-year-old COO of Wallack Holdings and one part of a father-son duo that owns/operates Mango's locations here and on South Florida's South Beach.

Somber celebration

The night of March 14 is clear in Wallack's memory. "That Saturday was busy, but we didn't know what to do because we didn't get the order to close and we had reservations," Wallack recalls.

"People were saying they were still coming. I was there with hundreds of people, but you could tell the mood was somber. The normal celebration wasn't there. It felt like right before Hurricane Irma [in 2017], those last days got bad, but everybody got in and wanted one more party before they ran for the hills."

Three days later, an executive order by Florida Gov. Ron DeSantis shut down all bars and nightclubs across the state.

The days since then have been nothing but brutal for Mango's.

Mango's has been through tough times before with the slowdowns caused by the Sept. 11, 2001, terrorist attacks and the 2008 Great Recession, but this is a completely different beast.

"In 9/11 and 2008, we went down maybe 20% in business. We've never gone down to zero," Wallack said. "There's going to be a Mango's on the other side of this, but people don't realize how bad small business has been crushed — it's an *extinction-level event.*"

The next move

With the spigot of tourism completely shut off and no revenue coming into the business, Wallack said he and his father, David Wallack, 71, quickly reacted.

"We put our hands on each other's shoulders, looked each other in the eyes, and went total John Rambo — we are going all in and will survive," he said, referring to the iconic protagonist from the Rambo action film series starring actor Sylvester Stallone.

It's going to be a difficult mission, as the company typically builds a solid foundation of revenue in the March and April timeframes. Spring break, warm weather, and strong travel seasons for the southern hemisphere make a perfect recipe for business.

And April bookings at Mango's were looking promising, with more than $1.5 million in pre-paid convention buyouts in Orlando. But now that's gone.

As a result, the Wallacks have been working with their local lender, City National Bank of Florida, to get the relief needed to maintain its properties including the Hollywood Plaza complex next door. Those discussions are ongoing, and it will be critical moving forward. "This is happening because of relationship banking. *The old school 'going-into-the-lobby-and-shaking-hands' types of relationships,*" he said.

These personal relationships he and his father made over several years — as well as owning the land the properties are on — help control costs. It's one less worry and barrier for a business owner.

It also has helped his company to focus more on continuing to keep staff on board, and most importantly, to pay for their health benefits. "We always over-engineered everything in regards to the benefits, so we can still provide benefits."

But the end of the virus can't come soon enough.

The lost and lonely feeling

Wallack is doing all he can to keep his sights clear as he navigates the storm caused by the coronavirus.

He equates the current climate as being lost at sea and trying to use the stars for guidance, but no one can see anything. "Being a leader feels lost and lonely, but you have to be strong and feel your instincts and convictions."

But the reality is while Mango's is on relatively solid ground right now, everything has its limits.

Reports of other countries experiencing second waves of infections from the virus are not comforting. China, the country where the virus first emerged, is putting areas back into lockdown due to flare-ups in cases, an April 2 Bloomberg report said.

That can't happen in Central Florida or even the U.S., Wallack said. The burden of unemployment is at historic levels and a further crunch to consumer confidence would be a nightmare.

The Sunshine State already has more than 227,000 unemployment benefit applications from this crisis this week alone, according to the U.S. Department of Labor. That beats the record set by the prior week's revised total of 74,313. Another shutdown very well could be the final nail in the coffin for many businesses.

"I don't know what will happen. We can't open until our major infrastructure opens up like the theme parks and hotels," Wallack said. "We don't have a second chance at this because we won't be able to reopen after a second closure – we would be finished."

Coronavirus Chronicles: Mango's co-owner works on $200M I-Drive biz plan

Printed April 10, 2020

In the business of fast dancing and loud music, it's hard for Joshua Wallack to slow down and be stuck in the silence that fell on his nightclub at the end of March due to the novel coronavirus' negative global economic impact.

That's why Wallack, co-owner of Mango's Tropical Cafe Orlando with his father David Wallack, has been trying to focus on how to diversify the future of his business and the International Drive district to not be as dependent on the bigger tourism players in the region moving forward.

That's not to say he doesn't appreciate being in the land of Walt Disney World, Universal Orlando Resort, the Orange County Convention Center, and other tourism draws, but the widespread shutdown the virus caused has opened his eyes to just how vulnerable tourism-dependent Central Florida truly is. It also reinforced his belief that when push comes to shove, he's got to be the one prepared to make the calls and bring about change for his business.

"The most important thing from a small business perspective is somebody has to be the wall, someone has to be where the buck stops. David and I are in charge of making decisions. It's about survival, and you have to take control of the situation," he told Orlando Business Journal.

For now, his company, which went into the slowdown with 500-plus employees, has been keeping a small crew on site to keep the venue ready for business, and overseeing the ongoing construction for his future tenant Mooyah Burgers, Fries & Shakes location at Hollywood Plaza, which is owned by Wallack Holdings.

"From a management standpoint, we have it at *'Seal Team 6'* levels for each location, with the capability from numerous paradigms in administrative and operational aspects to maintain in the current state," he told *OBJ*. "Then there must be an ability, when the time is right, safe, and appropriate, to start up both Mango's locations like they were two Apache choppers. Get off the ground and get some height going quickly, get some 'fierce start-up energy' going."

But while waiting to reopen, Wallack has spent some of his time working on an effort that can help businesses along International Drive recover from the impacts of the virus faster.

One more round

Orlando faces a lot of competition when it comes to the convention and events industry, a major revenue driver for I-Drive businesses. Competitor cities like Las Vegas and

Chicago always have posed a threat due to having facilities that rival the Orange County Convention Center.

For companies like Mango's, the business that trade shows and events bring to town each year is vital, responsible for millions of dollars in bookings in some months. The longer nightclubs, restaurants, and hotels can keep attendees in their venues, the more opportunity to increase that night's profit.

That's why Wallack said he's been working with other I-Drive businesses on an effort that would ask Orange County to offer a way to extend the hours of liquor sales in businesses on the popular tourist corridor. It's something Chicago businesses already are capable of doing. "Chicago venues can apply for a late-night liquor license where you can serve longer at businesses like a nightclub. What that could do here is create another layer of hours on top of what I-Drive has and give us that Miami Beach/South Beach feeling," he said.

Orange County would have to create a new license that businesses could apply for, but it could be a potential game changer for the corridor. It could allow license holders to go beyond the 2 a.m. cut-off time to maybe 3-4 a.m. Monday through Saturday and to 5 a.m. on Sunday.

Officials with Orange County were not available for comment.

If successful, Wallack said it could generate an additional $200 million in business along the corridor, including the nearby Sand Lake Road restaurants and businesses. It also may make the corridor more enticing to new investment as developers may view the opportunities for more revenue.

It also would encourage more business at restaurants, bars, and hotel dining spots from tourists or locals who are late diners and looking to spend longer nights out on the strip.

That could breathe new life into I-Drive-area businesses that will be hungry for customers once the government lockdowns end.

"This would be the lift we need like Star Wars' Luke Skywalker trying to lift his *X-wing* out of the bog on Dagobah. We could use some help from Yoda on this one," he said, referring to local leaders helping businesses be primed to recover.

And that could be the injection needed for many businesses.

Demand to diversity

But the timeline for that effort is unknown as of now. That's because the priority of local leaders is on getting the region past the threat of the coronavirus.

Wallack said he understands the need for the all-hands-on-deck approach from the government level to help the region heal.

So that's why he's also been keeping tabs on deals that are ready to close to keep the activity moving forward.

He is using this time to diversify his business, especially now that he's seen what life can be like when being dependent on theme parks and trade show traffic.

For example, he's speaking with prospective tenants for the 10,500-square-foot restaurant space on top of his Hollywood Plaza complex. That space, which is being marketed by CBRE Inc. (*NYSE: CBRE*), has been advertised as a prime spot for a unique restaurant user and includes a large patio space. He said the interested tenants are looking to complete the deal by October. "I'm OK with that. You have to be more flexible now than before."

Patience with some level of assertiveness is the best medicine right now.

Companies are more skittish to close deals due to the uncertainty of the market, so it's a good opportunity to work on deals that can be put on ice with future commitments, Wallack said. "The worst of times often can be the best time to make good deals, as far as pure business goes."

But Wallack isn't being reckless, either. He said he has doubled down on making the right moves and not being beggared.

"We have to be playing like Tom Brady or Joe Montana, putting the ball only where our guys can get it. Be a sharpshooter now, even if you've never shot before," he said. "Don't let fear cloud your ability to be brave — do what's right even when you are afraid."

Coronavirus Chronicles: Mango's strategy to survive pandemic started decades ago

Printed April 16, 2020

Joshua Wallack remembers years ago sitting in the green Lincoln owned by his grandparents, Irving and Florence Wallack, as they met with Blanca Parets, their relationship banker at Intercontinental Bank, to deposit $88 into their account.

For several decades, the Wallacks owned and operated a beachfront hotel, the Park Sea-Surf Sea, and they needed a banker they could trust. Today, that property is home to Mango's Tropical Cafe South Beach, one of two Mango's locations co-owned by father-son duo David and Joshua Wallack — the younger Wallack overseeing the Orlando location on International Drive.

The family still banks with Parets, who is now with City National Bank of Florida, and her colleague, Silvia Martin, to oversee all of the Wallack family's finances. And there are no plans to change that dynamic as the coronavirus pandemic ravages the country.

"David and I have always done everything with Mango's through City National Bank, even all of our home mortgages. It's been a very complete relationship," Wallack told Orlando Business Journal.

Those years invested between the Wallacks, Parets and City National Bank spanning 55 years are now paying huge dividends for Mango's Tropical Cafe as it faces one of the most devastating moments for small business. Since March, the COVID-19 novel coronavirus has completely shut down businesses across Central Florida, including bringing Mango's Tropical Cafe's operations to a grinding halt and temporarily shuttering its doors in mid-March.

Despite those challenges, the Wallacks have committed themselves to re-opening the Mango's locations and getting their 500-plus employees back to work. And that will require the help of City National Bank and the relationships Irving and Florence Wallack started decades ago.

Helping hand

Since the pandemic shut down Mango's, Wallack has been creating a recovery plan for re-opening his businesses, including the Hollywood Plaza parking garage and entertainment complex next to Mango's Orlando.

The later steps are still in development, but the first goal has already been completed: Putting Mangos to sleep. Doing so would minimize costs and conserve as much cash reserves as possible with practically no new business coming in.

"We put the company to sleep where it can survive — just like Ellen Ripley [was put to cryosleep] in the movie "*Alien*." If we can put Mango's to sleep and wake it up later, that's what I'll do. I wish we could do something else, but we are just a small business," Wallack said.

But shutting down the business doesn't generate any revenue to cover the bills or pay back lenders. That's where having a strong relationship with a bank can help build an understanding and relief for a small business.

"This is the kind of banking relationship you want with people who work for the bank and who are your partners in arms. They want to make loans, push deals through, and, ultimately, they know we are payers. They want their payers back at work and making payments on loans," Wallack said of his company's history with City National Bank.

Executives with City National Bank of Florida were not available for comment.

The bank has been in constant contact with him on how it can assist with the business's needs or how it can help with federal assistance applications from the U.S. Small Business Administration.

Wallack said his relationship with City National helped expedite Mango's application in hopes it may receive funds shortly. He pegs that to the bank valuing the business the Wallacks have brought City National over the years — so the bank stepped up when it was needed.

"If I were on trial, I'm not representing myself, I'm hiring the best attorney. Same thing here, I'm allowing my relationship bankers to represent us through this thing."

Unfortunately, the SBA announced on April 16 that the Paycheck Protection Program — the $349 billion lifeline to help businesses pay workers — has dried up. That program was heavily sought after by companies to help stave off potential furloughs.

A notice, posted on the SBA's website, states the "*SBA is currently unable to accept new applications for the Paycheck Protection Program based on available appropriations funding. Similarly, we are unable to enroll new PPP lenders at this time.*"

Discussions by federal leaders are in the works to provide more funding, but that only builds on the uncertainty companies like Mango's are living with every day.

Keeping upright

It's been six weeks since Mango's closure, and Wallack doesn't hold back on just how challenging it's been for his family's company.

"Remember, we've never been down to zero like this. We are flat out on our backs like *'Weekend at Bernie's'* here. I'm on International Drive and someone can come and film a movie — there's nobody here," he said.

He recollects how before Mango's on I-Drive opened, the family considered a Las Vegas location. "If I was in Las Vegas, we'd be done. We may have had investor money tied up in some club that would have become irrelevant because the Strip is now shut down," he said.

But thankfully that didn't happen. Being in Orlando since 2012 ended up being the smarter play, as Mango's has more control over its destiny here due to owning its property.

As far as the Mango's staff, Wallack said most of them are still in good spirits. Mango's employs many in the entertainment and food service industry, including cooks, servers, bartenders, dancers, trainers, and sales and administration staff.

Metro Orlando's restaurant industry alone is comprised of more than 98,000 workers across 3,744 establishments.

The local restaurant payroll exceeds $1.8 billion each year, or about $4.93 million in daily wages, based on 2018 U.S. Census data, compiled by American City Business Journals.

"Many of them are young and scared, but they remember when we took care of them or their families after Hurricane Irma. We got them through a lot," he said, noting the company helped pay for temporary housing for many impacted Mango's families while they got back on their feet after the 2017 hurricane-ravaged Puerto Rico, the Caribbean, and the U.S.

He has also done what he can to help the community. "We donated all of our in-house food a month ago. I don't have any more food at Mango's to donate. That is an empty building."

But Wallack reminds himself to remain confident and steadfast about the future of the company. Neither he nor his father can afford to waver in their convictions to come out of this in one piece.

"A lot of businesses may not have the strength or character to survive. Sometimes it's because they can't separate themselves from the emotion and do what's right. You either have to do what's right for business or you are out of business."

And that goes back to building the relationships needed to keep Mango's a success — whether it's the relationships with the family's banker, the employees it has helped through tough times, or the Orlando community that welcomed Mango's nearly a decade ago.

"This is where the past catches up to you. Those relationships, the leases you signed or terms you agreed to when times were good, this is where those deals will make or break you."

Coronavirus Chronicles: Mango's ready to fight back in new tourism world

Printed May 4, 2020

The scene of the economic devastation caused by the COVID-19 coronavirus in Orlando is all too familiar to Mango's Tropical Cafe Orlando co-owner Joshua Wallack.

He recalls those times growing up in Miami Beach when hurricanes would ravage the coast and inner cities of South Florida leaving a trail of death and destruction in its wake. Many Central Floridians who have experienced massive storms understand the strength and havoc that the forces of nature can cause on humanity.

"Right now, I feel like we are in a hurricane and we are in the house waiting," he told Orlando Business Journal of the shutdowns caused by the virus. "I remember years ago walking out of my aunt's house [after Hurricane Andrew struck southern Florida in 1992] and seeing houses destroyed, cars flipped over, and trees and roofs ripped off. It was the craziest thing I'd ever seen."

This time, those forces of nature took the shape of a microscopic organism that has completely wiped out most businesses across the region. The feeling of fear and uncertainty is eerily similar.

And while many buildings still stand tall across the International Drive corridor that Mango's calls home, its apparent business owners continue to experience a tumultuous storm within their walls, including Wallack's very own restaurant/nightclub establishment.

And while state and local leadership work to find ways to reopen the region, Wallack knows there's still too much storm and debris everywhere to feel safe to walk outside.

Needing Niagara Falls

When not spending time with family, Wallack is piecing together the plans for a future recovery for his business and I-Drive. He spends time combing through studies on the nightlife industries in various cities to see what strategies he can put together.

Even before the virus shut down his nightclub, Wallack had brainstormed an idea of extending the alcohol-serving hours along International Drive. A couple of extra hours tacked onto the 2 a.m. limit could result in hundreds of millions of dollars in additional business, he previously told OBJ.

His vision is asking Orange County to create a new license that businesses could apply for, allowing the license holders to go beyond the 2 a.m. cut-off time to maybe 3-4 a.m. Monday through Saturday and to 5 a.m. on Sunday.

He's looked at study after study of how the nightlife of various cities has resulted in billions of dollars in revenue and economic impact — and how certain districts, also known as Entertainment Zones, have played a role in bolstering local commerce in the shadows of the regular 9-5 business community.

And now that state and local reopening guidelines are suggesting some businesses can reopen at 25% to 50% capacity, a diversified way to make additional revenue is even more critical.

"Opening up Walt Disney World with social distancing and masks will get people back, but it's a trickle [of business] when you need Niagara Falls," he said, noting travel will be limited, and leisure travel is just one piece of the puzzle.

For example, there's the uncertainty of how the region's robust convention business returns. Before the virus, the region's convention and trade show sector generated more than $3 billion in economic impact, primarily from events hosted at the Orange County Convention Center.

But the future of conventions is shrouded in mystery as many leaders expect shows to come back with fewer attendees. "The person who is 52 years old may think twice about going to the PGA Show because of Covid-19," Wallack added.

That's why he's devoted so much downtime during the shutdown researching how to build I-Drive's nightlife into a self-sustaining machine — paving an alternate, quicker path for Mango's recovery.

Ready for Round 2

Wallack won't deny his business — like many in the industry — got rocked by the novel coronavirus. He's often referred to it as getting knocked down by legendary boxer Mike Tyson.

But now that the pain in his jaw has subsided, he's had a chance to collect himself and gather his thoughts on what it will take to restart the business headed by himself and his father, David Wallack, who oversees the Mango's location on South Beach.

"Yes, we have a problem and there are black holes [of business] coming [such as small conventions]. But you know how you knock out Tyson? You hit him back. You don't let his initial fury overwhelm you — weather the storm and start to generate your offense," he said. "Push your enemy back or he'll steamroll you."

He's not being naive about the post-coronavirus world his business will be in. It's almost a guarantee that demand to travel to Orlando will be low and the prices of products will be reduced to grab whatever business is available — making overall competition aggressive.

And he fully admits he doesn't expect much business at Mango's to return to any substantial level until the holiday season — months after what's expected for reopenings to get up to speed.

But that reminds him to remain focused on making sure the company remains on solid ground for its 500+ employees.

Wallack said his company still has financial reserves needed to cover employee health benefits and cash to restart the business when given the OK. But business needs to return because even reserves can only last so long.

"It's important we don't dole it all out. We have to be strategic on the money going out. We have 24-hour communication between Orlando and South Beach. We are doing what we can to hold onto everything so we can bring them all back at the appropriate time," he added.

Even so, the environment won't be the same for business. Wallack said the world Orlando knew before the virus is gone, and now a new paradigm is being built that all businesses will have to learn.

"It will never be like it was, and we will have to anticipate a new level of rules — the obstacle course has changed. Before, you had the muscle memory to compete at the highest level, but they just changed the whole course. I have to learn again, fall on my face, and get it covered in mud to get up and fight on."

Coronavirus Chronicles: How Joshua Wallack's daily routine went from partying to planting

Printed May 12, 2020

Nightclub owner Joshua Wallack has a green thumb when it comes to putting a mint leaf into a mojito. But the coronavirus pandemic's shuttering of his business in March has led him to find new ways to fill his time.

"My wife and I have a flower garden we are growing from seeds," said the co-owner of Mango's Tropical Cafe Orlando, who admits his horticulture skills are a work in progress. He said he and his wife planted the seeds seven weeks ago, and they now have 30 mature plants. "I have some flowers that have grown beautifully, some OK ones, and some 'failures to launch'. "

Miles away from his Windermere home, Mango's remains shuttered and empty due to the COVID-19 coronavirus, like thousands of other businesses across Central Florida that await a chance to reopen.

As he admires his new flower garden, he can't help but see the similarities between his new hobby and the way some area businesses are fighting to survive while others have closed permanently. "[The flower garden] is some type of microcosm of life right now. You can give a seed the same care, love, and water, and one grows and the other just doesn't and becomes compost."

Although Wallack continues to work on his business and care for the employees who are living through the worst economic recession in modern history, the tempo and general mood of his days are a stark contrast to how he lived before the virus struck two months ago.

Merengue and mojitos

Before the pandemic, being in the nightclub industry meant his days started a bit slower in the mornings before heading off to parties in the evenings.

Wallack's day would begin with making sure he saw his two teenage kids at breakfast. "Everyone wants Daddy out of bed. Then I walk the dogs, get the kids to school and then my wife and I have coffee and talk. I might organize emails and watch the headline news — we may also work out together," he said.

His day at the office typically doesn't start until most of the rest of Orlando's business community is enjoying lunch. "I don't go into the office until noon because I stay

late. I don't want to be the 20-hour-a-day type. I'm a 12-
to 14-hour type that hits it real hard, then goes home and
has something left for the family."

At the office, he makes time to visit his associates and
leadership staff to catch up with different aspects of the
business. He may spend as little as five minutes or as much
as two hours getting a feel for what's happening with his
employees and their portion of the business operations.

By 6 p.m., it's time to get the energy going. He will go
down to Mango's kitchen and meet with the staff to check
on the food for that night.

"I watch them work and see what comes in. I want to see
the plates and the presentation. I might try the Ropa Vieja
[a shredded meat dish], the soup, or garlic bread. If I bite
into a piece of garlic bread that doesn't crunch right or is
zesty enough, I may pull the chef into the office and ask
them what they think of it," he said, noting he makes sure
any critique on the dishes come from his head chef and not
directly from him.

He said he makes sure his leadership team handles
critiques, as it teaches the executives his expectations and,
thus, maintains the level of quality expected even when
he's not around.

"I'm trying to keep everything together and blasting forward toward the common goal: Another fun night at Mango's," he said.

By showtime, Wallack often is found near — if not on — the ground floor, monitoring the room's vibe. "You know when it's going to be a good party. I have a good barometer to feel that energy."

It's something he's learned from growing up in the business. "When I come home with merengue and salsa music ringing in my ears, and I'm making mojitos in my dreams, that's when I know I need a vacation."

Tired and horrified

However, now — during the business shutdown that began in March — Wallack's time spent planting flowers and being with his family more has been a silver lining to a generally cloudy situation.

His typical day now is far more erratic than it was before, as he's trying to keep up the momentum of his business, despite being closed for so long. "I don't sleep great or as soundly as I did before. I wake up through the night and look at the news, horrified by what's going on."

His days don't have an hourly structure like before. Sometimes he drives to Mango's and works in his office, but the building is oddly empty with only a handful of staff or security workers present. "I have slowed the 200 miles per hour I was running to 20 miles per hour, so I can focus on what's important — the safety of our employees, properties, and family members."

He now handles phone calls with his father, legal counsel, and business partners from home while tending to his flowers. He regularly speaks with other industry colleagues or government officials who may play a key role in the recovery of the popular International Drive tourist corridor where his business is located.

"I talk to my father on FaceTime every day. We are trying to one-up each other on creating and cultivating big ideas for both Mango's locations in the post-Covid world, including ideal spacing while keeping things warm and how our employees can thrive in it," he said, noting other topics they discuss include how to further refine dishes on the menu, recruiting new talent and maximizing operations.

He may have Zoom meetings to attend, but he's not a fan of that style of conversation. "I'm old school. I love being in the room. I don't want to stop shaking hands or giving hugs — but for the short term, I will. I don't want to stop being a warm person."

Sometimes he and his wife drive around the tourist corridor to check on the property and other nearby businesses. That drive happens three or four times a week nowadays. "I take pictures or video if I see graffiti and notify the appropriate parties. I find myself going all the way down to SeaWorld Orlando to see everything. It's just so weird now — it's empty. Billions of dollars here."

Wallack said he has to stay in touch with what's happening on the I-Drive corridor because it's integral to restarting it when ready. He stays in contact with local government officials to let them know his concerns and that he's ready to help with any plans that could relaunch commerce.

That could range from new alcohol licenses for late servings to new rules that let businesses operate on parking lots — which Orange County Mayor Jerry Demings nixed last week unless they get a permit — to helping refine the I-Drive 2040 Vision plan that was meant to make the corridor more urbanized.

The end of Wallack's day now involves spending more time with family. They take turns picking the movie or entertainment that night and no complaints from anyone are allowed — even if it means belting out tunes from *Grease*.

"When they go to sleep, I stay up and print up everything at Mango's and pore over anything," he said, noting his evenings end with more work to make sure he's ready to reopen. "Everybody's brain is getting rewired."

Coronavirus Chronicles: This nightclub's future depends on I-Drive's ability to reopen as 'a Netflix, not a Blockbuster Video'

Printed May 20, 2020

Every day Joshua Wallack sees businesses reopening across the state — but he isn't sure when customers will return.

The co-owner of Mango's Tropical Cafe Orlando spends many days looking at the barren International Drive and Sand Lake Road intersection — a corner that used to welcome at least 20,000 cars each day. What once was Orlando's hottest tourist corridor now is a ghost town since the COVID-19 pandemic shut everything down.

Nowadays, he sees a smattering of vehicles on the road — likely just business owners like him checking on their properties before returning home for the rest of the week.

"Even though the law says we can reopen, I can take a nap in the middle of I-Drive and [safely] wake up right now. That's how often a car is coming down the road," Wallack told Orlando Business Journal.

Week after week, he's watched government leaders and local businesspeople work diligently to find a way to reopen and revive the region's economy. And while he's thankful for that activity, it hasn't stopped his fears of what will happen to the nightlife industry.

Nightlife establishments like Mango's rely on huge crowds that show up to dance, drink, and eat while just six inches apart from each other — not today's recommended six feet for social distancing. It is a business built off intimacy and close encounters where people cut loose on the weekends after a long week at the office.

But those days may be long gone. Industry experts have said the nightlife industry may disappear in major cities such as Las Vegas and Orlando, for at least the rest of 2020. Casinos likely will make the return of gaming operations a priority before reopening nightclubs, so that may draw entertainers and nightlife aficionados back to other tourist epicenters like Florida.

That's why Wallack is taking methodical steps to ensure the family business his father started lives on for the next generation.

Left in limbo

As major hotels, attractions, and even Walt Disney World and Universal Orlando Resort slowly take steps toward reopening, bars and nightclubs remain in limbo, unsure of when they'll get to turn the music back on.

On May 15, Florida Gov. Ron DeSantis expanded his first phase reopening plan to allow restaurants and retailers to welcome more customers, and encouraged other businesses such as attractions to submit plans for reopening — but the nightlife industry was given no guidance. When asked specifically about bars, DeSantis said those establishments were not identified in the White House's official first phase reopening plan, "and I didn't see a need to jump over that."

While the frustration of not being able to open mounts, there's no point in dwelling on what can't be controlled, especially since tourists have yet to show any signs of returning, said Wallack. "There's nobody here except Orlando residents. Of course, businesses with high Orlando population [customer bases] can open, and Mango's has a high Orlando [customer base], but not enough for seven days a week."

That's why he has decided to be more strategic on Mango's reopening timeline and not open up the establishment immediately under the restaurant category that's currently allowed by the state. Mango's is part restaurant so it technically would qualify for reopening.

"Even though I can open by law, I am doing a favor to our employees and long-term business sustainability not to open. I can control the burn rate of losses when I'm closed — I can't when I'm open," he said.

That's because the cost to operate the business, outside of critical factors such as payroll, would mount too quickly and could be disastrous and dip into reserves needed to meet debt obligations and keep workers' benefits intact.

"I take it seriously that we furloughed workers. I think about them," he said. "I want to open badly, but I don't want to open and lose $1 million a month like everyone else. We are working with our accountants and working on plans with officials to reopen the clubs with a feasible plan to operate."

He and his father have been working on plans to host dual grand reopening celebrations of the Mango's locations in Orlando and South Beach in the future.

Be Netflix, not Blockbuster

In the meantime, Wallack has continued work on making sure the future landscape Mango's finds itself in after COVID-19 is one filled with promise and growth.

That starts with his work as part of the many business chambers and advisory groups along the I-Drive corridor. His goal is to make sure that as businesses leave the corridor, the next one to step in adds unique value to the strip. "I-Drive/Sand Lake Road right now is sacred. What's coming down the line has to be part of a vision," he said.

Wallack's concern is as some businesses fold due to the shutdown, there may be a rush for property on the corridor by large chains that may not add new flavors to the area. Since I-Drive needs to compete with highly themed and intricately refined tenant lineups at places like Walt Disney World's Disney Springs or Universal Orlando's CityWalk, it's key to bring in the best to I-Drive, he said.

Those efforts now, while businesses may be shuttering are critical to secure a more vibrant and successful I-Drive once the pandemic passes. And it staves off I-Drive mistakenly landing multi-decade leases from chains that have been in the region since the 1980s.

He likens the I-Drive of nearly 40 years ago to Blockbuster Video, the now-defunct video rental store, and the future of the corridor to Netflix, a dominant power in video streaming.

"To get guests back, we have to do *our* thing. That thing needs to evolve now, so we open with [I-Drive's version of] Netflix. Our old I-Drive model is about as relevant as Blockbuster and Blackberry phones. I want to deal with the latest iPhones, Disney+ and Netflix," he said. "We need to come back with that mentality or we are just delaying the inevitable."

But it's not going to be easy as businesses also are working to stave off the worst economic recession in decades.

"How do you go from Blockbuster Video to Netflix in weeks as opposed to years? We are trying to find that needle in a haystack and we have to do it in weeks."

Mango's Tropical Cafe remains closed while waiting for convention biz to return

Printed July 20, 2020

The eerie silence inside Mango's Tropical Cafe is never-ending for Joshua Wallack.

The co-owner of the International Drive nightclub said his business once boomed in the tourist corridor, drawing tourists and conventioneers with great music and food.

But the nightclub has been shuttered since March due to the pandemic despite other businesses re-opening as the number of Covid-19 cases rises. Wallack, Mango's co-owner, and his father, David Wallack, who is also co-owner overseeing the original South Beach nightclub, have stayed firm that the time is not right to re-open.

It's been a difficult choice, as Mango's technically qualifies as a restaurant and can restart business per Florida's re-opening plan. But the tourist corridor's traffic still is practically nonexistent.

And the lack of convention business, one of the nightclub's primary revenue sources, has solidified Wallack's decision to not turn the music back on just yet.

"We are in no hurry to open. We don't know what it's going to be like when we open. I'm not going to march myself, my family, my employees, Orange County and I Drive right off a cliff," he told *Orlando Business Journal.*

OBJ asked Wallack for insight on strategy, how the slowdown in visitation has affected his business, and how he is navigating through these challenging times. Here's what Wallack shared, in his own words:

On not reopening during Phase 2:

"When we reopened the state in Phases 1 and 2, we anticipated the virus would community-spread for a while from people who are quarantining as they went back to just basic parts of their life like getting a haircut or working out. Also, only a few months ago barely anybody could even get a test.

"Now we have caught up with testing somewhat, and younger people are testing positive even though they're not sick, [and] they can spread the virus. We're sort of all over the place going through adjusting to being open and having this thing part of our world.

"Even though in [Florida's] Phase 2, we could've opened Mango's Orlando as a restaurant with fairly decent occupancy, it was the last thing in the world we were ever going to do. David and I anticipated this type of erratic behavior by the virus during the state opening, and we also believe 2020 is not done with us yet — potentially an active storm season to further disrupt travelers who aren't here at all anyway in August/September, typically the slowest part of the year."

On new strategies:

"Mango's is working with [entertainment promoter] AEG Live on available A-list talent [to bring to the venue]. New Mango's General Manager Mike Palma has received a list of available dates and some of the most notable performers are willing to work for less than half of their last year [cost] because there is nowhere for them to perform.

"We will open Mango's when we are solidly in Phase 3, the numbers are going down and everybody is looking to drink passion fruit mojitos and dance all night. The economic disaster is untold, and we feel our economic initiative of keeping I-Drive open later is critical to Orange County's recovery as so many industries have changed in so many ways forever, and so much that we used to know is irrelevant."

On convention business:

"When we said this was an 'extinction-level event' for small business in March, we said it with a level of certainty due to decades of expertise. When you add that to the fact that teleworking and attending conventions virtually has been rocketed a decade into the future due to COVID-19, the actual physical market will suffer a double-digit contraction of convention visitors. The market must reach for the next generation and go high, or you slide into nothingness."

On the general market and the future:

"Leisure business at the [theme] parks, combined with a national interest in the phenomenon that is the 'Olympic Village' NBA Bubble at Walt Disney World, will grow to a fever pitch once the seasons are underway and people are watching from home. It will rekindle the desire to return to vacation.

"Conventioneers [are a] different visitor who visits for work, not with family on vacation. The Orange County Convention Center's convention business and the economy of South I-Drive have been altered irreversibly. The area must reinvent itself as a nightlife district with premium entertainment and work/live/play as outlined in I-Drive 2040. All good ideas must be accelerated now while we still have punches left."

Chapter 9:
The Main Street Loan and An Evolution that Didn't Evolve

Nearly four months had passed since the onslaught of COVID-19, causing both Mango's locations to shutter by order of the State. My wife and I, together and completely obsessed with each other, fell into a quiet routine, finding a second honeymoon at home with the kids. While in business, we had lost nearly everything, in love and family, we had renewed and regained everything.

Though Mia missed dance and longed for the studio's reopening, we embraced bike rides, leisurely walks, park workouts, and our dinners and game nights. Every waking moment was spent together. In the Summer of 2020, in the aftermath of George Floyd's murder and national protests that followed, COVID's wildfire surge had seized the nation. Lockdowns endured, and even with limited attractions opened, Orlando simply crumbled; I Drive stood desolate, and Miami Beach's pulse was flatlined. When I ventured out, the streets resembled ghost towns as I headed to 'essential businesses' like Publix or Walmart. Mango's, far from 'essential,' lay silent.

Amidst this pandemic whirl, I dubbed it *World War 'V,'* a global conflict against the Virus. On International Drive, I'd frequent Mango's on the premises daily, checking and safeguarding the building. A handful of staff kept our connection, but the reality was surreal and terrifying. No cars graced the roads, and businesses were shuttered. A handful of restaurants clung open, offering Uber Eats' takeout. Now and then, a solitary vehicle traversed the landscape, mostly delivery drivers headed to a pickup at Outback or McDonald's.

Hotels were on their backs at a mere 8 to 10% occupancy. The distress was tangible, as were the fading PPP funds. Our resolve wavered, yet through June 1st, we continued to fund our staff's health insurance, a safety net in uncertain times. In those initial throes, we couldn't foresee the storm ahead. Would there be mass hospitalizations and mass fatalities? We kept our people medically insured months after the forced closure.

Shortly, any hope of swift reopening vanished as the situation severely deteriorated. The PPP funds, totaling around $3.4 million from the initial round, became a loan. Since our businesses fell into the category of non-essential, with nightclubs and bars at the bottom rung and nearly demonized, the Governor's orders to shutter weighed heavy. We had zero coming in and checks going out. If this persisted, you're talking catastrophe, regardless of the Company.

On social media, we saw other clubs across America open underground and illegally for bored teens and irresponsible 20-somethings; operating at the time was synonymous with spreading the virus. There was nothing worse than being labeled a *"super spreader."* People were getting 'canceled' left and right for all kinds of irresponsible behavior.

We brainstormed alternative approaches, like using our parking garage for distanced gatherings, car-side service, and tunes, but nothing made sense. The only way to stem our losses was to stay locked in silence.

In retrospect, the situation was much worse than we knew; it would be almost another year before Mango's South Beach would open its doors and even longer for Orlando. As our PPP loan funds dwindled, an inevitable stalemate loomed. My income pretty much ceased, and mortgage forbearance became necessary.

My home life and work life were a contradiction. I was in an all-consuming romance with my wife, idyllic moments with my children, growing flower gardens, and woods exploration as if in the throes of a shared summer camp adventure together. Never had we been this close. I reveled in the simple joy of being alive and united with them each and every day, a stark contrast to the preceding year's nightmare.

Not counting the days became normal as we shared ideas, even launching a new venture, my wife's aspiration to start a candle business. Together, we birthed 'Casa Bella Candles,' as she crafted these incredibly scented gems under our roof. Our days were a medley of candle-making, games, shared movie nights, and amazing family time. Days of the week dissolved into obscurity; "yesterday, today, and tomorrow" were the guiding markers during the summer of 2020.

My attire had changed completely; months had gone by without slacks and a shirt. The paradox was glaring; as though our businesses were shut, this was our Summer of Love.

I, every day, lived a vital lesson; my wife and my children were the cornerstones that grounded me. The imbalance that led to my previous breakdown had been completely corrected, and I basked in the comfort of being home and well with them.

Finances, however, were another story. No money flowed in, just out, and the shadow of impending constraints loomed large. While few people were able to capitalize on the pandemic by adapting and reinventing their businesses, our non-essential status remained unchanged. Mango's couldn't be transformed into a mask-making factory; we were far from essential and potentially a hazardous 'super spreader' if operational.

Amid the embrace of our family's happy cocoon, the Company's fortunes were grim. Our furloughed employees faced hardships, some reaching out, begging for help. We did what we could for everyone, but the future was completely uncertain. The contradiction was glaring: a loving, heartwarming time with family set against the backdrop of business hardship. Though we contemplated possibilities, the PPP funds had run their course.

At this point, it was an all-out war against the annihilation of Mango's, and I believed we had to lean on our relationships. The bonds we shared with our lender, City National Bank, ran deep. Juan Esterripa and Carlos Ramos, our longtime bankers, and dear friends, stepped up when they could, and their guidance proved invaluable. After a well-timed article in the *Orlando Business Journal* emphasized our multigenerational relationship with them, their CEO, Jorge Gonzales, became intrigued. Large depositors had moved over to CNB after reading the story of my Grandparents and their building on Ocean Drive.

Summoned to Miami, their gratitude for the great press was evident. These pieces, where I praised their institution, had received widespread attention. Even more prospective clients wanted to bank with them after reading about our saga.

We arrived in Coral Gables, where my wife dropped me off at City National. During my visit, I found myself in an unexpected position, starring in the lender's new TV commercial. City National Bank had set up a full studio, complete with cameras and makeup, urging me to share our experience with their work on PPP loans. I obliged, and the producer was quick to commend my performance, declaring it the most engaging story they'd captured. Drawing on my TV experience, I attributed the success to my familiarity with such settings.

My motive was clear to me. With Cares Act funds exhausted, the thought was to secure a $5 million extension on the South Beach property's mortgage. With the pandemic showing no signs of abating, this seemed like the only move. I felt momentum with the Bank and was optimistic something would be on the table.

After the commercial shoot, we went into the conference room. Once we sat down, as with all wonderful relationships, you didn't just jump into business. The conversation began with catching up on family, Orlando, Miami Beach, and personal matters, which took up the first 18 minutes of what was a 20-minute meeting. At the right time, I knew Juan would broach the topic of business.

Before shooting the commercial, Carlos asked me to discuss not only our work with the Bank regarding PPP but also 'Main Street Lending.' A couple of months back, the Trump Administration had unveiled the *Main Street Lending Program*. Unlike forgivable PPP loans from the SBA, these were loans to midsize businesses to help them recover to their 2019 sales levels. The loans were then purchased by the Federal Reserve. It happened that out of the hundreds of lenders in America, City National Bank was the leading institution using Main Street Lending, a signature move by their brilliant CEO, Jorge Gonzales. In between takes of the commercial, I Googled everything I could about the MSLP, beginning with the Federal Reserve term sheet and then nearly a dozen articles describing the program and its impact.

What I found fascinating was that many banks and prospective borrowers had opted not to participate in MSLP due to certain regulations and the fact that the loans were not forgivable. Out of the $600 billion that had been allotted to the program, *less than $2 billion had been loaned.* Many called the whole thing a failure due to its unpopularity and for the program's cancellation so they could reallocate the funds to more PPP availability. The quick download told me immediately that this was a tiny pinhole of a window, if there was one at all.

After our initial conversation about how everyone was doing, Juan segued into strategy. By then, I felt that the MSLP was a much better and easier move than the mortgage increase, and I had just pitched it for a TV spot. I felt like they were going to offer it up, and I waited for Juan to bring it up. My dear friend and brother in so many battles didn't take long.

"So, we're doing Main Street, right?" he said, looking at me and then Carlos.

"Yes, we've already discussed logistics," Carlos replied.

"Great. We are good," Juan said, smiling.

Then he got up and said some other clients were coming in to do more PPP commercial shoots and had to meet someone in the lobby.

City National Bank was truly an innovator in this. By that point, only around 60 or 70 Main Street loans, total, had been approved across the nation. This was an unusual scenario, but it was completely intriguing to me. The concept of securing a Main Street loan felt like the government's vote of confidence in Mango's as a going concern.

With no clear end in sight for the pandemic's impact, I hoped for a substantial sum from the Main Street loan. I envisioned something akin to the $5 million mortgage extension we had considered. Conversing with my father on the phone after my wife picked me up, he found the whole thing surreal. "$5 million would do it," he said excitedly, after I told him about my day.

The beauty of the Main Street Loan Program was that it targeted the business's operational entity, bypassing the need to tap into property equity and undergo reappraisal and mortgage procedures. The process seemed to move swiftly. Given the scarcity of takers for Main Street loans, the federal government aimed to encourage more borrowers. City National Bank was the major player in the Main Street landscape, originating half of the program's loans in the entire United States.

A few days after our Miami meeting, I received a call from Juan and Carlos. They inquired about our plans for the Main Street loan. "So, we are doing $5 million?" they asked.

With all that had happened, every punch we had taken, and with our businesses, but most importantly, our employees in mind, I decided to make a big-time suggestion and just let it rip.

"Can we make it $10 million?" I asked strongly.

Juan's answer, as always, was perfect. "Yeah, we can do 10," I asked them to send the papers right away.

I was on cloud nine; I didn't even know how to tell my father what had just happened. Though the words eluded me, I dialed Richard Preston, who answered on the 2nd ring and relayed the news. To Richard's astonishment, I shared that we were on the brink of securing a $10 million loan from City National Bank through the Main Street Lending Program. "Are you serious?" was all he could say.

The weight of the situation wasn't lost on him, and he marveled at 'the miracle' unfolding before us. July 2020 was a time of grave national uncertainty, the Black Lives Matter protests, COVID's relentless surge, and the absence of any clear pandemic endgame. This development could get us back to 2019 sales levels when it was clear.

Amid the turbulence and uncertainties of the times, the Main Street loan felt like a beacon of hope. It was an unexpected twist in our story, one that testified to the power of timing, relationships, and bold moves.

The loan's structure included a two-year, interest-free grace period, granting the borrower time for the pandemic's uncertainty to weaken. Afterward, a third-year saw interest-only payments, at around 6%, while the following years required the full repayment of principal in substantial portions. Unlike PPP loans, it was not forgivable. It demanded businesses stand back on their feet within three years to start repaying.

As we huddled to review and sign the loan papers, Richard Preston couldn't help what he continued to consider a miracle. He sensed the gravity of the moment, recognizing how unique and crucial this opportunity was. He said to my father directly, "David, do you realize what happened here? What this means? What Josh did? It means Mango's will live while many others won't."

August 1st, 2020, marked the closure of the loan, as confirmed by the bank's attorney. The loan funds, net of fees and closing costs, arrived at a formidable $9.85 million, which aimed to restore us to 2019's sales. However, we were still under lockdown orders, having nearly exhausted the PPP funds. Suddenly, the scenario shifted dramatically. With our deal sealed, the Federal Reserve purchased the loan, and we became a Main Street borrower. This influx of loan funds provided a much-needed reprieve, letting us run the business properly, including addressing deferred payments, fulfilling obligations, and planning budgets. The breathing room had been unavailable for so long, yet now it was ours to manage.

City National's leadership in the MSLP had them the subject of a major *Wall Street Journal* article, with us featured. Mango's Main Street loan was also picked up by *The Financial Times* and was international news.

Though my personal life blossomed in love and happiness, the specter of business closure loomed each time I visited Mango's, my sanctuary against the harsh reality of a nightlife industry in trouble. I studied global nightclub enterprises, watching even the largest group in Britain surrender to bankruptcy, their once precious assets sold at distressed, rock-bottom prices.

But for us, the Main Street loan now made a grim outlook into a horizon of possibilities. The loan symbolized resilience, the ability to weather storms and emerge stronger. Through wise decisions, strong relationships, and favorable timing, we orchestrated a triumph against the odds.

After the closing, exhausted from stress and anticipation, I suggested to my wife that we take a break. We seized the chance to book a getaway, a rare luxury as

Florida's travel industry was almost dormant. We chose Captiva Island's *South Seas Resort*, a tranquil haven where oceanside villas offered a serene escape. Dolphins danced through sunsets, creating a peaceful backdrop.

During the drive to Captiva, a vision dawned upon me. As I sat there, contemplating the $10 million loan from the United States Government Federal Reserve, I couldn't help but feel the weight of the responsibility. Miami Beach, which we drove through when we closed the loan in Miami, resembled a desolate wasteland with boarded-up storefronts. We were in the midst of the pandemic's darkest phase; many businesses had gone broke, and the future was shrouded in uncertainty. Seeing Ocean Drive shuttered, Mango's boarded up, and the horrendous state of the Beach had us hysterically crying in the car back to Orlando.

Amidst this hopelessness, a daring idea began to take shape in my mind. What if we couldn't reopen Mango's Tropical Cafe? What if the worst-case scenario became reality? Our establishment wasn't a historic landmark or a building worth preserving; it was more about the experience we offered. I felt a big idea begin to emerge. What if I could secure options to purchase the buildings behind Mango's on Collins Avenue and 9th Street? Not to immediately buy them but to create a package of properties, a unified master site, which could entice a developer to transform the area and potentially change the course of South Beach.

This vision led me to assess the target buildings directly behind ours. We had a vacant, unused store and a small office in a newer building, both of which could be torn down. The potential of the land under these structures was fascinating. By combining the air space above the alley, we could create a sizable property.

With this concept taking shape in my mind, I shared it with my father. He responded with cautious optimism, suggesting we set aside a budget to explore the idea further. He encouraged me to delve into the process of acquiring these properties and gauge their interest in selling us options. While the idea had potential, the ultimate feasibility rested on securing the necessary properties.

My expertise lies in guiding complex property acquisitions and entitlements, understanding owners' motivations, and establishing meaningful connections. I believed in my ability to make this vision a reality, and I was determined to explore every avenue to turn our dire situation into a transformative opportunity. Our long-time attorney and friend Bruce Weil advised me, "*Just get it done. Don't take any prisoners, Joshua. Get that site under your thumb.*"

During the process of securing the option on 909 Collins Avenue, which I managed through a brokerage firm and with an owner in Italy, I found a unique opportunity. 909 Collins lacked a tenant and generated no income. I crafted a proposition: I offered to purchase the property for

$7 million while renting it via an option to purchase for four months. This arrangement was quickly accepted, as the owners had the choice of either selling it to me for $7 million and getting some immediate income or letting it remain vacant.

A similar strategy was employed with 919 Collins next door, although it posed some challenges due to the older landlord, Mervyn, and the complexities within his family dynamics regarding property management. I took a trip to New York, wearing a mask and taking precautions during the pandemic. Mervyn was a staunch Republican and committed Trump supporter, so he relished the in-person meeting. He came in a crisp suit and tie, and we had tea and sandwiches in the *Plaza Hotel's* Palm Court, where I presented the proposal. He agreed to continue renting the office space to us and granted us the option to purchase the building. He was also a great guy and happy to tell his wife. "He was getting out of the house to be normal that day," he said.

Recognizing the potential of a third building at 929 Collins Avenue, I reached out to its owners as well and was able to make the third deal. The property had a main new building and one historic structure that could potentially be moved to another location. This effort to secure options on these properties meant that, together with Mango's, we would possess approximately an acre of developable land, unheard of on Ocean Drive.

However, South Beach operated without progressive zoning law of any kind, and every project's approval was treated on a case-by-case basis. It was mostly a popularity contest, which introduced extreme uncertainty into the development process. I called the environment *'Dysfunction Junction.'*

Despite this, our motivation to explore the idea was fueled by the unprecedented disaster brought about by the pandemic. We believed that by creating remarkable vision drawings and generating positive publicity, we could approach the city and obtain support. This sentiment had worked before, and I reached out to Chris Ritter, a talented architect and land planner, who also happened to be my wife's high school boyfriend and a close friend of mine. Harvard-trained but raised in Miami, Chris's expertise was invaluable in shaping our plans.

While in Captiva, I worked with Chris, who was affiliated with the global firm DPZ and had his own practice. I shared my vision with him, and he immediately began sketching potential designs. After returning, he started sending over his initial sketches. The preliminary drawings were in pencil, but within three days, he had comprehended our vision and provided initial art that resonated perfectly. Even though he'd lived in Boston since Harvard, Chris grew up in Miami and loved Ocean Drive, so he could uniquely grasp the essence of our endeavor. This vision had the potential to redefine the entire area's character if the city allowed an upzoning and bought in.

The way I saw it generally, through *'adaptive reuse,'* developers could *preserve historic buildings on Ocean Drive while constructing adjacent structures on Collins Avenue that enhanced their value, hospitality offerings, and onsite parking and potentially gave the deco gems themselves another 100 years of use.* We aimed to preserve the authentic character of these older Art Deco buildings, which were built as low-cost accommodations and were not luxurious by modern standards at all, with new construction on Collins, if possible.

When Chris delivered the final art, I was just floored by it. We sent the file to a FedEx Office in Miami Beach to be printed on a giant placard. With the stunning rendering in hand, we arranged a meeting with Mayor Dan Gelber and his chief of staff, Michele Berger.

City Hall was deserted and guarded like an army base. They told me the mayor hadn't seen anyone in person for months, and that made us (my wife accompanied me on this business/family endeavor) very aware of what our meeting meant. Gelber allowed us to set up in his conference room, and when he came in, I could see him staring intensely at our vision. I conveyed that we had secured options on the three properties behind Mango's and Mango's itself, intending to present them as a unified development site. We sought the city's approval and support for this redevelopment endeavor.

Gelber, known for his cautious approach, listened intently as I explained our plans for the interconnected properties and our intent to bring this proposal, seeking the city's endorsement for the transformation.

Throughout the meeting, Gelber outwardly displayed keen interest, although his demeanor remained somewhat enigmatic. Despite his habit of snacking on sunflower seeds, he was engaged and receptive.

However, even with his interest in the meeting, Gelber didn't follow up with much enthusiasm. My father had a history of contentious interactions with misguided city officials and hospitality critics due to his staunch defense of Mango's against all challenges, large and small. I wasn't sure if the lack of immediate support was due to this or the uncertain times we were in. On the other hand, his chief of staff, Michele, saw the immense potential in the project and expressed genuine excitement.

Although I felt a lack of strong backing from the mayor, I interpreted Michele's positive response as an indication of the city's support for the transformative endeavor. Perhaps Michele's inside communication was the mayor's actual sentiment, which is what I tried to deduce.

At that juncture, after the Gelber meeting, I reached out to Michael McShea, a top executive at CBRE Global, to discuss the project. He was surprised by the opportunity we presented, describing it as a once-in-a-generation chance to redevelop the location at 9th and Ocean Drive. I explained that we aimed to create, perhaps, a luxury building with renowned brands similar to those found in Surfside, known for its lower rise, upscale developments and celebrity residents like Tom Brady. Not everything had to be Sunny Isles Beach, with its 500 buildings, there is a middle ground.

Despite the lack of clear zoning regulations, the idea gained traction among many interested parties. The luxury brands *Fendi, Armani and Bulgari,* among others, were being used to brand buildings. I felt a trend like this could produce the glamour of South Beach's 1990s glory days, attracting elegance, excitement, and allure. The enthusiasm was real, even though the absence of zoning meant that the process would involve a bidder going under contract, funding a political campaign, and eventually winning a special election or referendum for the rezoning. Compared to I Drive 2040 zoning, which was like The Jetsons, Miami Beach was the opposite, The Flintstones of land use code.

We recognized the risk and knew that if a bidder proceeded, they would continue paying the option payments on the 3 Collins Ave properties while we retained the ability to reopen Mango's at any time during the contract. This strategy put us in a favorable position, and we believed that the package's overall value could potentially reach a staggering $90 million, maybe more.

This encompassed approximately $21 million for the three buildings behind Mango's and around $70 million for Mango's itself.

In essence, we were laying the groundwork for a transformation that could redefine the very essence of the area, uniting historical preservation with contemporary luxury, all while navigating a complex web of city politics and development dynamics. With a potential value of $70 million for Mango's, I felt reassured that even if we were only to secure that amount, it would provide substantial financial stability. August and September 2020 were dark days before even Florida was opened by Governor DeSantis. This opportunity seemed to pull things in a positive direction.

Lee Anne Korst was McShea's local Florida expert at CBRE. Together, we meticulously examined the complex details of the project. Soon, CBRE crafted a visually stunning video and a comprehensive package of the opportunity, which we called "*The Evolution of Ocean Drive.*"

I decided to first share the package with the mayor, commissioners, and other key figures before releasing it more widely. I expected opposition from the local NIMBYs (Not In My Backyard), who find fault with even the most promising of projects. Their joy is complaining, irrespective of the issues, and they let everyone know it on their social media channels. If God came back to Earth handing out million-dollar cashier's checks, they'd have a problem with it. *Just don't confuse them with the facts.*

This is why having the right narrative right away was critical. Our strategy involved exclusive interviews with two major press outlets, *The Miami Herald* and a prominent blogger from *RE: Miami Beach* named Susan Askew. During these interviews, I candidly discussed our plans, offering insights alongside our attorney, Monika Entin. I wasn't sure how these articles would turn out, but I hoped they'd convey the depth of our vision and our commitment to revitalizing Ocean Drive and South Beach.

To my surprise, the *RE: Miami Beach* article showcased our 3-generation journey in the City and aspirations amazingly well, showcasing the emotional connection we held to the area and our desire to contribute positively. However, while the blog piece was heartfelt and going viral, it wasn't backed by the authoritative stature of a major publication.

Then came the *Miami Herald* article titled *"Mango's May Lead the Way in the Reinvention of South Beach."*

This headline was a game-changer, implying that our nightclub could spearhead the transformation of the entire area. The article's content was equally impressive, emphasizing how our company was taking proactive steps to reshape South Beach during such trying times. It was an incredible boost to our credibility and vision.

Through strategic media exposure, we were now in the spotlight as potential pioneers in the revival of South Beach, *again*, as my father was a prominent figure in Miami Beach's 1980s Art Deco revival and the early 90s hospitality boom. This recognition was crucial to supporting our redevelopment plans and securing the narrative, which could lead to an overall sentiment that created the future necessary votes for rezoning. However, as exciting as the media coverage was, it was merely the first step in a complex journey that would require careful negotiation and collaboration with city officials, developers, and the community.

The 'Evolution of Ocean Drive' RFP was officially launched on December 8, 2020. Chris Ritter's artistic renderings adorned prominent media outlets that carried the news. The buzz surrounding the project was amazing, and the sentiment was a mix of nostalgia for the bygone days and hope for a new era of South Beach. We stood at a crossroads, waiting to see if the ambitious vision we had crafted would resonate with potential bidders.

As word spread about our plans, we began to realize the gravity of the situation. The RFP had garnered immense attention, with thousands of views on CBRE's website. Astonishingly, 90 qualified bidders from six different continents emerged. The diversity of interest was staggering, reflecting the global appeal of the site.

However, even with the influx of potential bidders, I knew that guiding this process would be an extremely difficult journey. Miami Beach's complex political landscape had proven to be, at times, an overwhelming challenge. Even the most recognized developers, who came in with grand plans over the years, would lose millions in pre-development costs and be sent packing. The city's small voting population, combined with the influence of entrenched, well-funded special interest groups, created a highly combative environment. Some of the top groups in the world had been shown the door over and over. Achieving any form of rezoning, without any overlay and in this primitive regulatory environment, would require overcoming considerable obstacles.

Yet, amidst the suspense and uncertainty, a deeper emotional struggle was brewing within me. Nights became restless as I wrestled with a mix of emotions. Throughout the pandemic, I remained extremely content, finding solace in the time spent with my wife and family, and had a profound sense of unity in overcoming challenges. But now, as the RFP process advanced, I was plagued by a terribly unsettling feeling.

As the clock ticked, I couldn't shake the realization how deeply the history of this building ran within my family. The connection stretched back to my grandparents, who had acquired the property in 1955, transforming it into a motel that my father grew up in. Mango's Tropical Cafe had not only been a lucrative enterprise but also a symbol of our legacy, interwoven with the very fabric of Miami Beach.

The thought of potentially selling and tearing down the building that had provided us all with financial stability and personal growth was overwhelming. The weight of my family's history and the memories that echoed within its walls were in stark contrast to the decision to consider letting go of this piece of our identity. A flood of emotions engulfed me as I wrestled with the significance of this choice.

As January rolled in, Florida was undergoing a noticeable shift in its approach to the pandemic. With the Delta variant wave still on the horizon, Governor DeSantis had reopened the state to full capacity, which contrasted starkly with the more stringent measures in other regions. The state's relaxed stance on mask-wearing, especially in outdoor settings, created a narrative that Florida was embracing a new normal, even as the pandemic persisted. The virus was endemic, "not ever going away, so neither are we. Florida is opened for business," declared DeSantis.

This change in approach coincided with the new year, a time traditionally marked by grand festivities at Mango's. However, for the first time in nearly three decades, there was no Mango's open, and I found myself away from the venue during this significant moment. The absence was felt deeply, a reminder of the tremendous impact Mango's had on my life and how much it had become a part of all of us.

The media began capturing images of people in Florida dining outdoors without masks, showcasing a sense of normalcy that had been missing for so long. This juxtaposition was glaring when compared to the stricter measures still in place in many other states, particularly in the Northeast and California. The visual of people enjoying themselves unmasked began shaping perceptions of Florida as a place either completely devoid of intelligence or completely free and moving beyond the pandemic's woes.

As we guided through these shifting dynamics, I couldn't help but reflect on the significance of this moment. Our ambitious plans to transform Ocean Drive were unfolding in a landscape marked by contradictions. *The Evolution of Ocean Drive* RFP was gaining traction in the City while the State of Florida was undergoing a transformation of its own, one that seemed to mirror the resilience and adaptability we were aiming to capture in our redevelopment project.

As the RFP process continued, a series of events and developments unfolded that shaped the trajectory of our project. Spring Break 2021 was looming, and Miami–Dade County made an assertive move to attract tourists by investing millions of dollars in advertising that communicated the area's openness during a time when most of the country remained closed due to the pandemic. The move was aimed at capturing the Spring Break tourism market, as for more than a year, it had been in a deep Depression. As the beaches beckoned and Florida embraced this different approach to the pandemic, more and more young people began to arrive, bringing some degree of life back to the area.

The prospect of Mango's reopening for Valentine's Day and President's Day weekend was on the table, a strategic move to coincide with the beginning of Spring Break. However, this plan didn't come to fruition. Instead, our focus was primarily on the RFP, which progressed steadily through its various stages. The momentum built up over the past six months was now culminating in the final days before bids were due.

Throughout this process, I had been preparing myself mentally for what lay ahead. I anticipated dedicating a year to assisting the chosen developer with the intricate politics and negotiations required to bring our ambitious vision to life. My interactions with key influencers, including those within the Chamber of Commerce and other Miami Beach activists, had prepared the ground for navigating these complex dynamics.

Yet, amidst the growing enthusiasm, there were undercurrents of skepticism. Rumors began to circulate, especially among the top local land use attorneys such as former Miami Beach mayor Neisen Kasdin and others, who were sought after for their expertise. Monika was told that several bidders were reportedly receiving discouraging advice, suggesting that the hurdles posed by the city's development complexities, its lack of zoning, would make it difficult to achieve success with the project.

The sentiment was also that the City would find every possible way to impede progress, creating an air of doubt and discouragement among those considering bidding. This was Miami Beach's reputation in the global real estate community.

As the skepticism reached my ears, I instructed Monika to reach out to her colleagues and get real information. She reported back that attorneys were actively warning our potential bidders of the formidable obstacles that awaited, causing some to question whether it was worth embarking on such an effort. I conveyed these concerns to CBRE, and they shared that they were seeing that same thing, potential big players might be hesitant to engage in a deal under these conditions. All they were asked by the bidders, over and over, was, *"What can we build here?"* They did not have an answer.

The realization set in that even though our vision was bold and promising, the inherent complexities of Miami Beach were casting a shadow over the venture. The very essence of the project, breathing new life into Ocean Drive, would be revolutionary, and revolutions are risky and expensive, and you can also, without assistance, lose them. Most directly, Miami Beach's past farces with formidable groups were not lost on the world.

As the deadline for submitting bids for the Evolution of Ocean Drive RFP approached, uncertainty filled the air. CBRE was actively fielding more inquiries, engaging in conversations, and attempting to address the *"What can we build here?"* issue.

One large group that loved our idea of a *Fendi Chateau* building to join the Versace Mansion on Ocean Drive, we felt were on the cusp of a major bid, and we held initial design meetings with *Fendi Casa*, their luxe home décor brand and consultant, who would design interiors. Then Spring Break 2021 happened.

Once again, even with most of its businesses closed or reduced, the City of Miami Beach lost control of Ocean Drive and Spring Break. News reports were all over the world documenting the chaos unfolding. *Saturday Night Live's* cold open lampooned our city as buffoons.

If the lack of zoning was already bad, Spring Break 2021 in South Beach was a total disaster. Even more unbelievably, the irresponsible and disingenuous nature of some of the public officials that, *caught with their pants around their ankles yet again,* blamed the nightclubs, *businesses that were closed* (and had been so for 12 months or more). I thought *Saturday Night Live's* skit took it easy on them.

I called McShea for the big update, and what he relayed to me was astonishing and disheartening but, at that point, not the least bit surprising. Despite the initial excitement, the momentum, and the extensive coordination that had gone into it, not a single one of the 90 qualified bidders had submitted a formal bid. That's how bad the past had been for development in Miami Beach, and, coupled with its notorious reputation as a place deals go to die, the disastrous Spring Break and another curfew and lockdown of the city was the death knell.

The outcome, or lack thereof, still managed to send shockwaves through my system. On one hand, the notion of selling my grandmother's building, along with Mango's Tropical Cafe, had weighed heavily on me. I could barely sleep; I was having intense nightmares and waking up sweating through the bed. The prospect of seeing a cherished legacy transformed or dismantled was completely unsettling.

On the other hand, there was a glimmer of hope as tourism began to pick up in Florida, suggesting that recovery was indeed on the horizon. Mango's could potentially reopen soon, and the State of Florida's resilience could lead the way in the United States' recovery from the pandemic.

Reflecting on the journey, it was clear that the *Evolution of Ocean Drive* wasn't prepared to evolve at that moment. A few months later, as Miami experienced a surge of development by people fleeing lockdown states, I received feedback from several multi-billionaire developers who acknowledged the boldness of our endeavor. They suggested that we were ahead of our time, and 8-10 months later would have easily yielded a $100 million buyer.

While disheartened by the loss and the pivot away from *Evolution the Ocean Drive*, we resolved to close the chapter on this venture and focus on reopening Mango's. From the successful closure of the Main Street loan to the eventual realization that our grand vision wasn't ready for right now, it was a period marked by highs and lows, hope, and disappointment.

As this chapter ended, I found myself looking to the future, contemplating our next move, and the story of Mango's Tropical Cafe continued in uncharted waters. While one path, a move born in the most hopeless part of the pandemic, had reached its end, we were ready to move on.

The important thing was I had my family, my beautiful wife and kids, and Mango's still had the Main Street loan. While there was optimism for that aspect, opening South Beach and then Orlando was still unknown; what it would take, what was coming around the bend, and how it would play out, was still a mystery.

Chapter 10:
The Summer of SVOG

The lack of significant bids for the RFP was utterly shocking to me, to say the least. We showcased some of the world's most precious real estate on an incredible platform. We had 90 qualified bidders on six continents. A billion dollar REIT aligned with *Fendi* was in deep discussions. However, South Beach's lack of zoning, the knowledge I had gained during my early days in Orlando, was an undeniable factor. Miami Beach's notorious difficulty in development and its requirement for FAR increases to pass through public referendum added to the challenge. PACs formed against you at the drop of a hat, diverting attention from development's key issues and causing uncertainty and chaos that resulted in referendum losses.

Although DeSantis had reopened Florida a few months prior, a sense of life hadn't returned. Despite receiving remarkable initial support, the RFP's outcome had fallen flat. Amid the countless panic attacks and guilt-ridden thoughts from the notion of selling the Mango's building, even amidst the worst economy and the history-making pandemic, it was killing me. Thankfully, relief washed over as the ordeal concluded. Talk of some potential business during Spring Break was buzzing, and thoughts of reopening Mango's circulated. Despite everything, we had funds from the Main Street loan, offering a lifeline to get sales going.

Around three days after the RFP closed, CBRE proposed an extension to keep trying, so I said, *"This is it, kindly tell the Fendi people to submit a bid today."* When the word came back that they were still discussing but wouldn't have an answer 'for a few weeks,' I opted to shut it down. We just didn't want to continue funding the option payments for the 3 Collins Avenue properties, so the unified site assemblage was gone.

At that time, the Delta wave of the pandemic gripped America, bringing the real death toll from COVID-19. My wife's high fever marked my birthday, and as her health deteriorated, I felt a heavy concern.

Her COVID symptoms mirrored what we were seeing on the news. I couldn't bear the thought of her battling it alone, so I told her to please kiss me. As my lips met hers, I knew I was in it with her.

Soon, my symptoms emerged: fever, headache, and brain fog. Days blurred as we fought the virus together, seeking solace in each other's arms. The Delta wave proved ruthless, unlike anything before in 2020. The news reported thousands of deaths daily, desensitizing society to unimaginable loss. The pandemic's cruelty truly dulled the nation's collective shock.

Amid our shared struggle, we discussed what was going on with regard to Miami Beach's lack of support for the groundbreaking ideas we'd presented. Despite the uphill battle, we agreed the goal was clear: *saving Mango's.* It wasn't about this proposal or that, but the survival of our family and business amidst a pandemic and a government that deemed our company '*non-essential.*'

Using Main Street loan funds, my father began rehiring for South Beach. The looming prospect of additional PPP2 loans, this time capped at $2 million maximum, likely less, cast a shadow. Since late December 2020, however, I eyed a potential lifeline—a cultural grant program for venues that I felt were like ours. President Trump's bill allocated funds for cultural organizations, including theaters, zoos, museums, and entertainment venues. A grant program, not another loan, held tremendous promise.

The timing, just after the 2020 election, was critical. I kept watching, knowing the grant program could maybe offer a beacon of hope. After emerging from the haze of being extremely ill with COVID, this had now become my new mission and to save our family business. Both Mango's remained shuttered, and as we navigated uncertain terrain, I zeroed in on the potential of this emerging program.

After finally getting over COVID-19, we decided to visit our favorite Mexican restaurant. Utilitarian eateries in suburban areas like this one were flourishing, while places in dense tourism areas like Mango's remained closed. It was mid-February 2021, and as we left the restaurant, the clear-headedness induced by the good meal had me checking Google for any updates on the program.

Conducting my habitual search, I stumbled upon a brand new, well-written article on JD Supra, a legal blog, penned by a D.C.-based attorney named Alexander Ginsberg. The position paper discussed a recently released FAQ for the program, tentatively called "Grants for Shuttered Venues," a moniker that felt more relevant than ever. I connected strongly with how Ginsberg opined on the issue, feeling it aligned perfectly with our situation.

I began to feel more confident that this grant program may be tailor-made for Mango's. We were, in essence, a dinner theater and live music venue, which was the IRS classification that the article alluded to. My gut told me strongly that this was the avenue we should explore rather than another loan with PPP2.

With a newfound sense of determination, I reached out to Alex Ginsberg right there in the parking lot. Connecting that afternoon was a game-changer, transforming him from a name on a byline to my attorney in a matter of hours. It's in these decisive moments that pivotal decisions must be made, a philosophy that has always led me through intense challenges.

Our phone call established the collaboration. By the time I got home, Ginsberg's letter of engagement had arrived, which I executed immediately. I sent it back along with his retainer via wire transfer.

The next day, our inaugural meeting on Zoom brought me together with Alex and Toni Suh, our new lawyers who would hopefully guide us through the federal grant process. Though Toni was an associate and Alex was the seasoned partner, it was clear that she would be doing much of the legwork under his direction. Their deep expertise in US Government statutes, IRS regulations, SBA issues, and the intricacies and nuances of such programs was evident. Expertise with the strict rules surrounding this kind of law was just what we needed.

With their guidance, we went on the journey of gathering an extensive list of documentation, to say the least. It was insanely meticulous work; the first list from Toni was seven pages, front and back, of documentation requirements for both our Miami Beach and Orlando venues. But necessity breeds creativity, and with a small team due to ongoing COVID-19 constraints, I leaned heavily on the resources I had available.

The process proved time-consuming and extremely demanding, with constant back-and-forth interaction. Several long lead time items were paramount, such as securing a System Access Management (SAM) account for Mango's South Beach, since we already had one in Orlando from an event we had done for the US Postal Service. This SAM account, which took many weeks to get approved, was how we'd receive the federal grant funds if we were successful. It was a step toward preparation that had to be completed despite the prevailing uncertainties.

As we waited for further guidance from the Government, I relentlessly compiled documents based on the ever-evolving FAQs that the Small Business Administration (SBA) periodically released per Toni's instructions. Within our constant communication, she had me painstakingly fulfilling each issue on the growing lists she provided. Every update brought new challenges and fresh inquiries. However, my drive was unrelenting, and I poured in hours, inspired by the conviction that this opportunity could save Mango's.

As more information was released, our attorneys tried to keep us on track. Their insights into the ever-evolving regulations were invaluable. As they diligently negotiated the fluctuating obstacles, I felt we were in capable hands.

With the mercurial document process in motion, I watched as the grant program's potential value began to crystallize. For Mango's South Beach, it could amount to the max grant of $10 million, and the Orlando location's figures hinted at nearly $7 million. This was totally game-changing; it was a lifeline that could save our business, which had suffered so much when the time came for us to reopen.

While the future was still uncertain, my determination remained resolute. We had entered a phase where patience, precision, and a keen eye for detail were the only things that mattered. The process was onerous, demanding, and brimming with unknowns. Yet, within the maelstrom of challenges, the prospect of the program offered a glimmer of hope.

While I deeply felt this was the ticket to reclaiming our former stature, the rules surrounding our journey were strict: applying for the Shuttered Venue Operators Grant (*SVOG*) precluded us from pursuing PPP2 completely. Even applying for PPP2, regardless of your application's success or failure, would automatically nullify your SVOG application. The dilemma was that the SBA hadn't yet announced when the SVOG program would launch. Meanwhile, my relationship lender Carlos was offering, via email, a bird in the hand, it seemed, a link to quickly apply for PPP2 to reopen Mango's South Beach. The choice was almost too much: *take PPP2 now, or seek out the undefined SVOG.*

Some prominent voices in America were highly concerned with the situation. Tom Sullivan, Vice President of small business policy at the US Chamber of Commerce, strongly stated, *"That's a big deal to say to a small business owner, that you have to choose between the PPP and the possibility of a large grant, but the deadlines don't match, and you are going to have to roll the dice. That's not a risk I think Congress intended for small business to take."*

In that decisive moment, I made a resolute choice. Without seeking external opinions, I trusted my instincts and Ginsberg's counsel and opted for the SVOG. My conviction was unwavering; this was our path forward. It was clear, and I owned the resolution and its outcome.

Upon sharing the decision with my father, I was met with understanding and support. The potential benefits of the grant program were substantial, and my choice was met with approval. Our journey to recovery had taken many turns, and this step felt like another natural evolution; a beacon of progress would overshadow our hardships.

Through March 2021, I was consumed six days a week, ten hours a day, with document curation per the attorney's requests on a grant program that didn't yet exist. I meticulously worked on two hundred documents for each Mango's location, single ones sometimes taking many hours and ensuring they met the rigorous checklist and criteria outlined by Alex and Toni. With an intricate choreography, I organized, compiled, and uploaded these documents into Dropbox, one for each location. The Dropboxes grew quickly, swelling with crucial information required for our eventual grant applications.

I was fortunate to have a dedicated team still by my side. Although our staff had been reduced to a mere six individuals per location, their commitment was unwavering. Assignments were handed out, deadlines were set, and the team rallied to fulfill their tasks. Each contribution was essential, each document meticulously scrutinized by Toni, who proved to be a perfectionist, leaving no room for error, as was the case in the public sector. As many times as she pointed out this or that mistake with something I had just worked 9 hours on, I appreciated the razor-sharp, bullseye precision. At the highest level, even the tiniest error can always be fatal.

As March wore on, a significant development arrived in Washington, D.C. Isabella Guzman was appointed to the Biden Cabinet as the new Secretary of the Small Business Administration. The atmosphere, still in the wake of the January 6th events, remained charged and divisive. Yet, the law was on the books, and the SVOG program was supposedly underway. Amidst the shifting political landscape, the anticipation for clarity grew, a need for guidance amid the uncharted terrain. Secretary Guzman took to organizing the SBA after taking office.

Finally, via Twitter, rumors about the *Shuttered Venue Operators Grant* began to circulate, now coined the word 'SVOG.' The whispers regarding the grant's launch date grew louder until the SBA officially announced that the portal for SVOG applications would open on April 8, 2021, at noon. The program was designed as a first-come, first-served process, and the eligibility criteria were tiered: 90%, 60%, and 40% revenue loss. Our situation matched the highest tier, the 90% loss, underlining the depths of our struggle.

The clock ticked down to the day of reckoning as both suspense and tension scaled. I was fully aware that within minutes of the portal opening, funds could be drained by the multitude of applicants vying for a lifeline. A race against time was upon us; it was like the *Hunger Games*. The opportunity to secure the grants was tantalizing, but the possibility of missing out was nerve-wracking. This was the defining moment.

The approach I decided upon was strategic and deliberate. I shared my intentions with Alex and Toni; I wanted to be there with them at their office to work through the application process together. Nothing like being in the room when synergy and communication are needed. Their DC office was closed, but the firm's Tysons Corner location in Northern Virginia was open to us. I was fueled by the desire for undistracted focus, a day dedicated solely to navigating this intricate process we had prepared so hard for.

I informed my wife of the plan, a brief up-and-back trip to return late the same night. The weight of this endeavor was not lost on her; she completely understood the significance of the moment. With a kiss goodbye at 5 a.m., I set off to fly to Dulles International Airport before sunrise.

The experience of stepping into a city still gripped by early 2020 pandemic-induced caution and policy was eye-opening. The atmosphere was worlds apart from our situation in Florida, a reminder of the disparate approaches that various regions were still taking to the crisis.

My arrival at the Northern Virginia office of the Pillsbury Law firm was met with an eerie calm. The building was quiet, and the huge shopping mall nearby largely deserted. I walked in, greeted by a masked security guard behind a plastic shield, an embodiment of the cautious stance still prevailing in that part of the country.

Ascending to the 14th floor, I met Alex and Toni. The office was nearly empty, with a virtual work culture still prevailing. We had the conference room at our disposal, and I coordinated with my cousin Blaze (who resided in Maryland) to bring lunch. We focused on the critical task at hand, preparing to navigate the SVOG application process.

We aimed to set up Toni's laptop in the conference room with the overhead projector. The goal was to strategize and work through the process as a complete team. The clock was ticking, and I kept a close eye on Twitter, gauging the pulse of the situation as other applicants from coast to coast eagerly shared their experiences. The portal's impending launch was imminent, and the collective tension was stressful and electric.

As the countdown neared and the SBA portal was an hour from opening, a confounding twist befell us: another FAQ of colossal proportions, 58 pages in length, was released by the SBA. This monolithic document arrived as *the largest FAQ* since the inception of the program.

As the clock ticked toward the portal's expected noon opening, Toni and I found ourselves poring over this latest development. The FAQs unveiled a trove of novel requests, with all new details and complexity that had not been broached or asked for before.

Perhaps only an hour to go until the portal's unveiling, the urgent task was to quickly decide and prioritize what we could do to adapt to these brand-new standards. Swift action was required, and I was fortunate I had teams on standby in South Beach and Orlando. Without a moment's delay, I set the wheels in motion, sending a flurry of texts and emails, rallying the troops to action.

South Beach needed someone in the building urgently to send me clear pictures from their iPhone, and I dispatched a trusted manager who lived nearby to capture crucial images. The DJ booth, lighting rig, and sound system in clear, high-resolution pictures were needed. Time was of the essence, with the ticking clock gnawing away.

By 11:45 a.m., the photographic assets were in hand, and our collective focus shifted to updating our budget to their new criteria. Our comptroller and CPA were summoned to guide us through the intricate web of new needs. The mission was to align our application with these freshly moved goalposts, unwaveringly staying within the boundaries of the statute, no matter what. To me, these were not mere grant applications but a battle to secure our future, and live bullets were now flying.

In the ensuing fever, my leadership turned passionate. While it might have seemed tyrannical that day, my intent was driven by extreme urgency, not malice. The survival of Mango's hinged on this moment, and there was no room for anything but complete dedication. It was a shared work, a team united in pursuit of a common cause.

Time ticked on relentlessly. As the morning progressed, the looming opening of the portal induced an increasingly feverish, heart-pounding pace. Despite the turmoil, we managed to muster enough to forge ahead some, navigating through the complexities of the new FAQs. Yet, a pervasive question lingered: Why did they release an FAQ of such magnitude on the very day the portal would open? *Was it to brutally eliminate the groups who couldn't keep up?* It was a question that echoed across Twitter, a chorus of frustration among the applicants, especially the smaller ones, who were alone with little or no professional help.

The countdown reached its culmination: 11:58, 11:59, and then at noon, the portal was live. Swiftly, we launched our application journey, creating accounts for both entities. Our focus first turned to Mango's South Beach. The very first question confronted us: "What type of venue are you?" We had a clear choice to make, and we opted for "*live music venue*" from the drop-down menu.

And then, of course, the unexpected, as the road that had appeared clear, was suddenly vanishing under my feet. The upload of our first document, a floor plan showing the permanent stage at Mango's South Beach, resulted in an error message. Concern was quickly replaced by alarm, and reality hit me. There was a major technical problem; the portal had opened, but our grasp on the lifeline was slipping.

Desperation urged us to try again, but the outcome remained the same. The error messages persisted, thwarting our attempts to do even the application's first question. Panic set in, a sinking feeling as doubt spawned at the edge of hope. Were our files intercepted by a firewall? Could this be the result of the firm's security measures? Was this just us? If so, how long before the funds ran out?

A brief reprieve came from Twitter; my network of fellow SVOG applicants confirmed that they, too, were grappling with the same issue. It was a sigh of collective relief as we weren't alone in this unexpected struggle.

With renewed resolve, we took stock. After an hour of Twitter fervor, the SBA tweeted they were taking the portal offline to repair the bug and would advise soon. We had no idea when it would be back opened, perhaps later that day, so we revisited the new FAQs, hoping to work through the new standards. Alex retreated to his office while Toni meticulously combed through the issues with me. Time stood still as we waited, both frustrated and hopeful, for a resolution to the technical dilemma that had stained our initiation into the SVOG application process.

Hours stretched on, and Blaze arrived with lunch from a local restaurant. We took a short break, pondering over the situation as we ate. Yet, beneath the mealtime chatter was an unspoken understanding: the precious moments that ticked away could spell the difference between resurgence and despair. *Was the portal to reopen at any moment or what?*

As the afternoon progressed, the SBA again addressed the glitch via Twitter, a promise that they were working on the technical impediments. Hope flickered anew, a chance that the portal's doors might yet swing wide that day after all.

After 5 p.m., it was clear the portal wasn't opening that afternoon, but I held hope that maybe it would in the morning, so Toni promised to meet me at 9 a.m. There was a Marriott next to their office, and with near zero occupancy, they gave me a king suite for $100. Exhausted, I ordered room service, surrendered to fatigue, fading into sleep.

The early morning light revealed the portal was still locked in technical limbo. My optimism hesitated, but I clung to a faint glimmer of hope that when the workday opened, maybe the portal would too. Either way, I had a ton of work with Toni on the new FAQ requirements. My flight back to Orlando was scheduled for later in the day. Maybe, just maybe, the portal would reopen and give us another chance.

Reality set in, I was stranded in the same clothes as the previous day. A CVS run was necessary to procure essentials, a comical ordeal playing out outside the store, filled with a few homeless guys' curious gazes. A reminder of my early days, I applied deodorant in the parking lot as had been done so many times 15 years prior, after being stuck on an Amtrak train for 20 hours.

Returning to the hotel room, I freshened up and resumed the waiting game. The law office beckoned where my collaboration with Toni continued. Amidst the uncertainty, we delved solely into the expanded FAQs, unearthing new layers of complexity that we hadn't fully comprehended in our distracted state the day before.

The second day brought clarity, a revelation that in light of the new criteria, the portal's crash had been a silver lining, allowing us to fully digest the implications of the monumental FAQ update. Toni's careful attention to detail, as always, was evident. I returned home with a list larger than the original one had been.

Days blurred as I straddled the responsibilities and deliverables. The office in Mango's provided a backdrop for my relentless pursuit of compliance; the intricate dance with the lawyers and financial experts played out over Zoom calls to ensure every aspect of compliance with the statute.

And then, 16 days later, a tweet shattered the suspense, a revival on the horizon. The SBA announced the reopening of the SVOG portal. The next day, a Saturday, was set to be the day. Yet, as excitement built, conflict erupted on Twitter, and critics raised concerns about the timing, citing religious observances. A weekend reopening was met with guff, forcing the SBA to backtrack and delay the launch again until Monday.

The weekend was a whirlwind of final preparations. Toni and I left no stone unturned as we combed through the expanded FAQs, checking and rechecking our approach and the documents in our Dropboxes. Delays had their advantages; we were now better equipped and more comprehensively prepared. *Frankly, I was ready to retake Omaha Beach.*

The SVOG portal reopened on Monday, April 26, 2021, at noon, approximately 18 days after the initial launch's crash. Armed with precision, my apprehensions were somewhat eased. I didn't have a sense of urgency to return to Washington, D.C.; my team was again ready to assist me effectively. My lawyers and others were on standby, ready to lend their expertise should the need arise.

Still concerned with a first come, first served race, I was determined to tackle both applications in tandem, a parallel pursuit of securing our future. Yet, the moment the portal opened at noon, that plan was upended. Within a minute, the portal logged me out, disrupting my attempt to juggle both applications simultaneously. Frustration nearly boiled over.

Amid the mounting chaos, Mauricio, a longtime friend and employee, offered a much-needed lifeline. His calming presence and energy became my anchor, steadying me as I reset myself. He sensed my frustration, offering cold water and a Red Bull, a simple gesture that carried immeasurable support.

With Mauricio by my side, I shifted gears, focusing on completing one application before tackling the other. His steady encouragement became my bedrock as I methodically progressed through the South Beach application, uploading documents with precision. This time, everything was working.

The intense preparation was the saving grace. Each question was met with a well-orchestrated response as if Mango's life had depended on it because, in reality, it did. Every file was in its designated Dropbox, clearly marked, organized, and accessible. There was no desperate search for anything; it was all at my fingertips, ready to go.

Hour by hour, the process unfolded. I guided through the 26 pages of questions of the first application, uploading some 200 documents required. The challenge was relentless, demanding intense focus. Yet, with Mauricio's support and the clarity of purpose, each hurdle was somehow surmounted. The clock seemed both an ally and a foe, urging me forward while also raising concerns about potential mistakes.

As the Mango's South Beach application neared completion, an attestation page loomed, a solemn moment of truth. The gravity of the declaration hit me as I checked and rechecked each detail. Mauricio offered reassurance he, too, believed everything looked correct, and after we both triple-checked, with a deep breath, I clicked "SUBMIT." The moment held a blend of triumph and trepidation, the culmination of months of total dedication.

With Mango's South Beach submitted, I swiftly turned to the Mango's Orlando application. The lessons learned from the first attempt eased the process somewhat. As each question was addressed and each document attached, a sense of purpose infused every keystroke. I stuck to the same approach, triple-checking details obsessively to ensure complete accuracy.

The process was both brutal and exciting, a testament to the lengths we'd gone through. Finally, the Mango's Orlando application was completed as well, and with a deep sense of accomplishment, I signed the attestation page and clicked "SUBMIT" once more.

In the aftermath of the submissions, I sought any confirmation the applications were received, scouring my email for a sign that the SBA was in receipt of everything. There was no immediate verification at all, no acknowledgment of our monumental effort. Doubts swirled, threatening to undo the hard-fought composure. Then, I saw pending files appear in both account portals, which gave a measured sense that the applications were in.

As the virtual curtain fell on that monumental day, I couldn't help but marvel at the intricacy of circumstances that had brought me to that point, echoing the chaos of the past, the determination of the present, and the hope for the future. And as the hours passed, a sense of calm descended, replacing the unrest that had characterized the journey. For in that moment, as I guided through sheer uncertainty, I knew that no matter the outcome, we had fought with all we had, refusing to bow down in the face of overwhelming adversity.

Along with our legal team, I held a steadfast belief that our efforts were well within the statute and firmly grounded in our eligibility. There was no doubt in my mind that we fit the bill of the very entities the grants were intended for.

As the reality of having done all we could sunk in, I returned home, a sense of accomplishment mingling with the need to decompress. A moment of respite was in order, a chance to recharge before the results of our painstaking efforts began to trickle in.

The countdown to May, a month dedicated to the supposed distribution of grants, loomed large. The value of the approaching month wasn't lost on me, for we if approved, were part of the 90% loss group that was to receive funding. With May's arrival, an air of expectancy surrounded us, teasing me with the promise of answers.

Mango's South Beach had reopened on weekends, a very scaled-down version, offering a glimmer of hope as patrons cautiously ventured out. The nightlife had begun to stir, and even though the kitchen was yet to open, the bar saw some action. On the other hand, Orlando remained in a slower tempo, with the convention center lying motionless, its former buzz replaced by an eerie stillness.

As the days of May progressed and we sailed through the month to Memorial Day weekend, my optimism held its ground. The hope that had been kindled during our application process, but as if to remind me of life's unpredictability (as if I needed reminding), May came to an end without the expected breakthrough.

The June heat rolled in, marking the onset of 'The Summer of SVOG,' a relentless, unending period of anxiety, terror, and uncertainty, where I searched for any sign from anywhere.

In an attempt to divert my mind from the ceaseless panic of waiting, I immersed myself in the reopening of Mango's Orlando, focusing on its upcoming weekend-only operations. The leisurely activities of summer in Orlando held a semblance of normalcy as the theme parks began to draw visitors. Yet, apprehension persisted, and people were cautious about congregating indoors, their unease a reminder of the impact of the pandemic.

The Delta wave of COVID-19 and its continuing consequences were a testament to the uncertainty that still shrouded our lives. While there was a show of recovery, the trauma of the past months left an unforgettable mark, shaping our collective actions and perspectives.

As the summer progressed, my attention was squarely on the flurry of articles and updates on SVOG that began to flood the media. In particular, a *New York Times* business reporter, Stacy Cowley, began a series of articles on the program, with many she interviewed already referring to it at that point as a debacle. The nuances of the political theater echoed across the country, where senators from opposing sides of the aisle united to criticize the SBA's handling of SVOG, highlighting the gravity of the situation as their constituents begged for help.

With the efforts of individuals waiting for any word on the grants to keep their cultural spaces alive, they were met with silence, no information, and further setbacks.

Throughout this unbelievably stressful period, a lifeline emerged through a Facebook group full of people who were in my very position. There started to be some detailed updates posted by an NYC-based Broadway executive named Meredith Lynsey Schade, who was getting to join in on SBA Zoom meetings about SVOG and would then share what she heard with the group. With tireless dedication, she collated notes and insights, and her posts, brimming with any available details, began to shed at least some light on what was happening.

As The Summer of SVOG wore on, I clung to the belief that our preparation and strong work would pay off at some point, carrying the weight of our hopes and dreams. With my income still next to nothing, I sold our house, a home we loved. While Toops was extremely sad to sell, the unending support of my wife was a balm for my weary soul, providing solace and strength in the face of adversity. I appreciated her so much; she was, and is, everything to me.

The Summer of SVOG began to shift in late July, marked by a noticeable change in the tone of Meredith's updates. The collective voices of venues across the nation, each with unique stories of struggle, finally resonated with those in power. Senators and members of Congress, regardless of political affiliations, united to denounce the SBA's mismanagement of the program. Chuck Schumer and Roger Williams, total adversaries in every way, banded together to get the program going immediately, as many venues had already lost everything and closed forever.

In response, Secretary Guzman, still new to her appointment, acknowledged the program's shortcomings and wisely assigned the team that had handled the original PPP program to SVOG. The essential shift allowed for quicker distribution of funds and changed or streamlined many policies, including alleviating the need for receiving grants in pieces.

In this evolving landscape, Meredith's updates, which had once painted a gloomy picture, now started to reveal signs of real progress. Thousands of grants were being disbursed in a single week, a marked departure from the sluggish pace that had characterized the early and mid-summer. The pain and suffering that had defined the earlier days were being met with some tangible relief as venues across all 50 states began to receive the lifeline they so desperately needed.

Amid this newfound momentum, my wife's support remained a constant source of strength. Her reassurances echoed through our days, reminding me that even in the face of adversity, love and understanding were what truly mattered. She reminded me of how intensely I had prepared and would say, "No one could have done more for this to happen. Do you know how I know that, Honey?

Because it's not possible. It's not possible to be more consistent and dedicated than you were."

As July ended, the bloodbath of frustration gave way to a wave of hope as the updates continued to show more progress. Trying to find humor in the face of my stress and terror, I would tell my dad when he asked if we'd heard anything that "maybe our applications fell between the seats."

The doldrums of anxiety and uncertainty had taken their toll, and The Summer of SVOG just pulverized me. Amidst the migraines that lasted for days at a time, I found reprieve in engrossing myself in Mango's reopening assessments. One such meeting, I was on a conference call, sitting on a barstool in my kitchen.

It was August 10, 2021, at 3:14 pm.

As the Zoom ended, I glanced at my phone to find a series of new emails. Then, my eyes bugged out of my skull as I saw among them was one from '*noresponse@sba.gov*' with the subject line, "Your Shuttered Venue Operators Grant Application."

I had recognized this from dozens of posts and comments on the Facebook group page. My heart began to race, and I couldn't speak. Opening that email felt like opening a decision letter from Harvard, except this held the potential to save our business's future. Mango's employees, whom we so adored, had suffered immeasurably, with the venues being closed for 16 months; this was for their and everyone else's security.

I hesitated for a split second, torn between desperately wanting to know and being scared to death of the outcome, living every emotion of that moment. But then, almost involuntarily, my finger clicked to open the email. The first word I saw was "*Congratulations!*" punctuated with an exclamation mark. I hit the roof.

My son Brett raced downstairs, his face a mix of curiosity and excitement, hearing the screams of happiness. "Did you get it?" he asked eagerly. My reply, "We got it!" made my son beam. He went through The Summer of SVOG, too; he knew what it did to me and what this meant.

The email itself didn't specify the amount granted, but the word "Congratulations" was enough to make me believe that we had secured the maximum allocation. The application figures I had submitted for Mango's South Beach suggested a potential of around $14 million, which was capped at $10 million. So, I was almost certain that we had achieved that ceiling.

The email instructed me immediately to check my portal for two documents I needed to download, complete, and upload to receive the grant funds. Fueled by a mix of excitement and impatience, I dashed out of my home, hopped into my car, and drove to Mango's Orlando. Despite my desire to drive 160 mph, I kept to the speed limit. Arriving at the venue, I headed straight to my office, where I eagerly accessed my portal to commence the next steps. I was soaring, floating through the air. The managers caught wind of what was happening and drifted into my office with giant smiles.

In front of my computer, I began the process I had been waiting for every day of The Summer of SVOG. Downloading and printing the documents, I felt a sense of amazing accomplishment that words just couldn't capture. One document was the actual grant form for the funding, a tangible representation of all the hopes and dreams I had been nurturing. The other document was an additional attestation, a final affirmation that my journey had led me to this moment of truth.

As I stared at those forms, I continued living out what I had only fantasized about for months. It was no longer a distant hope; it was reality; it was here and now. I savored every detail: the texture of the paper, the weight of the pen in my hand, the forms themselves, and all their listed information. Following specific directions from Meredith, I signed everything in wet ink as opposed to digitally. *There would be no mistakes.*

After I executed the funding form and scanned the documents, frustration struck; my signature was half cut off, no way this would do. There was no room for error, no margin for anything less than perfection. So, I printed the forms again, this time signing at a slightly higher spot with even greater precision. When I scanned them again, it worked; my signature was bright and intact. I renamed each document with the exact name of the form and with the grant application number, no detail was spared.

I accessed the portal to upload the forms, once again triple-checking that the PDF files were the perfect scans. My portal accepted both documents and told me that my action items were completed. For the first time in 7 months, I breathed a little easier.

The next morning, a call from our comptroller, Sergio, disrupted the stillness of the morning. His voice crackled with excitement as he shared the news that a wire transfer had been received, and it appeared a substantial sum had entered our account. My heart raced as I contacted the bank, urging them to expedite the release of the funds. In a matter of moments, the confirmation arrived: $10 million had been wired through our SAM account to Mango's Tropical Cafe, LLC.

That August day marked the turning point. The Summer of SVOG had been a never-ending rollercoaster of emotions, brutally testing my patience, hope, and resilience. But on that day, the elation of success replaced the tension of uncertainty. I knew this achievement wasn't just for me, it was for my family, my team, and the future of Mango's South Beach and Mango's Orlando. As many times before, really my entire life, I embraced the deep realization that even amidst life's greatest challenges, persistence and intensity yield truly extraordinary results.

All the pain, the rage, and the anxiety were suddenly replaced by a profound relief. Our unyielding faith in this endeavor had worked beautifully, a moment of triumph amidst the trials. I couldn't help but share the news with my father, who had been by my side through every twist and turn, even as he, too, lost faith once or twice. The screenshot of the $10 million in our account spoke volumes, a testament to my relentless determination, my decision to pursue the grants in the first place, and the strength of our resolve. With this victory, a weight had lifted not only from my shoulders but from the backs of our entire team.

As I returned to work, there was a renewed sense of purpose and revitalized energy. The grant had provided a lifeline, a chance to breathe, to rebuild. With the funds at our disposal, a path forward emerged, illuminated by opportunities and resources.

Richard Preston, who had referred a year before to my obtaining the Main Street loan as a miracle, said this time, beside himself, that he truly couldn't believe it. Everyone was just elated.

Yet, the journey wasn't over. Another email from 'noresponse@sba.gov' 11 days later heralded the news of

Orlando's grant. The excitement that had become a welcome presence in our lives surged a second time. I called my wife, eager to share the news we had done it again. Her elation mirrored mine. Mango's and our family had turned the corner.

As before, I repeated the ritual, signing, scanning, and submitting the forms for Orlando like clockwork. Within a day, $6.4 million was wired into Mango's Tropical Cafe Orlando's account. The realization struck me like a tidal wave; we had received $16.4 million in tax-free Shuttered Venue Operator Grants. The struggle, the sacrifice, and the sleepless nights had all converged into this astounding outcome.

With the weight of uncertainty lifted, the dense fog of The Summer of SVOG began to dissipate. It was as if the storm clouds had finally parted, revealing blue skies and a future that gleamed with potential. As I looked back on the journey, I was overcome by a mix of emotions, from the despair that had tested the depths of my tolerance for anguish to the triumph that had made it all worthwhile.

But the story didn't end there. The SBA shared that Mango's Orlando was eligible for a supplemental grant. It was a testament to the relentlessness of my pursuit, a reflection of the value we had brought to our communities. The supplemental grant, another $3.3 million, was accepted on November 8, 2021. As forms were signed, the attestation reaffirmed and I submitted everything, I allowed myself to go back to August 10th, the day the pain turned to joy. I felt the moment again as I did the same process a 3rd time. My heart was full of thankfulness; I was so grateful to everyone, most especially to my wife, who every single day reminded me with her unending care, warmth, and love that I knew what I was fighting for.

A journey that began in a haze of confusion and terror as COVID struck us down had concluded with a triumphant clearing of the skies nearly 18 months later. We had emerged victorious, stronger, and more determined than ever. We had received $19.7 million in Shuttered Venue Operator Grants and couldn't have been more excited and enthusiastic about what tomorrow could be.

This was the legacy of The Summer of SVOG, a tale of navigating the darkest of storms, taking a vicious, merciless beating for 11 ½ rounds, and with only seconds left, throwing a punch for the ages that knocked the Heavyweight Champion of the World out cold.

Mango's and our Family, nearly upended forever, emerged with a radiant victory. Even though I was terrified, I pushed on. Being brave is not the absence of fear, but always doing the right thing even when you're afraid.

Love guided me, and my one hope is that it continues to guide everyone, anywhere and through anything.

Love, truly, is the answer.